Understanding Violence

David P. Barash

University of Washington

ALLYN AND BACON

Boston   London   Toronto   Sydney   Tokyo   Singapore

Executive Editor: *Carolyn Merrill*
Editorial Assistant: *Lara Zeises*
Marketing Manager: *Caroline Croley*
Editorial–Production Service: *Matrix Productions Inc.*
Composition and Prepress Buyer: *Linda Cox*
Manufacturing Buyer: *Megan Cochran*
Cover Administrator: *Jenny Hart*
Electronic Composition: *Omegatype Typography, Inc.*

Between the time Website information is gathered and then published, it is not unusual for some sites to have closed. Also, the transcription of URLs can result in unintended typographical errors. The publisher would appreciate notification where these occur so that they may be corrected in subsequent editions.

Library of Congress Cataloging-in-Publication Data

Barash, David P.
 Understanding violence / David P. Barash.—1st ed.
  p. cm.
 Includes index.
 ISBN 0-205-31662-X
 1. Violence. 2. Criminal psychology. I. Title.
HM1116 .B37 2000
303.6—dc21

                                        00-030598

Printed in the United States of America

10 9 8 7 6 5 4 3 2 1   05 04 03 02 01 00

Contents

3.   Sociology   100

4.   Anthropology   153

Introduction:
Understanding Violence?

If you set out to identify the various problems bedeviling humans, the resulting melancholy list would be long indeed—too long. It would probably include such things as war, poverty, crime, environmental destruction, overpopulation, intolerance, disease, child and spouse abuse, political tyranny, failures of social justice, and the denial of human rights as well as any number of more idiosyncratic complaints: cruelty toward animals, perhaps, or insufficient religious faith (alternatively, in the opinion of some people, maybe too much faith!), sexism, racism, personal alienation, and so forth. But perhaps the one item that would appear on just about everyone's list is violence.

What is violence? The word derives from the Latin root *vio,* referring to "force." Dictionary definitions include "rough, unjust, unwarranted and injurious physical force or treatment" as well as "immoderate vehemence, typically causing injury, pain or gross distortion." We might speak of a violent storm or an earthquake of exceptional violence, but the term is most usefully applied to human actions, in which case it generally carries the implication that pain or injury is intentionally inflicted on someone or something.

A distinction is sometimes made between violence and aggression, the latter coming from the Latin roots *ag* ("before") combined with *gred* ("to walk or step"). Hence, to aggress is to step before or in front of someone, to initiate something, commonly an attack. Aggression—whether by a state or an individual—thus refers to an unprovoked, offensive action against another. But unlike violence, aggression is not necessarily hurtful: One may aggressively promote a viewpoint, for example, which implies initiative, forcefulness, and assertiveness, but one may do so without injury. We may even seek, aggressively, to oppose violence!

For our purposes, precise definitions are less important than broad understanding. Indeed, we may even satisfy ourselves by ducking the issue, as with the noted jurist's observation about pornography: We may not be able to define it, but we know violence when we see it.

Most people, most of the time, have a gut-level recognition of violence, which is testimony to its significance. Moreover, violence is not new; it traces from the story of Cain and Abel in the Western tradition and the Upanishads of ancient India. It seems likely to be with us for a very long time. Communism has essentially bitten the dust, along with apartheid in South Africa, as well as the Cold War. As amazing as these changes have been, they would be as nothing compared with a world-wide cessation of violence generally. This, unfortunately, has not happened. Nor is it likely to, either soon or in the long term.

Such "realism" should not lead to despair, however, any more than a realistic recognition that we will not live forever is cause for giving up on medicine or medical research. Although perfect health is impossible, *better* health is always feasible. And although a world without aggression or aggressiveness is impossible, one with substantially reduced violence is no more unrealistic than one without major epidemic diseases.

Violence underpins many of the other ills we confront. Violence and war, for example, are almost synonymous. Violence toward the natural world is another way of describing pollution, the problem of endangered species, and even the exploitation of nonrenewable resources. As we will see, the stunting of human lives as a result of inadequate social structures can also be considered a kind of violence, not to mention the obvious connections between violence and crime, violence and family strife, violence and child abuse, violence and racism, violence and tyranny, and so forth.

Violence, in short, is ubiquitous. It is an immense global problem, huge in what we might call its *horizontal* dimension; that is, violence occurs widely throughout the world, among individuals, small groups, and nations. It also has a powerful hold on the human imagination, although it is universally reviled: Few people are in favor of violence (although this doesn't stop them, on occasion, from engaging in it).

Perhaps at some level, people are secretly fonder of violence than they generally acknowledge. After all, the entertainment industry has long known that violence sells. Newspaper headlines scream about the latest murder, rape, genocide, mutilation, abduction, arson, or robbery, never announcing that "No One Was Killed, Injured, or Threatened Today." As the great Indian nonviolence advocate Mohandas Gandhi pointed out, we ought to celebrate the nonviolent conflict resolution that goes on around us and the fact that nearly all disputes are settled without recourse to arms or, indeed, to violence of any sort. But whether it is a matter of rubbernecking at the scene of an automobile accident or playing computer games, people are drawn to violence.

Similarly, at the international level there are daily reports concerning "hot spots" and "armed incidents" around the globe, but never an announcement that, for example, "Venezuela and Brazil Did Not Go to War Today." Violence gets our attention, while its absence gets a shrug of indifference. Significantly, we have numerous war songs, war movies, and war novels, but precious few that comparably celebrate peace. We name the various wars, rebellions, and outrages of history, but only rarely do we identify "peaces," even though periods between wars are no less distinct (and considerably more extensive) than those brief episodes of violence that punctuate human history.

People confer names on things they care about: Bedouins, for instance, have dozens of different words for the English noun *camel* (depending on whether the animal in question is ill natured or friendly, easy to ride or bumpy, and so forth). The reason is clear: Bedouins care about camels, enough to make precise distinctions among them. The fact that we give names to specific wars, massacres, and other episodes of violence but consider "peace" to be so homogeneous—and uninteresting—that we usually do not bother to distinguish one peace from another, speaks eloquently about what *we* care about. When and if we are as concerned about peace as about war, as interested in the normal, humane conduct of daily life as in occasional outbreaks of violence, then perhaps such outbreaks will become rare aberrations.

For now, maybe violence and wars are simply more interesting than their alternatives. Is peace boring? For all the widespread abhorrence of violence, can it be that we like it?

Although it seems perverse that people are fascinated by violence, there may be some logic behind it. Thus, even though episodes of injury and pain—not to mention bloodletting, brutalization, and outright killing—are comparatively rare, they are nonetheless especially important when and if they occur. So it pays to take them seriously, to be particularly attuned to the circumstances and effects of violent outbreaks. Lightning storms, tornadoes, and earthquakes, for example, are rare, but very consequential when they happen. They cannot be prevented, but to varying degrees they can be prepared for. Violence, too, can be prepared for . . . and perhaps even prevented as well.

It is tempting but misleading—as well as potentially dangerous—to assume, just because violence sometimes happens, that it structures (or should be allowed to structure) much of our lives. But it may be equally misleading—as well as potentially dangerous—to assume that just because violence is extreme as well as uncommon, it should be ignored or its existence denied.

There is remarkably little agreement about the causes of violence (not to mention what to do about it). Let us therefore go beyond acknowledging the horizontal extent of violence and examine its *vertical* dimensions, starting perhaps with the smallest, most reductionist approach (at the level of genes, perhaps, or hormones, or brain regions), up to globe-girdling concerns such as political or religious ideology.

As with other big problems, which tend to be caused at different levels and in different ways, violence has a habit of eluding our best efforts at comprehension as well as control. Maybe violence is just too large, too complex, to be easily pigeonholed. This brings to mind the famous story of the blind men and the elephant, as told by the nineteenth-century American poet John Saxe:

> It was six men from Industan, to learning much inclined,
> Who went to see the elephant (though all of them were blind),
> That each by observation might satisfy his mind . . .

Not surprisingly, each blind man felt a different part of the elephant, so that the one touching its legs thought they were tree trunks, the one touching its tail thought it was a snake, and so on. At the end, they

> Disputed loud and long, each in his opinion stiff and strong,
> Though each was partly in the right, and all of them were wrong.

Violence, then, is a bit like an elephant: too complex to be easily tamed or readily understood, maybe even too large to be perceived accurately. (And also, of course, too big and too potentially dangerous to ignore!)

Hence this book.

And yet—suprisingly, perhaps—the goal of *Understanding Violence* is *not* to understand violence! Rather, it is one step removed: to understand some of the most important efforts at understanding violence. Each of the various chapters represents a sampling of the efforts of a different discipline, a different blind man, in a sense. Although no one discipline is blessed with 20-20 vision, it is hoped that pooling them in this way will provide a glimpse of the elephant's outlines.

Even this admittedly modest enterprise is fraught with controversy. There is, for example, the question of depth versus breadth: Ideally, both should be included in an overview such as this, but considerations of length (and cost) require compromises. So I have opted to include a relatively large number of different selections, but have had to edit them—in some cases, severely—in order to permit the inclusion of many different perspectives. I can only beg the indulgence of both authors/researchers and students/instructors and hope that I have been able to retain the crucial information and the key elements of each approach. In the process, I have also taken the liberty of deleting detailed presentation of data, generally of greater interest to other researchers than to students; similarly, I plead guilty to the scholarly sin of removing academic references from the various selections. This was done—albeit reluctantly—to save space and enhance readability and seems legitimate in what is, after all, an introductory survey text, intended as an overview and a starting point for learning.

There is also abundant room for disagreement over which disciplines to include. Thus, most experts agree that when it comes to understanding violence, substantial contributions have been made by specialists working from within biology, psychology, anthropology, criminology, sociology, and political science. Should psychiatry have been given its own chapter? And what about other fields, such as theology or economics? The Old Testament, for example, and Karl Marx's *Das Kapital* have much to teach us about violence.

And what of the humanities? The human imagination resonates to violence in complex ways, and literary depictions of violence are crucial and unique in touching the emotional centers that explain the extraordinary horror (as well as the perverse attraction) of this phenomenon. It may be, therefore, that any rounded attempt to sample efforts at understanding violence should also include a wide spectrum of the world's great literature, from *The Iliad* through Shakespeare's great tragedies, Dostoyevsky's *Crime and Punishment,* and Erich Maria Remarque's *All Quiet on the Western Front* as well as more recent accounts of World War II or the Vietnam War, such as Norman Mailer's *The Naked and the Dead* and Tim O'Brien's *The Things They Carried.*

"Beyond the scope of this book" is a frequent apology and excuse . . . but in this case, it is accurate. *Understanding Violence* is a beginning, not an end in itself. I hope that instructors will find it a convenient foundation text, complete enough to provide a meaningful yet diverse sampling of major approaches, while still allowing room for the assignment of additional, more specialized readings consistent with each instructor's personal orientation. I have sought to include readings that are important, representative of a major tradition, and at least moderately accessible to nonspecialists.

There is yet more room for controversy, however. Some people—notably many social and political conservatives—often argue against efforts to ferret out so-called root causes of violence in general or crime in particular, maintaining that society's attention and resources should instead be devoted to incarceration or, in extreme cases, execution. Similarly with war. The cause of war, they say, is simple: bad people doing bad things. And the response is equally simple, in both cases: more police, judges, jails, locked and gated communities, bulletproof vests, armies, tanks, and bombers.

Another problem exists: In the opinion of some people, to understand is to justify. The French have a saying: *Tout comprendre c'est tout pardonner*—"To understand all is to forgive all." Accordingly, perhaps we should struggle against too much "understanding," lest it preclude responsibility as well as punishment. It is far easier simply to condemn violence than to make the admittedly greater effort required to understand it. Forgiveness for offenders—whether criminal perpetrators or war makers—may or may not be possible, or desirable. But "understanding" need not imply sympathetic acceptance. It can also mean comprehension and the beginning of wisdom, with the goal not so much to forgive but, ultimately, to prevent. (Not that forgiveness is necessarily precluded, mind you.)

Finally, there are those who disparage the very idea of understanding violence, claiming that underlying causes simply do not exist or cannot be determined for some of the darker, deeper, danker aspects of human behavior. And yet an essential part of the Western worldview is that any effect (e.g., violent behavior) must have a cause. We all have one or more theories of what causes violence; the difference is whether we elect to make these theories explicit. Some blame "human nature." Others point to failures of self-control; to bad genes, bad wiring, bad chemistry, faulty neuroanatomy, or inappropriate parenting; to blunders by society, the vagaries of social and economic inequality or of competition; to failures of communication or of socialization; to just plain bad luck or even the work of the devil.

Whatever the underlying causes of violence, and whatever we as individuals and as society may choose to do about it, we have an obligation at least to consider what is understood thus far about it, if only as part of the Socratic injunction "Know thyself." Thus, even those who have been blessedly spared any direct experience of violence are likely to have "experienced" its horrors in some way or other, if only in dreams, fears, hidden fantasies, or simply by living in a society and a world of which violence is so large and regrettable a part.

The great philosopher Immanuel Kant proposed *Sapere aude* ("Dare to know") as a motto for the Enlightenment. It would also be a suitable subtitle for this book.

1

Biology

"Violence," announced 1960s Black Power advocate H. Rap Brown, "is as American as cherry pie." At that time, his words outraged many, who not only considered them unpatriotic but also a cynical justification of violence on the part of Brown's own group, the Black Panthers.

Several decades later, however, few will dispute that the United States is a very violent society, although when it comes to violence, this country does not have a monopoly. Violence is indeed as American as cherry pie, but also as British as boiled beef, as Russian as caviar, as Japanese as sushi. Not only is violence disturbingly widespread, but it also enjoys a very old pedigree. Thus, although it seems unlikely to be "inherently" American (or British, or Russian, or Japanese), the evidence strongly suggests that violence is "inherently" human. And animal as well.

Given that it is so broadly distributed, historically no less than geographically, violence seems likely to be deeply ensconced in our biological natures too. Furthermore, there is a solid logical reason for taking the biology of violence seriously: Scientific explanations are often most successful when most reductionistic, when they examine things at the smallest practical level (such as atoms, molecules, electrical charges, basic laws of physics, and so forth).

On the other hand, there are reasons for caution. For one, biological explanations for complex human behavior may be seductive but misleading. The philosopher Alfred North Whitehead advised: "Seek simplicity, and then distrust it." Along with the benefits of simplifying and thus focusing our attention, there comes the danger of *over-simplifying*, distracting attention from other important factors. In short, it is all too easy to conclude that biology explains everything, thus prematurely ending serious investigation into nuanced and complex causation.

A second and related reason for caution comes from the fact that biological explanations are often seen as rigidly deterministic. If people become convinced, for example, that violence, narrowly defined, is "caused" by genes, chemicals, or brain function, then it can be sorely tempting to lose hope of amelioration. Violent perpetrators may be abandoned as incorrigible while, ironically, freed of personal responsibility.

Overreliance on unitary biological "explanations" can lead to a kind of fatalism and hopelessness, with the despairing claim that the root of the trouble is "human nature," "in the genes," or a matter of "bad brains" or "raging hormones." It then becomes tempting to deny the possibility of effective social intervention, which becomes a self-fulfilling prophecy.

A final problem with efforts to link biology to violence is that despite the claim to scientific respectability (especially compared to the "softer" social sciences), attempts at "biologizing" violence have often been wrong, sometimes embarrassingly so. For literally centuries, for example, human personality was attributed to the balance of "vital fluids" known as *humors*. These included *choler* or "yellow bile," which was supposed to produce anger and irascibility; thus, people who were more choleric had a greater penchant for violence (as opposed to those with more phlegm, which produced a cooler or "phlegmatic" personality).

The undoubted connection between brain activity and behavior led to the pseudoscience of phrenology, based on the assumption that by examining skull shape, it was possible to infer the degree of underlying brain development. The nineteenth-century Italian forensic physician Cesare Lambroso held that certain facial and cranial features accurately predicted tendencies for criminality. For example, a sloping forehead indicated a degenerate ("atavistic") throwback to more primitive human types. Although misused for racist ends and now thoroughly discredited, such theories were immensely influential in their time and have sensitized people against the possible ideological appropriation of biology.

Yet despite these drawbacks, we are about to sample efforts to understand the biology of violence. Why? For one thing, the fact that something has been misused does not diminish its legitimacy; we simply must work all the harder to guard against misuse. Similarly, the fact that something has been empirically wrong in the past does not mean that it is incorrect now. The biology of violence offers many important and exciting leads that demand attention; in some cases, moreover, the connection between biology and violence is so straightforward as to be undeniable.

When it comes to the problem of excessive reductionism, the antidote is readily available: humility, recognizing that violence is so large and so multifaceted that no single explanatory dimension, taken alone, will suffice. In addition, the various narrowly defined "biological factors" such as genetics, hormones, and neuroanatomy do not act in a vacuum; they influence social processes, and, in turn, are influenced by them.

On War and Peace in Animals and Man

NIKO TINBERGEN

Ethology is the biological study of animal behavior. It emphasizes observation of animals in their natural environments, focusing especially on what is loosely called *instinct*—that is, behavior that requires essentially no learning, is rigidly stereotyped, and derives from relatively simple acts having a strong genetic component and involving little or no insight. Ethologists have also sought, on occasion, to extend their approach to human beings. When applied to aggression and violence (notably in Konrad Lorenz's influential book, *On Aggression*), ethology has tended to focus on an innate "need" for aggressive and violent behavior, which is sometimes thought to demand release, like steam building up pressure inside a closed, heated container.

Niko Tinbergen (1907–1988) was a Dutch biologist who worked for most of his professional life at Oxford University. Tinbergen shared a Nobel Prize with Lorenz and entomologist Karl von Frisch for seminal contributions to ethology. In the following selection, Tinbergen is particularly concerned to lay out a more nuanced and flexible research program for ethology than the Lorenzian paradigm, which is often caricatured as rigid, unchangeable instinctivism.

In 1935 Alexis Carrel published a best seller, *Man—The Unknown*. . . .   1
Today, more than 30 years later, we biologists have once more the duty to remind our fellowmen that in many respects we are still, to ourselves, unknown. It is true that we now understand a great deal of the way our bodies function. With this understanding came control: medicine.

The ignorance of ourselves which needs to be stressed today is igno-   2
rance about our behavior—lack of understanding of the causes and effects of the function of our brains. A scientific understanding of our behavior, leading to its control, may well be the most urgent task that faces mankind today. . . .

I am an ethologist, a zoologist studying animal behavior. What gives   3
a student of animal behavior the temerity to speak about problems of human behavior? Of course the history of medicine provides the answer. We all know that medical research uses animals on a large scale. This makes sense because animals, particularly vertebrates, are, in spite of all differences, so similar to us; they are our blood relations, however distant.

But this use of zoological research for a better understanding of our-   4
selves is, to most people, acceptable only when we have to do with

those bodily functions that we look upon as parts of our physiological machinery—the functions, for instance, of our kidneys, our liver, our hormone-producing glands. The majority of people bridle as soon as it is even suggested that studies of animal behavior could be useful for an understanding, let alone for the control, of our own behavior. They do not want to have their own behavior subjected to scientific scrutiny; they certainly resent being compared with animals, and these rejecting attitudes are both deep-rooted and of complex origin.

5   But now we are witnessing a turn in this tide of human thought. On the one hand the resistances are weakening, and on the other, a positive awareness is growing of the potentialities of a biology of behavior. . . .

6   I shall argue that we shall have to make a major research effort. I am of course fully aware of the fact that much research is already being devoted to problems of human, and even of animal, behavior. I know, for instance, that anthropologists, psychologists, psychiatrists, and others are approaching these problems from many angles. But I shall try to show that the research effort has so far made insufficient use of the potential of ethology. Anthropologists, for instance, are beginning to look at animals, but they restrict their work almost entirely to our nearest relatives, the apes and monkeys. Psychologists do study a larger variety of animals, but even they select mainly higher species. They also ignore certain major problems that we biologists think have to be studied. Psychiatrists, at least many of them, show a disturbing tendency to apply the *results* rather than the *methods* of ethology to man.

7   None of these sciences, not even their combined efforts, are as yet parts of one coherent science of behavior. Since behavior is a life process, its study ought to be part of the mainstream of biological research. That is why we zoologists ought to "join the fray." As an ethologist, I am going to try to sketch how my science could assist its sister sciences in their attempts, already well on their way, to make a united, broad-fronted, truly biological attack on the problems of behavior. . . .

8   The potential usefulness of ethology lies in the fact that, unlike other sciences of behavior, it applies the method or "approach" of biology to the phenomenon behavior. It has developed a set of concepts and terms that allow us to ask:

1. In what ways does this phenomenon (behavior) influence the survival, the success of the animal?
2. What makes behavior happen at any given moment? How does its "machinery" work?
3. How does the behavior machinery develop as the individual grows up?
4. How have the behavior systems of each species evolved until they became what they are now?

The first question, that of survival value, has to do with the effects of   9
behavior; the other three are, each on a different time scale, concerned
with its causes.

These four questions are, as many of my fellow biologists will rec-   10
ognize, the major questions that biology has been pursuing for a long
time. What ethology is doing could be simply described by saying that,
just as biology investigates the functioning of the organs responsible for
digestion, respiration, circulation, and so forth, so ethology begins now
to do the same with respect to behavior; it investigates the functioning
of organs responsible for movement. . . .

Having stated my case for animal ethology as an essential part of the   11
science of behavior, I will now have to sketch how this could be done.
For this I shall have to consider one concrete example, and I select aggression, the most directly lethal of our behaviors. And, for reasons that
will become clear, I shall also make a short excursion into problems of
education.

Let me first try to define what I mean by aggression. We all under-   12
stand the term in a vague, general way, but it is, after all, no more than
a catchword. In terms of actual behavior, aggression involves approaching an opponent, and, when within reach, pushing him away, inflicting damage of some kind, or at least forcing stimuli upon him that
subdue him. In this description the effect is already implicit: such behavior tends to remove the opponent, or at least to make him change his
behavior in such a way that he no longer interferes with the attacker.
The methods of attack differ from one species to another, and so do the
weapons that are used, the structures that contribute to the effect.

Since I am concentrating on men fighting men, I shall confine myself   13
to intraspecific fighting, and ignore, for instance, fighting between
predators and prey. Intraspecific fighting is very common among animals. Many of them fight in two different contexts, which we can call
"offensive" and "defensive." Defensive fighting is often shown as a last
resort by an animal that, instead of attacking, has been fleeing from an
attacker. If it is cornered, it may suddenly turn round upon its enemy
and "fight with the courage of despair."

Of the four questions I mentioned before, I shall consider that of the   14
survival value first. Here comparison faces us right at the start with a
striking paradox. On the one hand, man is akin to many species of animals in that he fights his own species. But on the other hand he is,
among the thousands of species that fight, the only one in which fighting is disruptive.

In animals, intraspecific fighting is usually of distinctive advantage.   15
In addition, all species manage as a rule to settle their disputes without
killing one another; in fact, even bloodshed is rare. Man is the only
species that is a mass murderer, the only misfit in his own society.

16   Why should this be so? For an answer, we shall have to turn to the question of causation: What makes animals and man fight their own species? And why is our species "the odd man out"? . . .

17   I have already indicated that when thinking of causation we have to distinguish between three subquestions, and that these three differ from one another in the stretch of time that is considered. We ask, first: Given an adult animal that fights now and then, what makes each outburst of fighting happen? The time scale in which we consider these recurrent events is usually one of seconds, or minutes. To use an analogy, this subquestion compares with asking what makes a car start or stop each time we use it.

18   But in asking this same general question of causation ("What makes an animal fight?") we may also be referring to a longer period of time; we may mean "How has the animal, as it grew up, developed this behavior?" This compares roughly with asking how a car has been constructed in the factory. The distinction between these two subquestions remains useful even though we know that many animals continue their development (much slowed down) even after they have attained adulthood. For instance, they may still continue to learn.

19   Finally, in biology, as in technology, we can extend this time scale even more, and ask: How have the animal species which we observe today—and which we know have evolved from ancestors that were different—how have they acquired their particular behavior systems during this evolution? Unfortunately, while we know the evolution of cars because they evolved so quickly and have been so fully recorded, the behavior of extinct animals cannot be observed, and has to be reconstructed by indirect methods. . . .

20   Fighting is started by a number of variables, of which some are internal and some external. What both authors know, and what cannot be doubted, is that fighting behavior is not like the simple slot machine that produces one platform ticket every time one threepenny bit is inserted. To mention one animal example: a male stickleback does not always show the full fighting behavior in response to an approaching standard opponent; its response varies from none at all to the optimal stimulus on some occasions, to full attack on even a crude dummy at other times. This means that its internal state varies and in this particular case we know . . . that the level of the male sex hormone is an important variable. . . .

21   We must remember that we are at the moment concerned with the human problem: "What makes men attack each other?" And for this problem the answer to the first stage of our question is of prime importance: Is our readiness to start an attack constant or not? If it were— if our aggressive behavior were the outcome of an apparatus with the

properties of the slot machine—all we would have to do would be to control the external situation: to stop providing threepenny bits. But since our readiness to start an attack is variable, further studies of both the external and the internal variables are vital to such issues as: Can we reduce fighting by lowering the population density, or by withholding provocative stimuli? Can we do so by changing the hormone balance or other physiological variables? Can we perhaps in addition control our development in such a way as to change the dependence on internal and external factors in adult man? However, before discussing development, I must first return to the fact that I have mentioned before, namely, that man is, among the thousands of other species that fight, the only mass murderer. How do animals in their intraspecific disputes avoid bloodshed? . . .

The clue to this problem is to recognize the simple fact that aggression in animals rarely occurs in pure form; it is only one of two components of an adaptive system. This is most clearly seen in territorial behavior, although it is also true of most other types of hostile behavior. Members of territorial species divide, among themselves, the available living space and opportunities by each individual defending its home range against competitors. Now in this system of parceling our living space, avoidance plays as important a part as attack. Put very briefly, animals of territorial species, once they have settled on a territory, attack intruders, but an animal that is still searching for a suitable territory or finds itself outside its home range withdraws when it meets with an already established owner. In terms of function, once you have taken possession of a territory, it pays to drive off competitors; but when you are still looking for a territory (or meet your neighbor at your common boundary), your chances of success are improved by avoiding such established owners. The ruthless fighter who "knows no fear" does not get very far. For an understanding of what follows, this fact, that hostile clashes are controlled by what we could call the "attack-avoidance system," is essential.

When neighboring territory owners meet near their common boundary, both attack behavior and withdrawal behavior are elicited in both animals; each of the two is in a state of motivational conflict. We know a great deal about the variety of movements that appear when these two conflicting, incompatible behaviors are elicited. Many of these expressions of a motivational conflict have, in the course of evolution, acquired signal function; in colloquial language, they signal "Keep out!" We deduce this from the fact that opponents respond to them in an appropriate way: instead of proceeding to intrude, which would require the use of force, trespassers withdraw, and neighbors are contained by each other. This is how such animals have managed to have all the advantages of

22

23

their hostile behavior without the disadvantages: they divide their living space in a bloodless way by using as distance-keeping devices these conflict movements ("threat") rather than actual fighting. . . .

24   So far I have discussed animal species that defend individual or at best pair territories. But there are also animals which possess and defend territories belonging to a group, or a clan. . . .

25   Now it is an essential aspect of group territorialism that the members of a group unite when in hostile confrontation with another group that approaches, or crosses into their feeding territory. The uniting and the aggression are equally important. It is essential to realize that group territorialism does not exclude hostile relations on lower levels when the group is on its own. For instance, within a group there is often a peck order. And within the group there may be individual or pair territories. But frictions due to these relationships fade away during a clash between groups. This temporary elimination is done by means of so-called appeasement and reassurance signals. They indicate "I am a friend," and so diminish the risk that, in the general flare-up of anger, any animal "takes it out" on a fellow member of the same group. . . . Clans meet clans as units, and each individual in an intergroup clash, while united with its fellow-members, is (as in interindividual clashes) torn between attack and withdrawal, and postures and shouts rather than attacks.

26   We must now examine the hypothesis (which I consider the most likely one) that man still carries with him the animal heritage of group territoriality. This is a question concerning man's evolutionary origin, and here we are, by the very nature of the subject, forced to speculate. Because I am going to say something about the behavior of our ancestors of, say, 100,000 years ago, I have to discuss briefly a matter of methodology. It is known to all biologists (but unfortunately unknown to most psychologists) that comparison of present-day species can give us a deep insight, with a probability closely approaching certainty, into the evolutionary history of animal species. Even where fossil evidence is lacking, this comparative method alone can do this. It has to be stressed that this comparison is a highly sophisticated method, and not merely a matter of saying that species A is different from species B. . . .

27   The basic procedure is this. We interpret differences between really allied species as the result of adaptive divergent evolution from common stock, and we interpret similarities between nonallied species as adaptive convergencies to similar ways of life. By studying the adaptive functions of species characteristics we understand how natural selection can have produced both these divergencies and convergencies. To mention one striking example: even if we had no fossil evidence, we could, by this method alone, recognize whales for what they are—mammals that have returned to the water, and, in doing so, have developed some similarities

to fish. This special type of comparison, which has been applied so successfully by students of the structure of animals, has now also been used, and with equal success, in several studies of animal behavior. . . .

Now, when we include the "Naked Ape" in our comparative studies, it becomes likely . . . that man is a "social Ape who has turned carnivore." . . . On the one hand he is a social primate; on the other, he has developed similarities to wolves, lions and hyenas. In our present context one thing seems to stand out clearly, a conclusion that seems to me of paramount importance to all of us, and yet has not yet been fully accepted as such. As a social, hunting primate, man must originally have been organized on the principle of group territories.

Ethologists tend to believe that we still carry with us a number of behavioral characteristics of our animal ancestors, which cannot be eliminated by different ways of upbringing, and that our group territorialism is one of those ancestral characters. . . . Most writers who have tried to apply ethology to man have . . . made the mistake, to which I objected before, of uncritically extrapolating the results of animal studies to man. They try to explain man's behavior by using facts that are valid only of some of the animals we studied. And, as ethologists keep stressing, no two species behave alike. Therefore, instead of taking this easy way out, we ought to study man in his own right. And I repeat that the message of the ethologists is that the methods, rather than the results, of ethology should be used for such a study.

Now, the notion of territory was developed by zoologists (to be precise, by ornithologists . . . and because individual and pair territories are found in so many more species than group territories (which are particularly rare among birds), most animal studies were concerned with such individual and pair territories. Now such low-level territories do occur in man, as does another form of hostile behavior, the peck order. But the problems created by such low-level frictions are not serious; they can, within a community, be kept in check by the apparatus of law and order; peace within national boundaries can be enforced. In order to understand what makes us go to war, we have to recognize that man behaves very much like a group-territorial species. We too unite in the face of an outside danger to the group; we "forget our differences." We too have threat gestures, for instance, angry facial expressions. And all of us use reassurance and appeasement signals, such as a friendly smile. And (unlike speech) these are universally understood; they are cross-cultural; they are species-specific. And, incidentally, even within a group sharing a common language, they are often more reliable guides to a man's intentions than speech, for speech (as we know now) rarely reflects our true motives, but our facial expressions often "give us away." . . .

28

29

30

31 Man has the ability, unparalleled in scale in the animal kingdom, of passing on his experiences from one generation to the next. By this accumulative and exponentially growing process, which we call cultural evolution, he has been able to change his environment progressively out of all recognition. And this includes the social environment. This new type of evolution proceeds at an incomparably faster pace than genetic evolution. Genetically we have not evolved very strikingly since Cro-Magnon man, but culturally we have changed beyond recognition, and are changing at an ever-increasing rate. It is of course true that we are highly adjustable individually, and so could hope to keep pace with these changes. But I am not alone in believing that this behavioral adjustability, like all types of modifiability, has its limits. These limits are imposed upon us by our hereditary constitution, a constitution which can only change with the far slower speed of genetic evolution. There are good grounds for the conclusion that man's limited behavioral adjustability has been outpaced by the culturally determined changes in his social environment, and that this is why man is now a misfit in his own society.

32 There a frightening, and ironical paradox . . . that the human brain, the finest life-preserving device created by evolution, has made our species so successful in mastering the outside world that it suddenly finds itself taken off guard. One could say that our cortex and our brainstem (our "reason" and our "instincts") are at loggerheads. Together they have created a new social environment in which, rather than ensuring our survival, they are about to do the opposite. The brain finds itself seriously threatened by an enemy of its own making. It is its own enemy. We simply have to understand this enemy. . . .

33 I must now leave the question of the moment-to-moment control of fighting, and, looking further back in time, turn to the development of aggressive behavior in the growing individual. Again we will start from the human problem. This, in the present context, is whether it is within our power to control development in such a way that we reduce or eliminate fighting among adults. Can or cannot education in the widest sense produce nonaggressive men?

34 The first step in the consideration of this problem is again to distinguish between external and internal influences, but now we must apply this to the growth, the changing, of the behavioral machinery during the individual's development. Here again the way in which we phrase our questions and our conclusions is of the utmost importance.

35 In order to discuss this issue fruitfully, I have to start once more by considering it in a wider context, which is now that of the "nature-nurture" problem with respect to behavior in general. . . . And there was a time, some 30 years ago, when the almost grotesquely environmentalist

bias of psychology made it imperative for ethologists to stress the extent to which behavior patterns could appear in perfect or near-perfect form without the aid of anything that could be properly called learning. But I now agree (however belatedly) . . . that we must extend our interest to earlier stages of development and embark on a full program of experimental embryology of behavior. When we do this, we discover that interactions with the environment can indeed occur at early stages. These interactions may concern small components of the total machinery of a fully functional behavior pattern, and many of them cannot possibly be called learning. But they are interactions with the environment, and must be taken into account if we follow in the footsteps of the experimental embryologists, and extend our field of interest to the entire sequence of events which lead from the blueprints contained in the zygote to the fully functioning, behaving animal. . . .

When we follow this procedure the rigid distinction between "innate" or unmodifiable and "acquired" or modifiable behavior patterns becomes far less sharp. This is owing to the discovery, on the one hand, that "innate" patterns may contain elements that at an early stage developed in interaction with the environment, and, on the other hand, that learning is, from step to step, limited by internally imposed restrictions. . . . Now it has been shown . . . that male sticklebacks reared from the egg in complete isolation from other animals will, when adult, show full fighting behavior to other males and courtship behavior to females when faced with them for the first time in their lives. This is admittedly an important fact, demonstrating that the various recognized forms of learning do not enter into the programing of these integrated patterns. This is a demonstration of what Lorenz calls an "innate response." But it does not exclude the possibility that parts of the machinery so employed may, at an earlier stage, have been influenced by the environment. . . .   36

Second, there are also behavior patterns which do appear in the inexperienced animal, but in an incomplete form, and which require additional development through learning. . . . When young male chaffinches reared alone begin to produce their song for the first time, they utter a very imperfect warble; this develops into the full song only if, at a certain sensitive stage, the young birds have heard the full song of an adult male. . . .   37

By far the most interesting aspect of such intermediates between innate and acquired behavior is the fact that learning is not indiscriminate, but is guided by a certain selectiveness on the part of the animal. This fact has been dimly recognized long ago; the early ethologists have often pointed out that different, even closely related, species learn different things even when developing the same behavior patterns. This   38 has been emphasized by Lorenz's use of the term "innate teaching mechanism." . . .

39   Whatever the causation of our aggression, the simple fact is that for the time being we are saddled with it. This means that there is a crying need for a crash program, for finding ways and means for keeping our intergroup aggression in check. This is of course in practice infinitely more difficult than controlling our intranational frictions; we have as yet not got a truly international police force. But there is hope for avoiding all-out war because, for the first time in history, we are afraid of killing ourselves by the lethal radiation effects even of bombs that we could drop in the enemy's territory. Our politicians know this. And as long as there is this hope, there is every reason to try and learn what we can from animal studies. Here again they can be of help. We have already seen that animal opponents meeting in a hostile clash avoid bloodshed by using the expressions of their motivational conflicts as intimidating signals. Ethologists have studied such conflict movements in some detail, and have found that they are of a variety of types. The most instructive of these is the redirected attack; instead of attacking the provoking, yet dreaded, opponent, animals often attack something else, often even an inanimate object. We ourselves bang the table with our fists. Redirection includes something like sublimation, a term attaching a value judgment to the redirection. As a species with group territories, humans, like hyenas, unite when meeting a common enemy. We do already sublimate our group aggression. The Dutch feel united in their fight against the sea. Scientists do attack their problems together. The space program—surely a mainly military effort—is an up-to-date example. I would not like to claim, as Lorenz does, that redirected attack exhausts the aggressive urge. We know from soccer matches and from animal work how aggressive behavior has two simultaneous, but opposite effects: a waning effect, and one of self-inflammation, of mass hysteria. . . . Of these two the inflammatory effect often wins. But if aggression were used successfully as the motive force behind nonkilling and even useful activities, self-stimulation need not be a danger; in our short-term cure we are not aiming at the elimination of aggressiveness, but at "taking the sting out of it."

40   Of all sublimated activities, scientific research would seem to offer the best opportunities for deflecting and sublimating our aggression. And, once we recognize that it is the disrupted relation between our own behavior and our environment that forms our most deadly enemy, what could be better than uniting, at the front or behind the lines, in the scientific attack on our own behavioral problems? . . .

41   Scientific research is one of the finest occupations of our mind. It is, with art and religion, one of the uniquely human ways of meeting nature, in fact, the most active way. If we are to succumb, and even if this

were to be ultimately due to our own stupidity, we could still, so to speak, redeem our species. We could at least go down with some dignity, by using our brain for one of its supreme tasks, by exploring to the end.

On Human Nature

EDWARD O. WILSON

Ethology is not the only biological approach to behavior that makes use of evolutionary insights. Ecology—specifically, behavioral ecology—is another. Its basic approach is to evaluate the adaptive consequences of various behavioral strategies—that is, the effect of different behavior on the *fitness* (the evolutionary success) of the organisms and genes in question. In simple terms, imagine that a given gene increases the likelihood of a particular behavior pattern, whereas an alternative gene is likely to lead to an alternative pattern. Over time, which gene—and thus, which behavior—will be more frequent? Answer: that which ultimately results in greater reproductive success for the individuals (really, the genes) in question.

An especially important concept in this regard is *optimality*. Each act carries a different array of benefits and costs. Living things are assumed to maximize the difference between these, such that under the influence of natural selection, organisms tend to behave in a way that results in a maximum number of surviving descendants and, more important, their constituent genes. Applied to violence, this process leads to such considerations as maximal efficiency, defensibility of resources, the resource needs of the creatures in question (presuming that violence is one of several tactics for achieving access to such resources). Resources, in turn, are important because—whether food, nest sites, mates, or whatever—they contribute to evolutionary success.

There is no implication here that violence is ethically "good," simply that living things are likely to be selected to behave with regard to violence—as with regard to other things, such as getting food, migrating, and rearing young—in a way that maximizes their success. It is then up to human beings, if they choose, to use this information to attribute "good" or "bad," or at least to learn more about the phenomenon.

Our next selection is from renowned biologist Edward O. Wilson, who first popularized the term *sociobiology*, referring to the biological study of complex behavior in animals and human beings. Wilson's book *Sociobiology* (1975) summarized many of the crucial findings in this field and was also very controversial, especially in its assertion that human behavior can be analyzed by an evolutionary/ecological/genetic perspective not unlike that employed in examining the behavior of animals.

1   Are human beings innately aggressive? This is a favorite question of college seminars and cocktail party conversations, and one that raises emotion in political ideologues of all stripes. The answer to it is yes. Throughout history, warfare, representing only the most organized technique of aggression, has been endemic to every form of society, from hunter-gatherer bands to industrial states. During the past three centuries a majority of the countries of Europe have been engaged in war during approximately half of all the years; few have ever seen a century of continuous peace. Virtually all societies have invented elaborate sanctions against rape, extortion, and murder, while regulating their daily commerce through complex customs and laws designed to minimize the subtler but inevitable forms of conflict. Most significantly of all, the human forms of aggressive behavior are species-specific: although basically primate in form, they contain features that distinguish them from aggression in all other species. Only by redefining the words "innateness" and "aggression" to the point of uselessness might we correctly say that human aggressiveness is not innate.

2   Theoreticians who wish to exonerate the genes and blame human aggressiveness wholly on perversities of the environment point to the tiny minority of societies that appear to be nearly or entirely pacific. They forget that innateness refers to the measurable probability that a trait will develop in a specified set of environments, not to the certainty that the trait will develop in all environments. By this criterion human beings have a marked hereditary predisposition to aggressive behavior. In fact, the matter is even more clear-cut than this qualification implies. The most peaceable tribes of today were often the ravagers of yesteryear and will probably again produce soldiers and murderers in the future. Among contemporary !Kung San violence in adults is almost unknown; Elizabeth Marshall Thomas has correctly named them the "harmless people." But as recently as fifty years ago, when these "Bushman" populations were denser and less rigidly controlled by the central government, their homicide rate per capita equalled that of Detroit and Houston. . . .

3   Like most other mammals, human beings display a behavioral scale, a spectrum of responses that appear or disappear according to particular circumstances. They differ genetically from many other animal species that lack such a pattern of behavior altogether. Because there is a complex scale instead of a simple, reflex-like response, psychoanalysts and zoologists alike have had an extraordinarily difficult time arriving at a satisfactory general characterization of human aggression. They would encounter exactly the same difficulty defining gorilla aggression or tiger aggression. . . . Like so many other forms of behavior and "instinct," aggression in any given species is actually an ill-defined array of different responses with separate controls in the nervous system. No

fewer than seven categories can be distinguished: the defense and conquest of territory, the assertion of dominance within well-organized
groups, sexual aggression, acts of hostility by which weaning is terminated, aggression against prey, defensive counterattacks against predators, and moralistic and disciplinary aggression used to enforce the rules
of society. Rattlesnakes provide an instructive example of the distinctions between these basic categories. When two males compete for access to females, they intertwine their necks and wrestle as though testing
each other's strength, but they do not bite, even though their venom is
as lethal to other rattlesnakes as it is to rabbits and mice. When a rattlesnake stalks its prey it strikes from any number of positions without
advance warning. But when the tables are turned and the snake is confronted by an animal large enough to threaten its safety, it coils, pulls its
head forward to the center of the coil in striking position, and raises and
shakes its rattle. Finally, if the intruder is a king snake, a species specialized for feeding on other snakes, the rattlesnake employs a wholly different maneuver: it coils, hides its head under its body, and slaps at the
king snake with one of the raised coils. So to understand the aggression
of rattlesnakes or human beings it is necessary to specify which of the
particular forms of aggressive behavior is of interest.

Continuing research in zoology has also established that none of the   4
categories of aggressive behavior exists in the form of a general instinct
over broad arrays of species. Each category can be added, modified, or
erased by an individual species during the course of its genetic evolution, in the same way that eye color can be altered from one shade to another or a particular skin gland added or eliminated. When natural
selection is intense, these changes can occur throughout an entire population in only a few generations. Aggressive behavior is in fact one of
the genetically most labile of all traits. We commonly find that one
species of bird or mammal is highly territorial, with every square meter
of habitable environment carefully staked out; the residents perform
spectacular dances or emit loud cries and noisome odors to repel rivals
of the same species from their private little domains. Yet coexisting in
the same habitats may be a second, otherwise similar species that shows
no trace of territorial behavior. Equally abrupt differences among
species commonly occur in the other categories of aggression. In short,
there is no evidence that a widespread unitary aggressive instinct exists.

The reason for the absence of a general aggressive instinct has been   5
revealed by research in ecology. Most kinds of aggressive behavior
among members of the same species are responsive to crowding in the
environment. Animals use aggression as a technique for gaining control
over necessities, ordinarily food or shelter, that are scarce or are likely to
become so at some time during the life cycle. They intensify their threats

and attack with increasing frequency as the population around them grows denser. As a result the behavior itself induces members of the population to spread out in space, raises the death rate, and lowers the birth rate. In such cases aggression is said to be a "density-dependent factor" in controlling population growth. As it gradually increases in intensity, it operates like a tightening valve to slow and finally shut off the increase in numbers. Other species, in contrast, seldom or never run short of the basic necessities of life. Their numbers are reduced instead by the density-dependent effects of predators, parasites, or emigration. Such animals are typically pacific toward each other, because they rarely grow numerous enough for aggressive behavior to be of any use to individuals. And if aggression confers no advantage, it is unlikely to be encoded through natural selection into the innate behavioral repertory of the species. . . .

6   Although markedly predisposed to aggressiveness, we are far from being the most violent animal. Recent studies of hyenas, lions, and langur monkeys, to take three familiar species, have disclosed that individuals engage in lethal fighting, infanticide, and even cannibalism at a rate far above that found in human societies. When a count is made of the number of murders committed per thousand individuals per year, human beings are well down on the list of violently aggressive creatures, and I am confident that this would still be the case even if our episodic wars were to be averaged in. Hyena packs even clash in deadly pitched battles that are virtually indistinguishable from primitive human warfare. . . . I suspect that if hamadryas baboons had nuclear weapons, they would destroy the world in a week. And alongside ants, which conduct assassinations, skirmishes, and pitched battles as routine business, men are all but tranquilized pacifists. For those who wish to confirm this statement directly, ant wars are very easy to observe in most towns and cities in the eastern United States. One simply looks for masses of small blackish brown ants struggling together on sidewalks or lawns. The combatants are members of rival colonies of the common pavement ant, *Tetramorium caespitum*. Thousands of individuals may be involved, and the battlefield typically occupies several square feet of the grassroots jungle.

7   Finally, the more violent forms of human aggression are not the manifestations of inborn drives that periodically break through dams of inhibition. The "drive-discharge" model created by Freud and Lorenz has been replaced by a more subtle explanation based on the interaction of genetic potential and learning. . . .

8   The clear perception of human aggressive behavior as a structured, predictable pattern of interaction between genes and environment is consistent with evolutionary theory. It should satisfy both camps in the

venerable nature-nurture controversy. On the one hand it is true that aggressive behavior, especially in its more dangerous forms of military action and criminal assault, is learned. But the learning is prepared . . . we are strongly predisposed to slide into deep, irrational hostility under certain definable conditions. With dangerous ease hostility feeds on itself and ignites runaway reactions that can swiftly progress to alienation and violence. Aggression does not resemble a fluid that continuously builds pressure against the walls of its containers, nor is it like a set of active ingredients poured into an empty vessel. It is more accurately compared to a preexisting mix of chemicals ready to be transformed by specific catalysts that are added, heated, and stirred at some later time.

The products of this neural chemistry are aggressive responses that 9 are distinctively human. Suppose that we could enumerate all of the possible kinds of actions in all species. In this imaginary example, there might be exactly twenty-three such responses, which could be labeled A through W. Human beings do not and cannot manifest every behavior; perhaps all of the societies in the world taken together employ A through P. Furthermore, they do not develop each of the options with equal facility; there is a strong tendency under all existing conditions of child rearing for behaviors A through G to appear, and consequently H through P are encountered in very few cultures. It is the *pattern* of such probabilities that is inherited. We say that for each environment there is a corresponding probability distribution of responses. To make the statistical characterization entirely meaningful, we must then go on to compare human beings with other species. We note that rhesus monkeys can perhaps develop only aggressive behaviors F through J, with a strong bias toward F and G, while one kind of termite can show only A and another kind of termite only B. Which behavior particular human beings display depends on what they experience within their own culture, but the total array of human possibilities, like the monkey array or termite array, is inherited. It is the evolution of each pattern that sociobiologists attempt to analyze.

Territoriality is one of the variants of aggressive behavior that can be 10 directly evaluated by the new insights of biology. Students of animal behavior define a territory as an area occupied more or less exclusively either directly by overt defense or indirectly through advertisement. This area invariably contains a scarce resource, usually a steady food supply, shelter, space for sexual display, or a site for laying eggs. Often the limitation on the availability of the resource to competing individuals secondarily affects population growth to the extent of also serving as a density-dependent factor, so that territorial defense intervenes as a buffering device against long-term changes in the environment. In other words, territoriality prevents the population from either exploding or crashing. Close studies by zoologists of the daily schedules, feeding behavior, and energy expenditures of individual animals have revealed that territorial behavior evolves in animal species only when the vital resource is *economically defensible*: the energy saved and the increase in survival and reproduction due to territorial defense outweigh the energy expended and the risk of injury and death. The researchers have been able to go further in some instances to prove that in the case of food territories the size of the defended area is at or just above the size required to yield enough food to keep the resident healthy and able to reproduce. Finally, territories contain an "invincible center." The resident animal defends the territory far more vigorously than intruders attempt to usurp it, and as a result the defender usually wins. In a special sense, it has the "moral advantage" over trespassers. . . .

11   The biological formula of territorialism translates easily into the rituals of modern property ownership. When described by means of generalizations clear of emotion and fictive embellishment this behavior acquires new flavor—at once intimacy familiar, because our own daily lives are controlled by it, and yet distinctive and even very peculiar, because it is after all a diagnostic trait of just one mammalian species. Each culture develops its own particular rules to safeguard personal property and space. . . .

12   The particular forms of organized violence are not inherited. No genes differentiate the practice of platform torture from pole and stake torture, headhunting from cannibalism, the duel of champions from genocide. Instead there is an innate predisposition to manufacture the cultural apparatus of aggression, in a way that separates the conscious mind from the raw biological processes that the genes encode. Culture gives a particular form to the aggression and sanctifies the uniformity of its practice by all members of the tribe.

13   The cultural evolution of aggression appears to be guided jointly by the following three forces: (1) genetic predisposition toward learning some form of communal aggression; (2) the necessities imposed by the environment in which the society finds itself; and (3) the previous history of the group, which biasses it toward the adoption of one cultural innovation as opposed to another. To return to the more general metaphor used in developmental biology, the society undergoing cultural evolution can be said to be moving down the slope of a very long developmental landscape. The channels of formalized aggression are deep; culture is likely to turn into one or the other but not to avoid them completely. These channels are shaped by interaction between the genetic predisposition to learn aggressive responses and the physical properties of the home range that favor particular forms of the re-

sponses. Society is influenced to take a particular direction by idiosyncratic features of its preexisting culture.

Thus the Mundurucu populations were apparently limited by   14
scarcity of high-grade protein, and they perfected headhunting as the
convention by which competition was diminished on the hunting
grounds. The Yanomamo of southern Venezuela and northern Brazil, in
contrast, are temporarily in the midst of rapid population growth and
range expansion. Reproduction by the men is limited not by food but
by the availability of women. A principle of animal sociobiology, still
only partly tested, is that in times of plenty and in the absence of effective predators females tend to become a density-dependent factor limiting population growth. As Napoleon Chagnon has shown, the
Yanomamo conduct their wars over women and in order to revenge
deaths that ultimately trace back to competition for women. This is not
a casual or frivolous preoccupation. They have been aptly called the
"fierce people." One village studied by Chagnon was raided twenty-five times in nineteen months by neighboring villages. One quarter of
all Yanomamo men die in battle, but the surviving warriors are often
wildly successful in the game of reproduction. The founder of one bloc
of villages had forty-five children by eight wives. His sons were also
prolific, so that approximately 75 percent of all of the sizable population
in the village bloc were his descendants.

It is obvious that the specific conventions of aggression—for example   15
ambush as opposed to open warfare, and ornamental stone axes as opposed to bamboo spears—are heavily influenced by the materials at
hand and the bits and pieces of past custom that can be conveniently
adapted. In Claude Lévi-Strauss's nice expression, culture uses the *bricologe* available to it. What is less obvious is the process that predisposes
people to fabricate aggressive cultures. Only by considering the determinants of aggression at the three levels—the ultimate, biological predisposition; the requirements of the present environment; and the
accidental details that contribute to cultural drift—can we fully comprehend its evolution in human societies.

Although the evidence suggests that the biological nature of hu-   16
mankind launched the evolution of organized aggression and roughly
directed its early history across many societies, the eventual outcome of
that evolution will be determined by cultural processes brought increasingly under the control of rational thought. The practice of war is
a straightforward example of a hypertrophied biological predisposition.
Primitive men cleaved their universe into friends and enemies and responded with quick, deep emotion to even the mildest threats emanating from outside the arbitrary boundary. With the rise of chiefdoms and
states, this tendency became institutionalized, war was adopted as an

instrument of policy of some of the new societies, and those that employed it best became—tragically—the most successful. The evolution of warfare was an autocatalytic reaction that could not be halted by any people, because to attempt to reverse the process unilaterally was to fall victim. A new mode of natural selection was operating at the level of entire societies. . . .

17   To recapitulate the total argument, human aggression cannot be explained as either a dark-angelic flaw or a bestial instinct. Nor is it the pathological symptom of upbringing in a cruel environment. Human beings are strongly predisposed to respond with unreasoning hatred to external threats and to escalate their hostility sufficiently to overwhelm the source of the threat by a respectably wide margin of safety. Our brains do appear to be programmed to the following extent: we are inclined to partition other people into friends and aliens, in the same sense that birds are inclined to learn territorial songs and to navigate by the polar constellations. We tend to fear deeply the actions of strangers and to solve conflict by aggression. These learning rules are most likely to have evolved during the past hundreds of thousands of years of human evolution and, thus, to have conferred a biological advantage on those who conformed to them with the greatest fidelity.

18   The learning rules of violent aggression are largely obsolete. We are no longer hunter-gatherers who settle disputes with spears, arrows, and stone axes. But to acknowledge the obsolescence of the rules is not to banish them. We can only work our way around them. To let them rest latent and unsummoned, we must consciously undertake those difficult and rarely travelled pathways in psychological development that lead to mastery over and reduction of the profound human tendency to learn violence. . . .

Making Sense of Sex

DAVID P. BARASH AND JUDITH EVE LIPTON

The fundamental principle of sociobiology (also sometimes called *evolutionary psychology*) is that living things will act so as to maximize their fitness: their success in projecting copies of their genes into the future. This does not imply conscious awareness of such goals, any more than a tree, for example, is aware that by flowering in the spring, it produces seeds that will germinate in the most favorable season. When it comes to violence, a significant sociobiological insight concerns male-female differences: In many species—including human beings—males are significantly more aggressive and violent than females. Please note, incidentally, that this distinction says nothing about male violence being "good" or "inevitable" any more than the fact that tuberculosis is "natural" means that it is good or inevitable.

A benefit of editing an anthology is the opportunity to include one's own writing. The following selection, from a book written by David P. Barash and psychiatrist Judith Eve Lipton, was intended for the general public. At the same time, it conveys some basic principles underlying the sociobiology of sex-specific violence, a provocative approach that has demonstrated considerable explanatory power.

Ultimately, it is the type of gamete—egg or sperm—an individual produces, rather than penis or vagina, breast or beard, color or costume, that determines the difference between maleness and femaleness. Herein lies the crucial difference between bulls and cows, stallions and mares, men and women. Eggs, which are large and relatively few in number, are produced only by females, whereas sperm, which are small and abundant, are produced only by males. . . . The size difference between eggs and sperm can be staggering, in fact, with some animals making eggs 100,000 times bigger than their sperm. Even in humans, eggs weigh 85,000 times as much as sperm. . . . Overall, males have little to do with the actual business of reproduction, beyond producing sperm packaged in seminal fluid. In contrast, all female mammals invest enormous resources in their offspring after fertilization occurs. They not only build a placenta and nourish the developing fetus but also nurse their young after birth. Admittedly, many women today do not breast-feed their children, but most human tendencies were established thousands of generations ago, long before modern technology and current cultural whims.

The notion that differences in parental investment, with females producing costly, nutrient-rich eggs and males producing cheap, near-naked sperm, account for behavioral differences between males and females was first articulated twenty years ago by Robert Trivers, a young evolutionary biologist then at Harvard University. He postulated that sexual competition is a replay of fertilization itself, in which numerous males, like small, hyperactive sperm, compete among themselves for access to females. Success crowns those who are pushy enough to outcompete their rivals yet have enough wanderlust to keep moving, searching for new conquests. But unlike fertilization, in which (as far as we know) the egg passively receives suitors, females are usually too invested in their potential offspring to mate with the first male that happens along.

3   *Roving Inseminators.*   As Trivers described it, the sex—in most cases, the female—that invests more in offspring becomes a limited resource, something for which the sex that invests less—usually, the male—must compete. Thus, in evolutionary terms, it behooves males, which can produce millions of sperm with relatively little effort, to mate with as many females as possible. But females, which produce far fewer offspring, benefit most by being selective—that is, by choosing mates that are healthy, strong, smart, wealthy, and so on. . . .

4   These different reproductive strategies—and the theory of parental investment that enables us to understand them—go a long way toward explaining male-female differences. Time and again, patterns of social and sexual behavior among animals have been found to correspond to the patterns predicted on the basis of differences in parental investment.

5   *Harem Masters.*   Consider elephant seals, well known for their gargantuan males, which at 6,000 pounds weigh four times as much as the average adult female. As is typical of species with striking sexual dimorphism, elephant seals form harems, in which a cluster of females mates exclusively with a dominant male. Parental investment on the part of the female is extremely high (an adult female weighing about 1,500 pounds typically gives birth to a 110-pound pup, which may then gain another 220 pounds from its mother's milk), and she is nearly always mated by a harem master.

6   As might be expected, the male elephant seal invests virtually none of his immense bulk in offspring. Instead, he throws his weight around in other ways, trying to inseminate as many females as possible. A successful bull elephant seal may have forty mates, each of which will probably bear one pup per season. But because the sex ratio is one to one, for every harem master there will be thirty-nine disappointed bachelors. Although a few males will be immensely successful, producing some forty pups per season, most will be reproductive failures, living their lives on the sidelines, with no mating prospects. In short, males operate within a system that is inherently unequal, divided between reproductive haves and have-nots. Because the stakes are so high, competition among males during mating season is intensely physical, often expressing itself in violent clashes that result in serious, though rarely fatal, head and chest wounds.

7   From a strictly biological point of view, human males are much like bull elephant seals and many other male mammals: they are larger and more aggressive than females, become sexually mature later, and have higher mortality rates. Such traits exist because of the evolutionary advantage they confer on their owners: larger size and heightened aggressiveness are likely to win more mates, by brute force, if nothing else,

and thus to produce larger numbers of surviving children. And delayed maturation enables males to avoid violent competition when they are too small, too inexperienced, too weak—that is, too young—to prevail. In humans, this particular sex difference is immediately apparent in any seventh-, eighth-, or ninth-grade classroom, where the more mature girls tower over boys who suddenly—if temporarily—seem several years younger than their classmates. . . .

When biologists see certain characteristics in other species—larger male size, greater aggressiveness, delayed maturation, and shorter life span—they know the males must be competing for access to females. Combined with the overwhelming cross-cultural data on *Homo sapiens*, we can safely conclude that in our history, human beings were polygynous. Even so, as with elephant seals, few men had what it took to become harem masters, so most had to settle for either monogamy or celibacy. But the end result was the same: men competed among themselves—as they do today—for women. When it comes to the biological whisperings within, humans still tend toward polygyny. And with polygyny comes competition. **8**

Fighting for Females. How much competition at the physiological level takes place in other species remains largely unknown. Biologists do know, however, that in most species males compete intensely for the sexual attention of females. In fact, as long ago as 1871, Charles Darwin introduced the concept of "sexual selection" to explain why males tend to be relatively large, conspicuous in color and behavior, and endowed with intimidating weapons (tusks, fangs, claws, antlers) and a willingness to employ them in their efforts to gain access to females. **9**

Darwin's idea—upheld today—is that sexual selection, which is a subset of natural selection, favors any attribute that enhances an individual's chances of reproduction. Traits such as a peacock's tail or a buck's antlers will be favored by sexual selection if the mating advantage they confer outweighs their survival disadvantage. The peacock's tail may become tangled in shrubbery and may draw the attention of predators, but if it charms the peahen—and it does—then on balance it will be favored by evolution. The same goes for weaponry in the form of tusks and other hefty adornments. Imagine the energetic costs to a male moose, which carries upward of 50 pounds of antlers on his head, or to a bull elephant, whose two tusks may have a combined weight of 200 pounds! **10**

But tusks, antlers, horns, and the like enable their bearers to outbattle lesser-adorned competitors, and with victory come more opportunities for reproduction. And large-tuskers beget more large-tuskers, and so on. Thus, over time, sexual selection has led to a remarkable preponderance of extraneous accoutrements among males, including **11** wattles, ruffs, collars, crests, iridescent patches of feathers, horny ex-crescences, bony shields, elaborate antlers, raspy noise makers, perfumed plumes, and an equally outlandish behavioral repertoire designed to defeat other males and attract females.

12   Such adornments would have little effect on reproduction, however, if their male bearers lacked behaviors to match or if they failed to evoke a response from females. Thus, sexual selection has two behavioral components: first, competition among members of the same sex for access to mates, and second the exercise of choice when members of the more desired sex choose mates from a competitive pool of suitors. Because of the male-female differences in parental investment, competition becomes predominantly a male activity and choice becomes a female prerogative, with fussy egg makers discriminating among pushy competing sperm makers.

13   Competition among males may be fierce, notably so in polygynous species such as elk, moose, elephant seals, and gorillas, for which being male means ending up either a harem master or an evolutionary failure. Not surprisingly, with such intense pressure, selection favors males that grow up to be large, tough, and well armed: unpleasant bullies, as befits a winner-take-all lifestyle. . . .

14   In most cases, noncompetitiveness among males results in reproductive failure. In the famous children's story of Ferdinand the Bull, this physically impressive creature preferred smelling flowers to fighting other bulls. But few Ferdinands occur in real life because such individuals would be less likely to promote themselves or, more to the point, project their peace-loving, flower-sniffing genes into the future. Regardless of his testes, if Ferdinand has no heart for male–male competition, his sperm—and thus his preference for flowers over fighting—will probably be replaced by that of his less docile rivals. . . .

Role Reversals

15   As with almost every facet of the living world, there are exceptions to the rule; in some animal species, the typical pattern of male-female differences is reversed, so that females are the pursuers and males the pursued. It is very revealing that in these species the usual pattern of parental investment is also reversed. For example, among pipefishes (close relatives of sea horses) males are smaller, less brightly colored, and more sexually coy than females, which are brightly adorned, physically aggressive, and sexually pushy. Although male pipefishes are clearly male (they make sperm, not eggs), they are uncannily like female mammals in their reproductive behavior: they nourish their offspring internally through a placentalike structure and eventually "give

birth," with abdominal contractions reminiscent of a female in labor. Among pipefishes, the *males* provide the bulk of parental investment and display what might be called "feminine" traits, whereas the *females* compete among themselves for the males and might be called "macho."

Traditional sexual roles are also reversed among several species of South American birds known as jacanas. Female jacanas act like harem masters: they maintain large territories within which are several males, each with his own nest. The dominant female mates with all her males, lays eggs in their nests, and then leaves them with child-rearing duties. Each dutiful jacana "husband" incubates his egg clutch and provisions his young after they hatch. Not surprisingly, female jacanas are remarkably malelike, being larger than their mates, brightly colored, and sexually aggressive. . . . Until a decade or two ago, it appeared that no other animal, apart from humans, killed members of its own species. But long-term field studies in animal behavior have since dispelled this myth. Chimpanzees kill others of their own kind, as do wolves, lions, elk, and bison. In fact, nearly every mammal species that has been carefully studied has sooner or later revealed a penchant for lethal violence. Biologists also know that when such events occur, the perpetrators are almost always male. **16**

Among human beings, biology has set the stage not only for the fabled "battle of the sexes" but also for battles *within* the sexes, especially those pitting males against males. As with other animals, violence among humans is by and large something men direct toward other men; they are disproportionately both the perpetrators and the victims. **17**

Men, in fact, are so much more violent and deadly than women that the difference is taken for granted. On hearing the term *suicide bomber* or *serial killer*, most people automatically—and correctly—assume that the individual in question is male. Across the board, the human "killing establishment"—soldiers, executioners, hunters, violent gangs, even slaughterhouse operators—is overwhelmingly male. From rampages in post offices and the infamous California schoolyard massacre to unprovoked, deadly shootings in a Texas restaurant, the Long Island Rail Road, and the Empire State Building, men—not women—are the mass murderers. Nor is this imbalance limited to the United States. When killings take place, whether in Bosnia, Rwanda, Cambodia, El Salvador, or Israel, the culprits are nearly always men. . . . Violence may or may not be as American as cherry pie, but it is certainly a male proclivity. It would not be realistic to romanticize or idealize women or to deny that they too can sometimes be violent and deadly, but when it comes to brutal behavior, the two sexes simply are not in the same league. Why? **18**

Before answering this question, we must emphatically state that by looking to evolution to explain the violence and conflict that rocks our **19** society, we are in no way attempting to justify or legitimize such behavior. On the contrary, we hope that by bringing to the fore the evolutionary logic that is inherent in human conflict worldwide, that we may help bring about a better understanding of our species and so ultimately *reduce* the toll of human violence. To deny the connection, we think, is akin to putting one's head in the sand. The reality is that all social animals—whether parrots, peacocks, or people—engage in conflict. Add sex differences to the equation and the stage is set for even more trouble. . . .

20   The difference in reproductive strategies between males and females—with males varying greatly in the number of offspring they produce and females varying not much at all—holds the key to patterns of violence. In a nutshell, males must compete for access to females either through song, coloration, or display or by engaging in direct battle with their competitors, and thus evolution has strongly favored aggression over timidity. . . .

21   Among monogamous nonhuman species, such as geese, eagles, foxes, gibbons, and most songbirds, males and females produce nearly equal numbers of offspring and also are nearly equal in physical size and aggressiveness. Among polygynous species, however, the bigger and nastier a male is, the more likely he will be to fend off his competitors successfully and win the mating game. Accordingly, it is the James Bonds and the Rambos, not their more pacific brothers, whose genes are projected into the future, thus giving rise to succeeding generations that are likely to be, if anything, more violent.

22   When does this arms race stop? Only when the overall disadvantages of such behavior exceed its evolutionary benefits. At some point, highly aggressive individuals either run too great a risk of injury or death or lose out in other ways. For example, among some birds, males occasionally spend so much time singing, posturing, threatening, and fighting with their male neighbors that they neglect their own offspring. Overall, however, natural selection smiles on behavior—any behavior—that contributes to reproductive success. For males, that smile has been especially broad and toothsome when it comes to aggressiveness.

23   This link between gender and aggression is clearly seen in the strange case of the blue-headed wrasse, a polygynous species of coral reef fish. Breeding groups consist of a relatively large male associated with a bevy of females. But there are no bachelor males skulking resentfully in the coral crevices, as there are, for example, unsuccessful harem master wannabes among elephant seals. Instead, blue-headed wrasse populations start off as all female. On maturity, the largest and most aggressive individuals become male—in this species, sex is not determined by the X or Y chromosome but by hormonal changes triggered by behavioral events. Remove the male from a breeding group and the largest, most

aggressive female will stop producing eggs and turn into a sperm-producing male. Within a week, egg-making ovaries become sperm-making testes, and the newly transformed male mates with his bevy of females. For our purposes, this bizarre example of transsexualism demonstrates, almost diagramatically, the essence of the relationship between maleness, aggressiveness, and biology. A blueheaded wrasse is biologically rewarded for being male *if* it is large enough and tough enough to dominate the others. Otherwise, it remains meek and female. . . .

Why has evolution favored such a distinct gender gap? Simply put, males succeed reproductively at the expense of fellow males, whereas a female's reproductive success is unlikely to be enhanced by knocking fellow females out of the way. If anything, females with a penchant for ferocity are more likely to suffer injury with little or no reproductive gain to show for their efforts.   24

On occasion, of course, females can be violently competitive. Dominant female African hunting dogs may kill the offspring of lower-ranking females; female red howler monkeys push around other females; and female groove-billed anis (ravenlike tropical birds) sometimes evict rivals' eggs from their communal nest. Female-female competition is undoubtedly more widespread than many people realize, but in almost all cases it is less direct, less boisterous, and certainly less violent than its male-male counterpart. . . . If violent behavior reflected the vagaries of culture, we would expect female-initiated violence to be as frequent and intense as its male counterpart; it assuredly is not. The evidence is overwhelming that men and women are fundamentally, biologically different.   25

Studies of prosecution and imprisonment records in Europe going back several centuries, as well as examinations of modern crime statistics from the United States and around the world, show that men consistently outstrip women when it comes to violent crime by a ratio of at least three or four to one. The same applies to crimes against property. Men (especially those who are impoverished) are far more likely than women to rob their victims face to face, in a manner reminiscent of dominant-subordinate upmanship. The only areas in which women commit more crimes than men are prostitution (which some say is not a criminal activity but an act between consenting adults) and shoplifting, which is nonconfrontational.   26

When women are aggressive, their behavior tends to be defensive, as when a woman kills a man who abuses her or her children or when she "fights" to have her child's murderer condemned to death. Among animals, a mother bear with cubs, for example, is notoriously fierce, as are other females when defending their young. Thus, women's aggression tends to be reactive, whereas that of men tends to be truly "offensive." . . .   27

28   To make matters worse, males are to some extent caught in a vicious circle: their penchant for violence makes them vulnerable to get more violence. Thus the male proclivity for risk taking and competition often results in accidents, fights, and drug and alcohol binges. Yet when a person's brain is injured, as by physical damage or the effects of drugs or alcohol, his or her behavior becomes less thoughtful and more violent. There even exists a term, *dementia pugilistica*, that refers to brain damage from repeated blows to the head. Ironically, then, not only are males more aggressive than females, but their aggressiveness also makes them more likely to sustain brain injury, which in turn further increases their chances of resorting to violence.

29   Although the precise mechanism remains obscure, men are more known to be vulnerable than women to mental illnesses that produce violence. For example, adolescent boys suffer more than do adolescent girls from what is descriptively labeled "oppositional defiant disorder" as well as "general conduct disorder." And in a wide range of impulse control disorders, including intermittent explosive disorder, pathological gambling, and pyromania, males greatly outnumber females. It is noteworthy that men who lack impulse control are likely to be violent, whereas women tend toward kleptomania or trichotillomania—that is, they shoplift or pull out their hair. . . .

30   After reviewing murder records over a wide historical range and from around the world, psychology professors Martin Daly and Margo Wilson of McMaster University in Ontario, Canada, concluded "There is no known human society in which the level of lethal violence among women even begins to approach that among men." More specifically, they found that a man is about twenty times more likely to be killed by another man than a woman is by another woman. This finding holds true for societies as different from one another as modern-day urban America (Philadelphia, Detroit, and Chicago), rural Brazil, and traditional villages in India, Zaire (now the Democratic Republic of Congo), and Uganda. This is not to say that murder rates are equivalent in these places. In modern Iceland, for example, 0.5 homicides occur per 1 million people per year, whereas in most of Europe the figure rises to 10 murders per million per year, and in the United States it soars to more than 100. In all cases, however, male-male homicide exceeds its female-female counterpart by a whopping margin. The fact that the pattern of violence remains remarkably consistent from place to place and parallels male-male competition seen in other species argues forcefully for its biological underpinnings.

31   During 1995 in the United States, for example, 3,329 men were convicted of murder, compared with 226 women. What's more, the victims

were predominantly men: 3,051 men versus 508 women, numbers that clearly show men's tendency to kill other men. Moreover, around the world and throughout history, the age of most male murderers (that is to say, most murderers) has remained remarkably constant, in the early twenties. Put another way, those most likely to kill are men at their physical peak who are trying to establish themselves socially and reproductively. Today's proliferation of guns has changed these statistics, but not dramatically. In the United States, for example, the age group with the highest arrest rate for murder is currently those from eighteen to twenty-two. . . .

Violence at the Bottom

Male-male competition doesn't always afflict the winners. Men can be   32
as ferocious when trying to avoid the bottom of the sociosexual hierarchy as when trying to rise to the top. In fact, battles at the lower end of the competitive ladder are often more vicious than those among the elite. This is probably because men at the bottom have little to lose and thus are drawn to no-holds-barred fighting, a last-ditch bravado involving risky and deadly tactics.

Data gathered in the United States confirm this notion of violence at   33
the bottom. Across the board, killers are more likely to be unmarried, unemployed, less educated, and of lower socioeconomic status than nonkillers. In addition, young men, especially those from disadvantaged social and ethnic groups, are overrepresented when it comes to drug addiction, violent crime, absentee fatherhood, and the like.

The proliferation of violent gangs speaks to the desperation of the   34
have-nots. A young man must prove he is tough enough to fight his rivals and willing to defend his gang at all times. Thus, gang members engage in an endless series of offensive attacks and retaliation, battling those who wrong them or get in their way. It is not unusual in some inner-city neighborhoods to see guns brandished from car windows as gang members career through the streets displaying their bravado and willingness to fight. . . .

Another aspect of male violence is the ease with which it is triggered.   35
After interviewing convicted killers in Philadelphia, sociologist Marvin Wolfgang identified twelve categories of motive. Far and away the largest, accounting for fully 37 percent of all murders, was what he designated "altercation of relatively trivial origin; insult, curse, jostling, etc." In such cases, people got into an argument over something as unimportant as a sports game, who paid for a drink, an offhand remark, or a casual insult. . . .

36   To die over something so inconsequential as a casual comment or a dispute about some distant event or ill-chosen word seems the height of irony and caprice. But in a sense, disputes of this sort are not trivial, for they reflect our evolutionary past, when personal altercations were the stuff on which prestige and social success (and ultimately biological success) were based. In this context, it is very upsetting to be "dissed." Thus, it is not surprising that young men today fight and die over who said what to whom, whose prestige has been challenged, or whose clothing is offensive. . . .

Explanations Are Not Excuses

37   It is one thing to understand the male penchant for violence and entirely another thing to condone it. We consider violence to be the greatest problem confronting our species, whether it is directed toward women, men, children, larger social groups, or the natural environment. We do not believe that because violence comes more naturally to men than to women it is somehow pardonable, as if the fault lay entirely with evolution. It would be terribly perverse to use the material presented here to justify men's violence or to diminish its horror in any way. As Katherine Hepburn remarks sternly to Humphrey Bogart in the movie *The African Queen,* "Nature . . . is something we are put on earth to rise above."

38   At the same time, it serves no purpose to ignore the important sex differences that exist in aggressiveness and violence or to claim that these differences arise exclusively from faulty upbringing and ill-conceived social norms, although, to be sure, upbringing and experiences can exacerbate tendencies to which humans are already predisposed. When it comes to violent crime, social factors such as rage, retaliation, lack of positive role models, broken families, economic victimization, social despair, and outright ethnic and racial bigotry are undeniable. But evolution suggests that such factors only increase the likelihood that biological factors—*present in all people*—will be activated. No useful purpose is served by denying the existence of unpleasant things or sweeping them under the rug. (As linguist Deborah Tannen has suggested, this only makes for a lumpy rug.) Instead, let us employ biology's insights to make sense of why sperm makers are so prone to be troublemakers. On a more positive note, these findings may speak to the possible effect of enhanced socioeconomic opportunities for those—especially men—who are most excluded, disenfranchised, and alienated.

39   To some extent, it may be that violence, like poverty and disease, will always be with us. If such is the case, we have all the more reason to understand it.

An Overview of Biological Influences on Violent Behavior

KLAUS A. MICZEK, ALLAN F. MIRSKY, GREGORY CAREY, JOSEPH DEBOLD, AND ADRIAN RAINE

Biologists recognize two complementary ways of asking questions about behavior: ultimate or *why* questions, and proximate or *how* questions. Thus far, we have considered violence from the perspective of the former. To ask *why* an individual is violent is, essentially, to ask about the evolutionary, adaptive significance of the behavior in question. This leaves *proximate causation*—namely, the immediate mechanisms responsible for causing violence. For example, it may be adaptive—favored by natural selection—for males in certain situations to be especially violent, or for individuals to defend territories when resources are scarce, but this does not explain *how* such behavior is brought about. At the level of biological explanation, we are led, therefore, to brain mechanisms, hormones and other neurochemicals, and genetic factors. Insights from these, although substantial and promising, are also surprisingly incomplete, and have a checkered past.

For example, evidence of direct genetic influences on human behavior in general—and on violence in particular—is remarkably scarce. Some time ago, it was reported that men with a genetic XYY anomaly (so-called "supermales") were overrepresented among convicted criminals. Afterward, it was discovered that such individuals are also somewhat lower in intelligence, more likely to be confused about their sexual identity, as well as taller than average . . . any of which factors *might* predispose toward crime or a greater tendency to be apprehended afterward. It is an important cautionary tale, especially when combined with the ever-present danger that genetic factors predisposing to violence—if identified—will be used in support of social discrimination.

On the other hand, given the clear association of genetic factors with certain mental illnesses such as paranoid schizophrenia, which are in turn correlated with violence, it seems probable that genes and violence are also connected, albeit in a complex and roundabout manner. Genes "for" violence may never be identified; more likely are genetic "risk factors," analogous to risk factors for diseases such as cancer, which don't cause the outcome in a direct, deterministic manner but presumably interact with environmental conditions, influencing thresholds for irritability, perhaps, or for levels of behavioral inhibition. There is much to be learned in this regard, and just as it is important to avoid misuse and abuse of such concepts, it is also important to keep an open mind.

Similarly, there can be no doubt that the brain controls behavior. Certain brain regions have been shown to be especially involved with certain types of motor control, just as other brain regions are especially involved with certain types of sensory perception. This finding leads to the question of whether violent behavior is associated with abnormal activity in brain regions controlling such actions. Such speculation was given a boost, in the nineteenth century, when an American named Nicholas Gage suffered a severe injury to part of his brain (the prefrontal cortex), after which, although he survived and recovered physically, Mr. Gage's personality was dramatically changed: He became irresponsible and prone to sudden outbursts of verbal and even physical violence. In the twentieth century, brain regions were identified in animals, which, when subjected to electrical stimulation via surgically implanted electrodes, evoked so-called "sham rage" and apparently genuine attacks. Comparable regions have not been reliably identified in human beings. Nonetheless, this lack of evidence has not prevented ill-conceived efforts at psychosurgery in the hope of curing excessive violence.

The next selection is the introductory overview chapter of a major volume commissioned by the National Research Council concerned with "biobehavioral influences" on violence. It provides a basic introduction to a very complex and detailed literature, with particular emphasis on chemical factors.

1   Even the most complex social environmental influences on an individual's propensity to engage in violent behavior may eventually be traced to their biologic bases. In order to sketch such an interactive model, it is useful to begin with a consideration of the genetic influences on violent behavior as studied in animals as well as humans. Steroid and peptide hormones as well as peptides and biogenic amines are critically important in the neural and physiologic mechanisms initiating, executing, and coping with violent behavior. It is here that important endocrine and pharmacologic interventions are targeted. These neurochemical systems mediating violent behavior are specific to discrete neuroanatomic networks. Indirect measures of neural mechanisms of violent behavior may be obtained via neuroimaging and functional neuropsychologic assessments.

Genetic Mechanisms

2   Behavioral genetic research has shown that genes influence individual differences in a wide range of human behaviors—cognition, academic achievement, personality and temperament (including such traits as aggression and hostility), psychopathology, and even vocational interests and social attitudes. Hence, a research finding that criminal or violent behavior had some heritable component would come as no surprise— especially since violent and criminal behaviors are themselves correlated with some of the other behaviors for which genetic relationships

have been established. Beyond confirming the existence of heritability in violent behavior, the more interesting intellectual challenges are

1. isolating the precise nature of the mechanisms through which an individual's propensity to engage in or refrain from violent behavior may be inherited;
2. using quantitative methodology to control for heritable influences so that conclusions about environmental influences on violent behavior can be clarified; and
3. quantifying the genetic effect in terms of its importance or triviality in explaining human behavior and the magnitude of its correlation with risk factors for violence.

On the first challenge, quantitative genetic studies have not isolated any simple genetic syndrome, either Mendelian or chromosomal, that is invariably associated with violence or, more broadly, with antisocial behavior. Like inherited propensities for other behaviors, a genetic liability toward violence is likely to involve many genes and substantial environmental variation. The existence of such mechanisms may well be confirmed by future quantitative genetic research, but knowledge of their precise nature must await progress in detecting genes—and markers linked to them—that account for small variations in behavior, a problem in molecular biology that lies beyond the scope of this paper.

The second challenge suggests a more promising line of research than the reiteration of long-standing, sterile "nature versus nurture" debates—that genetic research designs may clarify environmental effects. This can best be illustrated by a hypothetical example. Suppose that a propensity toward violent behavior is transmitted from parent to offspring by two mechanisms: one operating through the genes and the other through social learning. How can these two mechanisms be detected and quantified in a study of intact nuclear families? If the parent-offspring correlation is interpreted solely in terms of social learning, then the environmental transmission will be overestimated. On the other hand, if the correlation is interpreted solely in terms of genetic transmission, then the social learning of aggression will be overlooked. Twin studies, studies of adoptive parent-offspring pairs, and studies of the biologic parents of adoptees are required to untangle the joint effects of genetic and family environmental transmission. Although such designs are becoming routine in the study of cognitive development, they are rare in the study of violent behavior.

The third challenge aims at determining whether a genetic propensity to violence is substantial or trivial and the extent to which it is correlated with other behaviors. Does the genetic influence on intelligence and on alcohol abuse explain genetic liability toward aggression?

Studies of Humans

6   Studies of the inheritance of violent behavior in humans rely on adoption or twin designs to tease apart the effects of shared family environment from those of shared genes. The adoption design capitalizes on the fact that an adoptee does not receive environmental transmission from a biological parent or genetic transmission from an adoptive parent. Similarly, adoptive siblings share environments but not genes, whereas biological siblings raised apart share genes but not environments. Twin studies rely on the fact that identical twins have all genes in common, whereas fraternal pairs share on average only half their genes (plus a small effect from assortative mating). In both kinds of studies, heritability coefficients—the proportion of observed variation due to genetic variation—may be calculated. As with all human behaviors, the interpretation of these coefficients may be confounded by several factors—selective placement in adoptions, and imitation and co-offending in twins. In addition, the study of violence presents problems of its own. Not only is the base rate for violence low, but it is also more poorly measured than most behaviors studied by behavior geneticists.

7   Despite methodologic weaknesses in the early twin studies, later twin and adoption research suggests important heritability for *adult* antisocial behavior with perhaps a smaller genetic influence on *juvenile* criminality. . . . Heritability estimates range from a low of about .20 to a high of almost .70 in Danish samples. Needless to say, such estimates cannot be easily extrapolated to other cultures.

8   In contrast to these data, the evidence for a genetic basis to *violent* offending is much weaker. Only three samples permit one to assess the role of genetics in violent offending, and two of the three produced nonsignificant results.

9   These findings suggest at most a weak role for heredity in violent behavior. But studies that use samples at high risk for violent behavior or that measure violent behavior through self-reports rather than arrest records may yet discover genetic relationships that have so far remained hidden—or underestimated—because arrests for violent offenses are rare in samples of the general population. One positive lead is the correlation between violence in biological parents and alcohol abuse in adopted-away sons. This suggests a genetic relationship between the two, an important link given the well-established correlation between alcohol and violent behavior as discussed below (see Miczek et al., Volume 3). Because many violent offenders also commit nonviolent offenses, heritability for criminality per se provides another possible link between genes and violence. Finally and perhaps most importantly, the gene-environment interaction reported for antisocial behavior may also extend to violence.

The principles of quantitative genetics raise strong cautions about the   10
extrapolation of empirical research findings on violence. First, evidence
for the heritability of individual differences *within* a population cannot
be used to explain average differences *between* populations or even
within the same population *over* time. It is unlikely that genetic differences could account for anything but a small fraction of the change in
violence over the twentieth century, differences in violent crimes among
nations, or variance in rates among certain subgroups within a nation.
Second, heritability cannot predict or explain an individual's culpabil-
ity in a particular violent event. Third, many estimates of heritability are
based on data from the Scandinavian countries, where the necessary
data are routinely collected in national registries. Because the environmental variance relevant to violence may not be the same in the Scandinavian countries and in the United States, for example, the heritability
estimates cannot be readily extrapolated.

Studies of Animals

A large number of strain comparisons and the successful establish-   11
ment of selected lines demonstrate significant heritability for rodent
aggression. . . .

   Although there is controversy over the extent to which the genetic   12
mechanisms are the same for male and female aggression in *Mus*, the
testing situation can change the rank order of selected lines—females
from high-aggression lines exhibit their agonistic behavior mostly in
sex-appropriate settings (e.g., postpartum tests). Similarly, studies of selected lines show that aggression may be modified by experience. Thus,
although agonistic behavior shows *some* developmental continuity and
cross-situational generality in inbred or selected strains, it is clearly not
a single genetic phenomenon that can be studied in isolation from specific contextual cues, social environment, and development.

   The recent trend in behavior genetic research is less toward demon-   13
strating the fact of the heritability of aggression and more on elucidat-
ing its genetic correlates and identifying genetic loci that underlie
agonistic behavior. Here, the Y chromosome may contribute to individual differences in male aggression in the mouse, at least in some strains.
There also appears to be genetic sensitivity to the effects of early neona-
tal androgens on aggression in mice.

Neurochemical Mechanisms

Endocrine Mechanisms and Violent Behavior

Steroids.   Research suggests that testosterone and its androgenic and es-   14
trogenic metabolites influence the probability of aggressive responding

to environmental events and stimuli through *organizational* as well as *activational* mechanisms. Organizational effects are traditionally those exerted, generally permanently, by a hormone during some sensitive period of development. This type of mechanism appears to explain sex differences in anatomy and some aspects of sex differences in behavior. For example, testosterone present during a particular period of fetal development in mammals induces the development of the male reproductive tract and genitalia. If androgen levels are low, as is normally the case in females, this development does not occur and female genitalia develop instead. A similar control for male aggression has been demonstrated in a number of laboratory animal species. For example, female mice given a single injection of testosterone at birth become much more sensitive to the aggression-enhancing effects of androgens as adults. Prenatal treatment of female rhesus monkeys with testosterone results in females that are male-like in their higher level of "rough and tumble" play as juveniles and more aggressive as adults. In humans, there is evidence for a similar, but reduced in magnitude, modulation of aggression by androgens. This research uses children that were accidentally exposed to inappropriate steroids during fetal development and assesses their behavior though observations, interviews, and psychologic assessments. In girls prenatally exposed to heightened levels of androgens, there is a trend for increased levels of aggression. In boys exposed to estrogens or antiandrogenic steroids during pregnancy, there is a trend for decreased aggressiveness. However, generally these steroids also have had some effect on genital development and the behavioral differences may be due to altered body image or to the affected children being treated differently by parents or peers. Interestingly, prenatal testosterone also alters the development of parts of the preoptic area of the brain. Preoptic area structure and neurochemistry are sexually dimorphic in animals and in humans, and this brain area is also thought to have a role in aggressive behavior. However, a direct link between the sexual dimorphism of the preoptic area and human violent behavior remains elusive.

15   In animals, testosterone (or its metabolites) has effects on the probability of aggressive response to conspecifics or other environmental events. This is frequently referred to as an activational effect although, mechanistically, androgens are not stimulating aggressive behavior *in vacuo*; more accurately, they appear to be altering the response to aggression-provoking stimuli. In laboratory animals, particularly rodents, there is research that demonstrates the brain sites involved in this action and the importance of the biochemical mechanisms by which testosterone can alter neural activity. The strength of the modulation that testosterone exerts on aggressive behavior seems to decrease in more

complex social animals. In nonhuman primates, the correlation between testosterone and aggressiveness or dominance frequently, but not in all studies, exists, but the activational effect of testosterone is more variable and harder to demonstrate. This trend is perhaps more exaggerated in humans. Positive correlations have been reported between androgen levels and aggressive or violent behavior in adolescent boys and in men, but these correlations are not high, they are sometimes difficult to replicate, and importantly, they do not demonstrate causation. In fact there is better evidence for the reverse relationship (behavior altering hormonal levels). Stress (e.g., from being subject to aggression or being defeated) decreases androgen levels, and winning—even in innocuous laboratory competitions—can increase testosterone.

The results of manipulating androgens with antiandrogen therapy in violent offenders are also mixed and difficult to interpret because of confounding influences on the data collection. Some critical reviews have concluded that antiandrogens show promise as an adjunct therapy for violent sex offenders. These may be relying more on the clearer relationship between testosterone and sexual motivation than between testosterone and violence. Another interesting approach will be to study the effects of anabolic steroids, but these studies have just begun and face very difficult methodologic problems. In general, most investigators conclude that there can be an influence of androgens on violence but that it is only one component accounting for a small amount of the variance. 16

Gonadal steroids have also been postulated to be involved in the increased irritability and hostility seen in some women with premenstrual syndrome (PMS). However, the endocrine evidence in support of this view is weak, and most recent papers find that individual differences in estrogens, progestins, and other hormones across the menstrual cycle do not explain the variability in intensity of PMS symptoms. 17

Adrenal steroids (glucocorticoids, such as cortisol and corticosterone) and the pituitary hormone ACTH (adrenocorticotropic hormone) have also been found to be related to aggressive behavior in animals. However, the strongest relationship is a negative one. Chronically increased levels of corticosteroids decrease aggressiveness, and ACTH increases submissiveness and avoidance of attack. These two effects are difficult to separate endocrinologically, but they appear to be mediated by different mechanisms. Correlations between dominance and corticosteroid levels in primates may more directly reflect variations in the ability to adapt to stress. 18

In summary, there is no simple relationship between steroids and aggression, much less violence. The strongest conclusion is that in humans, androgens can influence and be influenced by aggressive behavior. 19

However, they are only one of many influences and *not* the determining factor. The opposite relationship (i.e., the environment and behavior influencing hormone secretion) is the stronger of the two linkages.

20   *Other Hormones.*   Steroids are not the only hormones that have been related to aggression and violence, but other hormones appear to have less direct or less specific effects. For example, adrenal norepinephrine secretion has been related to the commission of violent crime, but norepinephrine and epinephrine are released in response to a wide variety of arousing or emotional conditions and are important in coping with stress. Animal and clinical studies have found evidence for a role of central nervous system (CNS) norepinephrine in aggressiveness—but when it acts as a neurotransmitter, not as a hormone. Because hormones can alter many aspects of cellular activity and because aggressive behavior involves so many areas of the brain, the potential for indirect or secondary effects of hormones is high.

21   In summary, there is no simple relationship between hormones and aggression, much less violence. The strongest conclusion is that in humans, steroids can influence and be influenced by aggressive behavior. However, they are only one influence of many and *not* the determining factor. The opposite relationship (i.e., the environment and behavior influence on hormone secretion) is the stronger of the two linkages.

Neurotransmitters and Receptors

22   *Dopamine.*   Evidence from animal studies points to large changes in brain dopamine systems during aggressive or defensive behavior. At present, evidence for similarly altered dopamine activity in brain regions of violent humans is not available. It is possible that brain dopamine systems are particularly significant in the rewarding aspects of violent and aggressive behavior. However, at present, a "marker" for some aspect of brain dopamine activity that is selective to a specific kind of aggression or violent behavior has not been identified in any of the accessible bodily fluids or via imaging methods in the brain.

23   The most frequently used treatment of violent outbursts in emergency situations and also in long-term medication of violence-prone individuals employs drugs that act principally at dopamine receptors. Particularly, drugs that antagonize the D2 subtype of dopamine receptors represent widely used antipsychotics with frequent application to violent patients. Evidence from animal and human studies emphasizes the many debilitating side effects of these drugs that render them problematic as treatment options, representing little more than a form of

"chemical restraint." Antipsychotic drugs that are antagonists at D2 dopamine receptors show a wide range of behavioral activities and, when used chronically, lead to various neurologic problems.

Cocaine and amphetamine activate behavior and engender euphoria   24
in all likelihood via action on brain dopamine receptors. The broad spectrum of behavioral and mood-elevating effects of these drugs may also include the aggression-enhancing effects that are seen in animals under certain conditions and that may be relevant to the occasional incidence of human violence after psychomotor stimulants. More important, however, are the psychopathic conditions that *precede* chronic amphetamine or cocaine use in predicting violent outbursts. Whether the paranoid psychosis due to amphetamine or cocaine use represents the causative condition for occasional violent behavior or the psychopathology preceding drug use is unclear at present. The relatively infrequent occurrences of violent activities in stimulant abusers appear to result from brain dopamine changes that are counteracted by treatment with antipsychotic drugs.

Norepinephrine.   Behavioral events involving intense affect are accompanied by adrenergic activity, in both the peripheral and the central nervous system. For several decades, the adrenergic contribution to the "flight-fight" syndrome in the form of increased sympathetic innervation as well as adrenal output has been well established. More recently, large changes in noradrenergic neurotransmitter activity in limbic, diencephalic, and mesencephalic regions, while preparing for, executing, and recovering from highly arousing activities—among them aggressive and violent behavior—have been documented. So far, in neither animal nor human studies have noradrenergic "markers" emerged that selectively identify the propensity to engage in an aggressive or violent act. Rather, noradrenergic activity, either measured in the form of metabolite levels in a bodily fluid or indirectly assessed in a sympathetically innervated end organ, is correlated with the level of general arousal, degree of behavioral exertion and activation, and either positive or negative affect, but not with a specific behavior or mood change such as a violent act.

The most significant development during the past dozen years in applying noradrenergic drugs in the management and treatment of retarded, schizophrenic, or autistic patients with a high rate of violent behavior is the use of beta-blockers primarily for their effects on the central nervous system rather than for their autonomic effects. Drugs that block adrenergic beta-receptors also act on certain subtypes of serotonin receptors, and their aggression-reducing effects may be derived from their action on these latter sites. Beta-blockers have not been compared in effectiveness and side effects, particularly during long-term treatment, with other therapeutic agents that reduce aggressive and violent activities.

27   Clonidine, an adrenergic drug that targets a specific alphareceptor subtype, has been used with success in managing withdrawal from alcohol, nicotine, and opiate addiction. Evidence from animal and human studies demonstrates that withdrawal states are often associated with irritability and a higher incidence of aggressive and defensive acts.

28   The application of therapeutic agents with increasing selectivity for adrenergic receptor subtypes to managing and treating patients with violent outbursts represents an important therapeutic alternative to the classic antipsychotics.

29   *Serotonin (5-Hydroxytryptamine)*   For the past 30 years, the most intensively studied amine in violent individuals has been serotonin. Evidence from studies ranging from invertebrates to primates highlights marked changes in aspects of serotonin activity in bodily fluids or neural tissue in individuals that have engaged in violent and aggressive behavior on repeated occasions. There is considerable evolutionary variation in the role of serotonin in mediating aggressive or violent behavior across animal species, functionally divergent roles even being represented at the nonhuman primate level. In psychiatric studies, deficits in serotonin synthesis, release, and metabolism have been explored as potential "markers" for certain types of alcoholic and personality disorders with poor impulse control. It is very difficult to extract, from single measures of whole brain serotonin or blood levels, activity information that is specific to past violent behavior, or represents a risk for future propensity, without also considering seasonal and circadian rhythmicity, level of arousal, nutritional status, or past drug history, particularly alcohol abuse. No single type or class of violent activity has emerged as being specifically linked to a "trait" serotonin metabolite level. However, challenges with pharmacologic probes and physiologic or environmental stresses begin to reveal an important profile of serotonin-mediated response patterns.

30   During the past decade, remarkable advances in serotonin receptor pharmacology have promised to yield important new therapeutic options. Evidence from animal studies suggest that drugs with specific actions at certain serotonin receptors selectively decrease several types of aggressive behavior. A new class of antianxiety drugs that target certain serotonin receptors is currently finding acceptance in clinical practice. However, specific antiaggressive effects have not been demonstrated for the serotonin anxiolytics. In humans, brain imaging of serotonin receptors begins to point to distinct alterations in serotonin receptor pop-

ulations in subgroups of affectively disordered patients. These ongoing developments promise to be significant for diagnostic and therapeutic applications to violent individuals.

Sensational incidents of violence have been linked to the use of hallucinogens that act at distinct serotonin receptor subtypes. However, little is known as to whether or not the action at serotonin receptors is the actual mechanism by which these substances engender violent outbursts in rare, possibly psychopathic individuals.   31

Gamma-Aminobutyric Acid—Benzodiazepine Receptors. Thirty percent of all synapses in the brain use gamma-aminobutyric acid (GABA), and many of the GABA-containing neurons are inhibitory in nature. This cellular inhibitory role has been postulated to apply also to the physiologic and behavioral levels, including aggression. However, the present neurochemical evidence from animal studies finds inhibitory as well as excitatory influences of GABA manipulations on different aggressive patterns in discrete brain regions.   32

Interest in GABA is currently intense because one subtype of GABA receptor (GABA-A) forms a supramolecular complex that also localizes benzodiazepine receptors and that also is the site of action for certain alcohol effects. These receptors are the site of action for the most important antianxiety substances that have also been used for their anti-aggressive properties. Evidence from animal and human studies documents the effectiveness of benzodiazepine anxiolytic for their calming and quieting effects. However, under certain pharmacologic and physiologic conditions, at low doses benzodiazepine anxiolytics may increase aggressive behavior in animals and humans, leading sometimes to violent outbursts that are termed "paradoxical rage."   33

The study of the benzodiazepine-GABA-A receptor complex in individuals with a high rate of violent behavior promises to enhance the currently available diagnostic and therapeutic tools for the management of violence.

Brain Mechanisms and Violent Behavior

Neuroanatomic Approach

Physiologic research on aggression in animals has discovered that different neural circuits appear to underlie "predatory attack" behavior as opposed to "affective defense" in animals. Sites in which electrical stimulation elicits predatory attack behavior in the cat include midbrain periaqueductal gray matter, the locus ceruleus, substantia innominata, and central nucleus of the amygdala. Brain sites that mediate affective defense reactions in the cat include the medial hypothalamus and the dorsal   34 aspect of periaqueductal gray matter. In general, limbic structures such as the amygdala, hypothalamus, midbrain periaqueductal gray, and septal area, as well as cortical areas such as the prefrontal cortex and the anterior cingulate gyrus, contain networks of excitatory and inhibitory processes of different kinds of aggressive and defensive behavior.

35   Aggression in animals largely reflects an adaptive response when viewed within an evolutionary framework. Whether or not violent offending in humans constitutes an instrumental act that can be viewed as adaptive is open to question. Nevertheless, the distinction between quiet, predatory, planned attack, on the one hand, and affective, explosive aggression occurring in the context of high autonomic arousal may be of heuristic value for understanding human violence. Possibly, cat (or rat) models could serve as effective screening methods to identify new drugs—some for control of "cold calculated" aggression, others for control of "explosive" aggression. Neuroanatomic and neuropsychologic studies are needed, however, to determine whether disruption of different brain mechanisms is indeed implicated in these two forms of aggression in humans.

36   Data on the neuroanatomy of violence in humans stem largely from clinical studies of the effects of epileptic activity and other forms of brain damage on behavior, as well as from reports of the effects of brain resections on control of violent behavior (i.e., psychosurgery). Psychosurgical studies in Japan, India, and the United States have aimed at destroying portions of the limbic system, especially the amygdala and medial hypothalamus, in cases of patients with uncontrollable violence. Other symptoms have been targeted for psychosurgical treatment, as well. Favorable outcomes are reported, but clinical improvement has been variable; moreover, the basis for assessing success is controversial. Several studies suggest a link between violence and temporal lobe epilepsy, although violence occurring during a seizure is extremely rare. The question remains unanswered as to whether some patients with seizure disorders are more violence prone (because of their putative heightened emotionality) than other persons. Another important question that remains unanswered to date concerns whether these limbic system structures (portions of the temporal lobe, hippocampus, amygdala, hypothalamus) are also implicated in ostensibly "normal" criminally violent offenders who are not preselected under the suspicion of neural abnormalities. Brain imaging techniques constitute one relatively new methodology for addressing such questions.

37   Clinical case studies of patients with damage to the prefrontal lobes provide some support for a link between this area and features of psychopathic behavior; however, the overlap between these two syndromes is only partial. Given the animal data implicating the prefrontal

cortex in the inhibition of aggression, together with neuropsychologic data on frontal dysfunction in violence, it would seem important to pursue research linking this brain site with violence. Studies are needed that combine brain imaging and social, cognitive, emotional or affective measures in order to assess both direct and indirect relationships between the prefrontal cortex and violence in humans.

Neuropsychologic Approach

A large number of studies have found that violent offenders have brain dysfunction as reflected in deficits on neuropsychologic tests. Although the etiological implications of these deficits are not fully understood, there is converging evidence that cognitive deficits may underlie early school failure, dropouts, alcohol and drug use, and ultimately, encounters with the legal system as violent offenders.   38

An important issue requiring resolution concerns whether neuropsychologic disturbances are a cause or an effect of violence. Left-hemisphere dysfunction that disrupts linguistic processing may be causal with respect to violence in that poorer verbal comprehension and communication may contribute to a misinterpretation of events and motives in an interpersonal encounter; this in turn could precipitate a violent encounter. Similarly, poor verbal abilities and communication skills could contribute to peer rejection in childhood, which in combination with other later social and situational factors could predispose to alienation and, ultimately, to violence. Alternatively, left-hemisphere dysfunction could result in verbal deficits that lead to school failure, which in turn could lead to violence. Left-hemisphere dysfunction may, however, be a result (rather than the cause) of violent behavior, since blows to the head and falls may result in concussion and damage to the cortex.   39

Another major source of damage to the brain that may have profound and irreversible consequences for adaptive behavior is in environmental toxins. Maternal use of ethanol (as in beverage alcohol) has effects on the fetus that may persist for many years, and are manifest in poorer attention at ages 4, 7, and older. The effects of lead on cognitive and social adaptation have been the focus of investigation by Needleman and collaborators. Even relatively "small" elevations of lead in the body are associated with poor attention, academic failure, and other impairment in life success. Maternal use of cocaine, opiates, and tobacco has also been shown to have a deleterious effect on the neurobehavioral capacities of the infant and developing child. These early effects may be associated, as well, with long-term academic and social failures.   40

Large-scale epidemiologic and prospective studies are required in order to help elucidate the etiologic significance of neuropsychologic   41 impairment for violence. One limitation of neuropsychologic studies, however, is that they are only indirect measures of brain dysfunction; additional statements regarding brain dysfunction in violence can be made on the basis of future studies that combine neuropsychologic testing with electroencephalogram (EEG) and positron emission tomography (PET) measures of brain activity.

Psychophysiologic Approach

42   Neurochemical, neuroanatomic, and neurophysiologic research on violent behavior faces formidable difficulties. Measurement of the central neurologic processes is costly, often invasive, and difficult to implement so as to observe the processes during reactions to transitory situations in the social environment. To cope with these difficulties, an alternative approach to the study of some types of violent offenders has been provided by the measurement of psychophysiologic variables (i.e., assaying autonomic and CNS functions by means of recordings from the periphery of the body). Included among these variables are heart rate and skin conductance autonomic nervous system variables), as well as EEG and event-related brain potentials (central nervous system variables). Differences among criminals, delinquents and conduct-disordered children on the one hand, and control subjects, on the other, have been shown to exist in resting heart rate (lower in offenders and in persons characterized as fearless). Some offenders have also been shown to have lower skin conductance responses to orienting stimuli than controls, although the reverse may be true for criminal offenders designated as psychopathic.

43   With respect to EEG studies, many have reported an excess of slow wave activity in the records of incarcerated criminal offenders. It is unclear whether this is best interpreted as the effects of underarousal in the prison setting, developmental anomalies, or the sequela of brain damage.

44   Event-related brain potentials (ERPs), in particular the P300 component, have been studied in a number of disordered populations. The P300 wave, which is an index of the allocation of attention to a stimulus is an example of a "cognitive" component of the ERP. These components vary as a function of some information processing requirement or task administered to the subjects. The P300 has been found to be larger in some groups of psychopathic criminals. The interpretation of this finding is unclear, although it suggests that these persons process information differently from normal subjects.

Neuroimaging Approach

45   Perhaps the most recent technical development in research into the antecedents of violence involves the application of new brain imaging techniques. Positron emission tomography and regional cerebral blood flow

(RCBF) techniques allow direct and indirect assessments of glucose metabolism (or blood flow in the case of RCBF) throughout the brain either during a resting state or during performance of a certain task. As such, PET and RCBF techniques assess brain *function*. Conversely, computerized tomography and magnetic resonance imaging (MRI) techniques, while providing detailed images, assess brain *structure* only.

Although studies suggest differences between violent and nonviolent offenders, sample sizes have been relatively small, and findings should be viewed as preliminary. Nevertheless, brain imaging is clearly a new field that has enormous potential for addressing questions concerning altered brain structure and function in violent offenders. For example, PET studies would be capable of directly assessing differential effects of alcohol administration on brain glucose metabolism in violent and nonviolent offender groups, and could help address the issue of whether some violent offenders constitute a subgroup that is particularly susceptible to the disinhibitory effects of alcohol on specific brain areas. Studies that combine both MRI and PET techniques are clearly desirable in that assessments of both structure and function would allow more complete statements to be made with regard to brain dysfunction in violence. Studies that combine brain imaging assessment with neuropsychologic, cognitive-psychophysiologic, and hormonal assessments in violent and nonviolent subjects would allow us to address the potentially important interactions between different biologic systems in predisposing to violence. 46

Hypoglycemia, Diet, and Violent Behavior

Some studies have observed that violent offenders, particularly those with a history of alcohol abuse, are characterized by reactive hypoglycemia. Although there have been no demonstrations to date that violent individuals are hypoglycemic at the time of the commission of violence, it is possible that low blood glucose levels (hypoglycemia) could be conducive to aggressive behavior. Increased irritability is one symptom of hypoglycemia, and this could be the first step in the development of a full-blown aggressive outburst. Anthropologic studies, studies of aggressive personality in "normal" subjects, and experimental studies in animals all support a link between hypoglycemia and aggression. 47

Acute symptoms of hypoglycemia are reported as maximal at 11:00–11:30 A.M. and this time corresponds to peaks in assaults on both staff and other inmates in prison, both of which reach their maximum at 11:00–11:30 A.M. 48

A number of studies have claimed that dietary changes aimed at reducing sugar consumption reduce institutional antisocial behavior in juvenile offenders, but these studies have methodological weaknesses 49 that preclude drawing any firm conclusions at the present time. There is also some limited evidence that food additives may contribute to hyperactivity, although the data on sugar intake and hyperactivity are inconclusive. There have been reports however that home environment mediates dietary effects on behavior.

50   Although data are limited at the present time, further double-blind studies into the effects of dietary manipulation on aggression and violence in institutions seem warranted. Furthermore, investigation of the interconnections between hypoglycemia or diet and other factors at both biological and social levels seems warranted. Since alcohol increases the susceptibility to hypoglycemia through its capacity to increase insulin secretion . . . , it may well be that predispositions to both hypoglycemia and alcohol abuse would make an individual particularly predisposed to violence. Hypoglycemia has also been theoretically linked to both low heart rate and EEG slowing, factors that have been found to characterize violent offenders. The fact that children from a supportive home environment show more dietary improvement than those from an unsupportive home also suggests an interaction between diet and family environment in antisocial behavior. Clearly, diet and hypoglycemia should not be studied independently of interactions with factors at other levels.

SUGGESTIONS FOR FURTHER READING

Archer, John. *The Behavioral Biology of Aggression.* New York: Oxford University, 1989. A wide-ranging review, by an expert on the behavioral effects of hormones, that includes a variety of animal studies as well as explanations of some applications of mathematical game theory.

Ghiglieri, Michael. *The Dark Side of Man: Tracing the Origins of Male Violence.* Reading, MA: Perseus, 1999. A solid layperson's guide to recent findings in the evolutionary psychology of male-female differences and how these differences relate to violence.

Niehoff, Debra. *The Biology of Violence.* New York: Free Press, 1999. A neurobiologist turned journalist integrates laboratory studies of animals with an especially strong treatment of neurochemistry to present a coherent picture of how biology and environment interact to produce violence.

Volavka, Jan. *Neurobiology of Violence.* Washington, DC: American Psychiatric Press, 1995. A psychiatrist describes the biological origins of violence, emphasizing behavioral pathology, substance abuse, and biomedical treatment options.

Wrangam, Richard, and Dale Peterson. *Demonic Males: Apes and the Origins of Human Violence.* Boston, MA: Houghton Mifflin, 1996. An excellent discussion of violent behavior, emphasizing its occurrence among nonhuman primates as well as its notable absence in at least one species.

STUDY QUESTIONS

1. Discuss the potential for abuse and misuse of biological aspects of violence. Compare these with possible abuse and misuse of nonbiological approaches: psychological, anthopological, sociological, and others.

2. To some extent, any scientific accounts of human behavior are likely to oppose basic conceptions of free will; that is, if behavior is "caused"—by neurochemicals, genes, brain regions, and so forth—it is not spontaneous or free. Is there any way out of this dilemma?

3. Propose a possible integration of neurochemistry, genetics, and neuroanatomy in the causation of violence, showing how environmental factors would necessarily be involved as well.

4. Identify and develop other biological approaches to the causation of violence that were not presented (or presented only sketchily) in this chapter.

5. Make an argument either for or against the relevance of animal studies for a deeper understanding of human violence.

6. Summarize the sociobiological explanation for the strong male bias of violence.

7. Distinguish among ethological, sociobiological, and strictly genetic explanations for violence.

8. Describe some similarities and differences when it comes to explaining violence in terms of neurochemicals, brain regions, and genetics.

9. To what extent are the various explanations of violence presented in this chapter specific to interpersonal violence (especially crime) as compared to international violence (war)? To what extent are they generally applicable?

10. Where do you think future breakthroughs in understanding the biology of violence are most needed? Where do you think they are most likely to occur?

2

Psychology

Psychology is the study of behavior. As such, it is concerned with such things as perception; cognition; abnormal mental conditions; normal "motivational" states such as hunger, thirst, and sex; personality theories; individual differences; the manifold interactions among individuals in society; and so forth. Not surprisingly, people have looked especially to psychologists for explanations of troublesome behavior, including violence. The answers have been as diverse as the discipline itself.

Early psychological interpretations of violence emphasized inherent factors, allied to early enthusiasm for "instinct" as a catch-all explanation for behavior that remained essentially unknown. Early psychoanalytic thinking was also consistent with this approach, notably Sigmund Freud's theorizing about the need for aggression as a means of reducing hostility and turning a supposed innate "death wish" away from oneself.

But psychology eventually moved away from philosophizing and pure theorizing to a more empirical stance, seeking testable propositions as well as opportunities to improve the human condition. Of special interest was an understanding of so-called normal aggression and violence as opposed to the extremes of psychosis or intractable rage.

Numerous theories have been developed, many if not all of them "true" to varying degrees. Indeed, consistent with our earlier metaphor of the blind men and the elephant, the one safe generalization about violence seems to be that it is multiply caused. As with Mark Twain's comment that it was easy to stop smoking—after all, he had done it hundreds of times!—it has been easy for psychologists to "explain" violence: they have dozens of explanations. Each, it appears, captures a part of the truth.

Aside from instinctivist theories, the one consistent pattern shared by psychological approaches to violence has been emphasis on the role of situation and circumstance—that is, appreciation of the importance of "nurture" as compared to "nature." Not that psychologists don't recognize the contributions of biology; there is a growing field of evolutionary psychology as well as continued focus on behavior genetics along with the organic underpinnings of pathological disorders. By and large, however, psychologists tend to take an *environmental* perspective, emphasizing that human beings are remarkably flexible in their behavior, typically adjusting it as a result of experience. (There is also something especially optimistic about this orientation, since it offers the prospect that by modifying the experience of individuals and/or engaging in enlightened social engineering, it should be possible to reduce propensities for violence.)

Psychological research has also emphasized a useful distinction, between impulsive and instrumental violence. Violence is *impulsive* when it takes place in the heat of the moment, typically a reaction to immediate circumstances: someone loses his temper, for example, and hits another person. It was not planned; it happened on impulse. By contrast, *instrumental* violence occurs as a result of premeditation: for instance, if someone intends to hit a victim on the head and steal her purse and then does so, such actions are not impulsive but rather instrumental; that is, they serve as "instruments," as means toward a particular end. Individuals are believed to be predisposed toward one or the other (or to neither) by their personality types, but also by the situations in which they find themselves.

Many such situations have been identified, including feeling wronged, experiencing unpleasant emotional or even physical sensations, observing violence (or nonviolence) modeled by others, the nature of one's association with family and a larger social group (including the behavioral norms of that group), one's perceived level of satisfaction or deprivation, internalized codes of what is acceptable and what is unacceptable behavior, learned (but often unconscious) associations between situations and preferred responses, differing tendencies for irritability and arousal, differences in capacity for self-inhibition, and the degree to which one has experienced violence directed toward oneself. The list is long, a fact that could be seen as suggesting the weakness of psychological theories of violence and aggression . . . or, alternatively, its strength.

The Psychoanalytic Approach to the Understanding of Aggression

ERICH FROMM

Our first selection represents a distinct and somewhat isolated tradition within psychology: psychoanalysis. The founder and major voice in this respect is doubtless Sigmund Freud, although his concern with the origins of aggression and violence was secondary to his interest in the role of other factors in the unconscious, notably sexual motivation. When

Freud addressed himself to aggression and violence, he argued for the existence of

> *erotic instincts which are always trying to collect living substances together into even larger unities, and the death instincts, which act against that tendency and try to bring living matter back into an inorganic condition. The cooperation and opposition of these two forces produce the phenomena of life to which death puts an end.*

Although it is conceptually tidy to envision a "life instinct" (*eros*), which is balanced by a "death instinct" (*thanatos*), it is difficult to imagine how the latter could have evolved, or be maintained. In addition, such a formulation is difficult, if not impossible, to prove or disprove. Nonetheless, Freud's formulation is important not only for historical reasons, but because it leads to rich philosophical and literary interpretations.

Numerous psychoanalysts have wrestled with the question of what causes human violence, often in the context of seeking to understand war. For example, in *The Psychoanalysis of War*, Franco Fornari examined the "curative" aspects of war, notably its potential function in reducing anxieties, especially fear that the enemy in some way threatens the warrior's "love object."

Erich Fromm was trained as a psychoanalyst, although he achieved renown as an author and social/psychological philosopher. In his much-noticed book *The Anatomy of Human Destructiveness*, Fromm reviewed and criticized various theories of violence (including Freud's) while also presenting his own. Fromm distinguished between *defensive* or *benign* aggression and what he called *malignant* aggression, arguing that the latter is unique to human beings and is especially dreadful and dangerous. Fromm's own work is notably connected to philosophy (especially existentialism) as well as literature and history. For a detailed consideration of certain case studies in malignant aggression—including Joseph Stalin and Adolf Hitler—readers are urged to consult Fromm's monumental book. In the following selection, Erich Fromm reviews traditional psychoanalytic approaches to aggression and violence.

1   Does the *psychoanalytic approach* offer a method for understanding aggression that avoids the shortcomings both of the behavioristic and the instinctivistic approaches? At first glance, it seems as if psychoanalysis not only has avoided their shortcomings, but that it is afflicted, in fact, by a combination of them. Psychoanalytic theory is at the same time instinctivistic in its general theoretical concepts and environmentalistic in its therapeutic orientation.

2   That Freud's theory is instinctivistic, explaining human behavior as the result of the struggle between the instinct for self-preservation and the sexual instinct (and in his later theory between the life and death instincts) is too well known to require any documentation. The envi-

ronmentalist framework can also be easily recognized when one considers that analytic therapy attempts to explain the development of a person by the specific environmental constellation of infancy, i.e., the impact of the family. This aspect, however, is reconciled with instinctivism by the assumption that the modifying influence of the environment occurs via the influence of the libidinous structure.

In practice, however, patients, the public, and frequently analysts themselves pay only lip service to the specific vicissitudes of the sexual instincts (very often these vicissitudes are reconstructed on the basis of "evidence" which in itself is often a construction based on the system of theoretical expectations) and take a totally environmentalistic position. Their axiom is that every negative development in the patient is to be understood as the result of damaging influences in early childhood. This has led sometimes to irrational self-accusation on the part of parents who feel guilty for every undesirable or pathological trait that appears in a child after birth, and to a tendency of people in analysis to put the blame for all their troubles on their parents, and to avoid confronting themselves with the problem of their own responsibility.

In the light of all this, it would seem legitimate for psychologists to classify psychoanalysis as *theory* under the category of instinctivistic theories, and thus their argument against Lorenz is *eo ipso* an argument against psychoanalysis. But caution is necessary here; the question is: How should one define psychoanalysis? Is it the sum total of Freud's theories, or can we distinguish between the original and creative and the accidental, time-conditioned parts of the system, a distinction that can be made in the work of all great pioneers of thought? If such a distinction is legitimate, we must ask whether the libido theory belongs to the core of Freud's work or whether it is simply the form in which he organized his new insights because there was no other way to think of and to express his basic findings, given his philosophical and scientific environment.

Freud himself never claimed that the libido theory was a scientific certainty. He called it "our mythology," and replaced it with the theory of the Eros and death "instincts." It is equally significant that he defined psychoanalysis as a theory based on resistance and transference—and by omission, not on the libido theory.

But perhaps more important than Freud's own statements is to keep in mind what gave his discoveries their unique historical significance. Surely it could not have been the instinctivistic theory as such; instinct theories had been quite popular since the nineteenth century. That he singled out the *sexual* instinct as the source of all passions (aside from the instinct for self-preservation) was, of course, new and revolutionary at a time still ruled by Victorian middle-class morality. But even this special version of the instinct theory would probably not have made such a powerful and lasting impact. It seems to me that what gave Freud his historical significance was the discovery of unconscious processes, not philosophically or speculatively, but empirically, as he demonstrated in some of his case histories, and most of all in his fundamental opus, *The Interpretation of Dreams* (1900). If it can be shown, for instance, that a consciously peaceful and conscientious man has powerful impulses to kill, it is a secondary question whether one explains these impulses as being derived from his "Oedipal" hate against his father, as a manifestation of his death instinct, as a result of his wounded narcissism, or as due to other reasons. Freud's revolution was to make us recognize the unconscious aspect of man's mind and the energy which man uses to repress the awareness of undesirable desires. He showed that good intentions mean nothing if they cover up the unconscious intentions; he unmasked "honest" dishonesty by demonstrating that it is not enough to have "meant" well *consciously*. He was the first scientist to explore the depth, the underworld in man, and that is why his ideas had such an impact on artists and writers at a time when most psychiatrists still refused to take his theories seriously.

7   But Freud went further. He not only showed that forces operate in man of which he is not aware and that rationalizations protect him from awareness; he also explained that these unconscious forces are integrated in a system to which he gave the name "character" in a new, dynamic sense.

8   Freud began to develop this concept in his first paper on the "anal character." (S. Freud, 1908.) Certain behavior traits, such as stubbornness, orderliness, and parsimony, he pointed out, were more often than not to be found together as a syndrome of traits. Furthermore, wherever that syndrome existed, one could find peculiarities in the sphere of toilet training and in the vicissitudes of sphincter control and in certain behavioral traits related to bowel movements and feces. Thus Freud's first step was to discover a syndrome of behavioral traits and to relate them to the way the child acted (in part as a response to certain demands by those who trained him) in the sphere of bowel movements. His brilliant and creative next step was to relate these two sets of behavioral patterns by a theoretical consideration based on a previous assumption about the evolution of the libido. This assumption was that during an early phase of childhood development, after the mouth has ceased to be the main organ of lust and satisfaction, the anus becomes an important erogenous zone, and most libidinal wishes are centered around the process of the retention and evacuation of the excrements. His conclusion was to explain the syndrome of behavioral traits as sublimation of, or reaction formation against the libidinous satisfaction or frustration of anality. Stubbornness and parsimony were supposed to be the subli-

mation of the original refusal to give up the pleasure of retaining the stool; orderliness, the reaction formation against the original desire of the infant to evacuate whenever he pleased. Freud showed that the three original traits of the syndrome, which until then had appeared to be quite unrelated to each other, formed part of a structure, or system, because they were all rooted in the same source of anal libido which manifests itself in these traits, either directly or by reaction formation or by sublimation. In this way Freud was able to explain why these traits are charged with energy and, in fact, very resistant to change.

One of the most important additions was the concept of the "oral-   9
sadistic" character (the exploitative character, in my terms). There are other concepts of character formation, depending on what aspects one wants to stress: such as the authoritarian (sadomasochistic) character, the rebellious and the revolutionary character, the narcissistic and the incestuous character. These latter concepts, most of which do not form part of classic psychoanalytic thinking, are related to each other and overlap; by combining them one can get a still fuller description of a certain character.

Freud's theoretical explanation for character structure was the notion   10
that the libido (oral, anal, genital) was the source that gave energy to the various character traits. But even if one discounts the libido theory, his discovery loses none of its importance for the clinical observation of the syndromes, and the fact that a common source of energy feeds them remains equally true. I have attempted to demonstrate that the character syndromes are rooted and nourished in the particular forms of relatedness of the individual to the outside world and himself; furthermore, that inasmuch as the social group shares a common character structure ("social character") the socioeconomic conditions shared by all members of a group mold the social character. . . .

The extraordinary importance of the concept of character is that it   11
transcends the old dichotomy: instinct-environment. The sexual instinct in Freud's system was supposed to be very malleable, and to a large extent molded by environmental influences. Thus character was understood as being the outcome of the interaction between instinct and environment. This new position was possible only because Freud had subsumed all instincts under one, i.e., sexuality (aside from the instinct for self-preservation). The many instincts we find in the lists of the older instinctivists were relatively fixed, because each motive of behavior was attributed to a special kind of innate drive. But in Freud's scheme the various motivating forces and the differences were explained as the result of environmental influence on the libido. Paradoxically, then, Freud's enlargement of the concept of sexuality enabled him to open the door to the acceptance of environmental influences far beyond what

was possible for the pre-Freudian instinct theory. Love, tenderness, sadism, masochism, ambition, curiosity, anxiety, rivalry—these and many other drives were no longer each attributed to a special instinct, but to the influence of the environment (essentially the significant persons in early childhood), via the libido. Freud consciously remained loyal to the philosophy of his teachers, but by the assumption of a super-instinct he transcended his own instinctivistic viewpoint. It is true he still hobbled his thought by the predominance of the libido theory, and it is time to leave this instinctive baggage behind altogether. What I want to stress at this point is that Freud's "instinctivism" was very different from traditional instinctivism.

12   The description given thus far suggests that "character determines behavior," that the character trait, whether loving or destroying, drives man to behave in a certain way, and that man in acting according to his character feels satisfied. Indeed, the character trait tells us how a person would *like* to behave. But we must add an important qualification: *if he could.*

13   What does this "if he could" mean?

14   We must return here to one of the most fundamental of Freud's notions, the concept of the "reality principle," based on the instinct for self-preservation, versus the "pleasure principle," based on the sexual instinct. Whether we are driven by the sexual instinct or by a nonsexual passion in which a character trait is rooted, the conflict between what we would like to do and the demands of self-interest remains crucial. We cannot always behave as we are driven to by our passions, because we have to modify our behavior to some extent in order to remain alive. The average person tries to find a compromise between what his character would make him want to do and what he must do in order not to suffer more or less harmful consequences. The degree to which a person follows the dictates of self-preservation (ego interest) varies, of course. At the one extreme the weight of ego interests is zero; this holds true for the martyr and a certain type of fanatical killer. At the other extreme is the "opportunist" for whom self-interest includes everything that could make him more successful, popular, or comfortable. Between these two extremes all people can be arranged, characterized by a specific blend of self-interest and character-rooted passions.

15   How much a person represses his passionate desires depends not only on factors within himself but on the situation; if the situation changes, repressed desires become conscious and are acted out. This holds true, for instance, for the person with a sadistic-masochistic character. Everybody knows the type of person who is submissive to his boss and sadistically domineering to his wife and children. Another case in point is the change that occurs in character when the total social

situation changes. The sadistic character who may have posed as a meek or even friendly individual may become a fiend in a terroristic society in which sadism is valued rather than deplored. Another may suppress sadistic behavior in all visible actions, while showing it in a subtle expression of the face or in seemingly harmless and marginal remarks.

Repression of character traits also occurs with regard to the most noble impulses. In spite of the fact that the teachings of Jesus are still part of our moral ideology, a man acting in accordance with them is generally considered a fool or a "neurotic"; hence many people still rationalize their generous impulses as being motivated by self-interest.   16

These considerations show that the motivating power of character traits is influenced by self-interest in varying degrees. They imply that character constitutes the main motivation of human behavior, but restricted and modified by the demands of self-interest under varying conditions. It is the great achievement of Freud not only to have discovered the character traits which underlie behavior, but also to have devised means to study them, such as the interpretation of dreams, free association, and slips of the tongue.   17

Here lies the fundamental difference between behaviorism and psychoanalytic characterology. Conditioning works through its appeal to self-interest, such as the desire for food, security, praise, avoidance of pain. In animals, self-interest proves to be so strong that by repeated and optimally spaced reinforcements the interest for self-preservation proves to be stronger than other instincts like sex or aggression. Man of course also behaves in accordance with his self-interest; but not always, and not necessarily so. He often acts according to his passions, his meanest and his noblest, and is often willing—and able—to risk his self-interest, his fortune, his freedom, and his life in the pursuit of love, truth, and integrity—or for hate, greed, sadism, and destructiveness. In this very difference lies the reason conditioning cannot be a sufficient explanation for human behavior.   18

To Sum Up

What was epoch-making in Freud's findings was that he found the key to the understanding of the system of forces which make up man's character system and to the contradictions within the system. The discovery of unconscious processes and of the dynamic concept of character were radical because they went to the roots of human behavior; they were disquieting because nobody can hide any longer behind his good intentions; they were dangerous, because if everybody *were* to know what he *could* know about himself and others, society would be shaken to its very foundations.   19

20   As psychoanalysis became successful and respectable it shed its core and emphasized that which is generally acceptable. It kept that part of the unconscious which Freud had emphasized, the sexual strivings. The consumer society did away with many of the Victorian taboos (not because of the influence of psychoanalysis but for a number of reasons inherent in its structure). To discover one's incestuous wishes, "castration fear," "penis envy," was no longer upsetting. But to discover repressed character traits such as narcissism, sadism, omnipotence, submission, alienation, indifference, the unconscious betrayal of one's integrity, the illusory nature of one's concept of reality, to discover all this in oneself, in the social fabric, in the leaders one follows—this indeed is "social dynamite." Freud only dealt with an instinctual id; that was quite satisfactory at a time when he did not see any other way to explain human passion except in terms of instincts. But what was revolutionary then is conventional today. The instinct theory instead of being considered a hypothesis, needed at a certain period, became the center and the straitjacket of orthodox psychoanalytic theory and slowed down the further development of the understanding of man's passions, which had been Freud's central interest.

21   It is for these reasons that I propose that the classification of psychoanalysis as "instinctivistic" theory, which is correct in a formal sense, does not really refer to the substance of psychoanalysis. Psychoanalysis is essentially a theory of unconscious strivings, of resistance, of falsification of reality according to one's subjective needs and expectations (transference), of character, and of conflicts between passionate strivings embodied in character traits and the demands for self-preservation.

Frustration and Aggression

JOHN DOLLARD, NEAL E. MILLER, LEONARD W. DOOB, O. H. MOWRER, AND ROBERT R. SEARS

We turn next to the major (and in some ways, only) scientific psychological theory for the origin of aggression and violence promulgated during the early twentieth century: so-called *frustration-aggression theory*. It was first presented in a brief but highly influential book published in 1939. The basic idea is simple, intuitively appealing, and has lent itself to a range of empirical tests. It was couched in terms that were consistent with the dominant paradigm in American psychology at the time: *Behaviorism*, which sought to interpret behavior as a strict consequence of connections between stimulus and response. Frustration-aggression theory received widespread acceptance and generated an enormous amount of research (some, but not all, of which has been supportive).

There is some ambiguity, however, as to the meaning of *frustration* (e.g., whether it involves actual interruption of a goal-directed response, or the negation of a desire or wish). Shortly after publication of the book, it was also recognized that frustration could generate other responses besides aggression, depending on the individual, the precise nature of the frustration, and the social situation. Moreover, aggression and violence sometimes arise in the absence of any discernible frustration. These criticisms aside, frustration-aggression theory enjoys an honored place among psychological concepts, as a pathbreaking effort to integrate aggression and violence with the real experiences of actual people.

The problem of aggression has many facets. The individual experiences difficulty in controlling his own temper and often sees others carrying on an unwitting struggle with their hostilities. He fears justified revenge or writhes at the blow or taunt that appears from an unexpected source. Children are often expert at annoying their elders by sly mischief or a sudden tantrum. Helpless minorities are persecuted. The lynching mob has a grimness and cruelty not to be expected from people who are so gentle and kind in other situations. Primitive tribesmen slay one another and even civilized people are frightened by the prospect of new and increasingly destructive wars. This book represents an attempt to bring a degree of systematic order into such apparently chaotic phenomena. 1

The Basic Postulate

This study takes as its point of departure the assumption that *aggression is always a consequence of frustration.* More specifically the proposition is that the occurrence of aggressive behavior always presupposes the existence of frustration and, contrariwise, that the existence of frustration always leads to some form of aggression. From the point of view of daily observation, it does not seem unreasonable to assume that aggressive behavior of the usually recognized varieties is always traceable to and produced by some form of frustration. But it is by no means so immediately evident that, whenever frustration occurs, aggression of some kind and in some degree will inevitably result. In many adults and even children, frustration may be followed so promptly by an apparent acceptance of the situation and readjustment thereto that one looks in vain for the relatively gross criteria ordinarily thought of as characterizing aggressive action. It must be kept in mind, however, that one of the earliest lessons human beings learn as a result of social living 2 is to suppress and restrain their overtly aggressive reactions. This does not mean, however, that such reaction tendencies are thereby annihilated; rather it has been found that, although these reactions may be temporally compressed, delayed, disguised, displaced, or otherwise deflected from their immediate and logical goal, they are not destroyed. With this assumption of the inevitability of aggression following frustration, it is possible to bring a new measure of integration into a variety of types of facts which have hitherto been considered more or less isolated phenomena and to consider reasonable many instances of human conduct that have commonly been regarded and lightly dismissed as simply irrational, perverse, or abnormal. . . .

Fundamental Concepts

3   At three-thirty on a hot afternoon the bell of an ice-cream vendor is heard on the street. James, aged four, runs toward his mother and announces: "Mother, the ice-cream man! I want an ice-cream cone!" Then he looks up very appealingly, puckers his lips, grasps his mother's skirt, and starts tugging her toward the front door.

4   At this point an observer who had been studying the behavior of this family might make a prediction. He might say: "Now James is going to try to take his mother out to the push cart. He may attempt to take her down the right or the left branch of the walk. In either case we can say that, unless something stops him, he will be holding a cone in his hand within three minutes and will have consumed it within ten. The act of consuming the cone will put an end to the sequence which I am predicting."

5   It is probable, however, that such an observer would find it more convenient for his purpose to deal abstractly with some of the significant aspects of the situation than with the actual events themselves. In referring to the origin of James' behavior sequence he might say, in the terminology to be used in this book, that James is *instigated* to take his mother out to buy him an ice-cream cone. An *instigator* is some antecedent condition of which the predicted response is the consequence, It may be directly observable as in the case of the vendor's bell; or it may be an internal condition that can only be inferred—in this instance from James' statement that he wants ice cream. The statement itself is not the instigator, of course, but it may be used to indicate that an instigator exists because on previous occasions the statement has been observed to be correlated with the predicted response. The bell and the vendor are likewise interpreted as instigators because of such a previously observed correlation. The concept of instigator is clearly much broader than that of stimulus; whereas the latter refers only to energy

(as physically defined) exerted on a sense-organ, the former refers to any antecedent condition, either observed or inferred, from which the response can be predicted, whether this condition be a stimulus, a verbally reported image, idea, or motive, or a state of deprivation.

The directly observable instigators to James' behavior are the bell and the ice-cream vendor. But the presence of internal instigators not directly observed could be inferred from what James says and does. To the extent that specific predictions could be made from the *appealing look*, the *puckering of the lips*, the *tugging on the skirt*, and the *statement* "I want an ice-cream cone!" that efforts would be made to get the ice cream, there would be justification for inferring the existence of instigators. All that is necessary, in order to infer their presence, is for the organism to have revealed some measurable, or at least denotable, behavior which has been shown previously to be correlated with the occurrence of the predicted response. Any refinements in either observational technique or theoretical analysis that enable one to predict responses more accurately also improve the inferences concerning the presence of instigators. 6

Several instigators to a certain response may operate simultaneously, and their combined effect represents the total amount of instigation to the response. Instigation, therefore, is a quantitative concept and so some consideration must be given to the problem of *strength of instigation.* This strength is measured by the degree to which the instigated response competes successfully with simultaneously instigated incompatible responses, or in different technical words, by the prepotency of the instigated responses. 7

James might notice that the lawn sprinkler was spraying water in such a way as to cut off his path to the ice-cream vendor. He might say that he did not want to get wet or display other behavior from which it could be inferred that there was instigation to avoid the sprinkler. Owing to the position of the sprinkler, this instigation would be incompatible with the instigation to get an ice-cream cone. On one occasion James might walk in the path of the sprinkler and on another he might not; the instigation to have an ice-cream cone would have competed successfully with the same simultaneous instigation to an incompatible response in the first case and not in the second. The instigation to obtain a cone, therefore, might be said to have been stronger when James ran through the water than when he did not. Any conditions which allow one to predict that James will run through more or less water to reach the cone are conditions from which an increase or decrease in the strength of instigation may be inferred. 8

In many instances of everyday behavior it is impractical to determine directly by an obstruction technique the degree to which simultanously 9 instigated incompatible responses can be overcome. In such instances it is desirable to use certain subsidiary measures for inferring the strength of instigation to the predicted response. The speed, duration, force, and probability of occurrence of a given response are presumably functions of the degree to which the response competes successfully with simultaneously instigated incompatible responses. Under properly constant conditions, these indicators may be used in lieu of the more exact measure. If James ran immediately and very rapidly toward the ice-cream vendor, it would be proper to assume that the instigation to this response was fairly strong. If, on the contrary, he dawdled, it would be reasonable to assume that the instigation to get ice cream was relatively weak.

10   In the example that has been cited, it has been said that the act of consuming the cone would put an end to the predicted sequence of behavior. This means that James is known, from observation of previous ice-cream episodes, to be very much less likely to respond to the ringing of the bell with the predicted sequence of behavior for some time after he has had an ice-cream cone than he was before eating the cone. An act which terminates a predicted sequence will be called a *goal-response*. The goal-response may be defined as that reaction which reduces the strength of instigation to a degree at which it no longer has as much of a tendency to produce the predicted behavior sequence. The hungry rat eats and no longer seeks food; because the behavior sequence is terminated, the eating is considered to be the goal-response. The ticket-buyer reaches the box-office, purchases his ticket, and no longer stands in line; the purchase of the ticket is therefore said to be the goal-response.

11   Later on, however, James may give the same appealing look, may tug his mother's skirt again, and announce he wants another ice-cream cone; thus he will be giving further evidence from which instigation can be inferred. The termination of a behavior sequence is frequently only temporary. If there is reason to believe that the instigation exists again, James will be expected to perform the predicted sequence a second time. In fact, he will be expected to be even more apt to repeat the previous acts which had led successfully to the ice cream, since goal-responses have a *reinforcing effect* that induces the learning of the acts preceding them.

12   So far it has been assumed that nothing goes wrong to stop James. His mother, however, may insist that he wait until dinner time for his ice cream. His father may arrive on the scene, reprimand the mother for being so indulgent, and threaten to spank James for going to the cart. Or the ice-cream man may not have any more cones. In any of these cases the expected sequence of action will be interrupted and James will

be prevented from consuming the cone. Such an interference with the occurrence of an instigated goal-response at its proper time in the behavior sequence is called a *frustration*.

Normally a series of acts ripples through without interruption, but interference may occur through punishment incident to the goal-seeking activities or through inaccessibility of the goal itself. The interference may be slight, as when a mosquito hums near a person absorbed in thought, or great, as when an individual suffers the effects of kidney disease. It is, nevertheless, the same form of interference that induces the frustration. Such expressions as "to disappoint a person," "to let someone down," "to cause pain to someone," and "to block somebody in carrying out an act" indicate that one person is imposing a frustration on another.   13

Neither the nature nor the origin of the interrupted behavior sequence need be considered here. It is essential only that it can be identified as in the process of occurring and that the mode of interference be specified. The goal-response may involve gross overt activity such as the manipulation of a physical object or it may involve but little overt activity as in the case of receiving congratulations for work well done. And it is irrelevant whether thumb-sucking in an eighteen-months-old child occurs as an unlearned response, or whether the physical integrations necessary to it have been learned in other stimulus contexts. To have the object-manipulation or the receiving of congratulations or the thumb-sucking blocked, however, constitutes a frustration. The instigations remain and the adequate goal-responses are interdicted. In order to say that a frustration exists, then, one must be able to specify two things: (1) that the organism could have been expected to perform certain acts, and (2) that these acts have been prevented from occurring.   14

It must be noted here that either the goal-response of eating the ice cream or a degree of prevention caused by an interfering agent can terminate James' activity; it may be difficult to tell whether the behavior sequence has stopped because of the first or the second circumstance. This is especially true when the interfering agent is an emotional conflict within the organism itself. From an operational standpoint, however, an infallible criterion exists. A goal-response reinforces the behavior sequence leading up to it, while interference does not. If it were not known from previous experience that eating ice cream was the goal-response to James' behavior sequence, it might be difficult to tell, if interference be assumed, whether the last act carried out (e.g., giving an appealing look) before the sequence was terminated was a goal-response or not; but by determining whether this act produced a stronger tendency for James to carry out the sequence a second time a decision could be reached.   15

16   Still another concept can be gleaned from this overworked example. In the past James might always have consumed vanilla cones. Interference with this response by the fact that the vendor had no vanilla ice cream would be a frustration. A chocolate cone, however, might be found to be a more or less acceptable substitute for vanilla. A response which substitutes for the goal-response, in that it also tends to terminate and reinforce the same preceding action, is called a substitute response. . . .

17   At times James may kick or scream or say he hates his mother. Any such sequence of behavior, the goal-response to which is the injury of the person toward whom it is directed, is called *aggression*. According to the hypothesis, this is the primary and characteristic reaction to frustration, and will occur when something happens to interfere with James' efforts to get the ice-cream cone.

18   Many of the common forms of aggression can be instantly recognized by almost any observer who belongs to Western society. Acts of physical violence are perhaps the most obvious. Phantasies of "getting even" with galling superiors or rivals, calculated forays against frustrating persons (whether the weapon is a business deal, a gun, a malicious rumor, or a verbal castigation is of little moment), and generalized destructive or remonstrative outbursts like lynchings, strikes, and certain reformist campaigns are clearly forms of aggression as well. It hardly needs special emphasis that tremendously complex learned skills, such as the use of the boomerang and machine gun, may occur in these aggressive behavior sequences.

19   Aggression is not always manifested in overt movements but may exist as the content of a phantasy or dream or even a well thought-out plan of revenge. It may be directed at the object which is perceived as causing the frustration or it may be displaced to some altogether innocent source or even toward the self, as in masochism, martyrdom, and suicide. The target of aggression quite as readily may be inanimate as animate, provided that the acts would be expected to produce injury were the object animate. In fact, the aggression may be undirected toward any object—a man swears after striking his thumb with a hammer—when the action would cause pain if it were directed toward a person. Such nouns as anger, resentment, hatred, hostility, animus, exasperation, irritation, and annoyance carry something of the meaning of the concept. Verbs such as destroy, damage, torment, retaliate, hurt, blow up, humiliate, insult, threaten, and intimidate refer to actions of an aggressive nature.

20   Although the frustration-aggression hypothesis assumes a universal causal relation between frustration and aggression, it is important to note that the two concepts have been defined *independently* as well as *dependently*. The dependent definition of aggression is *that response which*

follows frustration, reduces only the secondary, frustration-produced instiga-
tion, and leaves the strength of the original instigation unaffected. Frustration
is independently defined as *that condition which exists when a goal-*
response suffers interference. Aggression is independently defined as *an*
act whose goal-response is injury to an organism (or *organism-surrogate*).

Examples of the Frustration-Aggression Sequence

It is not necessary for the purpose of this discussion to take the posi- 21
tion that frustration originally (in a genetic sense) produces aggressive
behavior. Frustration is possible as soon as unlearned or learned reaction sequences are in operation in the child. It would seem, therefore,
that frustration can conceivably occur during the birth process itself
and at any time thereafter. This need not be the case, however, with aggressive responses as here defined. The first reactions to frustration
may indeed be of a random character and may lack that destructiveness which is here posited for aggression. It may also be that out of a
battery of random responses to frustration certain ones are learned as
effective in reducing the strength of the frustration-induced instigation
(though not the strength of the original instigation) and that these later
appear as aggression. Whether the relationship be learned or innate,
when the curtain rises on the theoretical scene which is surveyed in
this volume, frustration and aggression are already joined as response
sequences.

Since frustrations and aggressions are familiar elements in the im- 22
mediate experience of most persons in Western society, the task of de-
noting the phenomena to which these terms refer is relatively easy.
The following examples of frustration-aggression sequences are presented with a view to giving somewhat fuller connotation to the definitions which have been presented in the foregoing pages. They are
presented, the reader is reminded again, for purposes of illustration,
not proof.

1. A college student was driving to a distant city to attend a foot- 23
ball game. It was the Big Game of the season and represented an important event in the season's social festivities. He was accompanied by
a girl whose good opinion he valued highly and whom he wished to
impress with his extensive plans for a weekend of parties and amuse-
ment. They became very gay and hilarious during the course of the
drive and he was silently congratulating himself on the successful
arrangements he had made. Suddenly a siren sounded behind him
and, when he stopped, the traffic officer reprimanded him severely and
in a very insulting manner for "driving like a high-school kid." The
sound of the siren and the officer's intrusion immediately destroyed

both his rapport with the girl and the happy anticipations he had had. As soon as he was permitted to drive ahead, he began berating the manners of the officer and telling the girl that the police in that state were notorious for their bullying methods. During the remainder of the drive he seemed to have difficulty with his car; he grated the gears frequently in shifting, refused to let other cars pass him, and made insulting comments about every policeman who came in sight (though, of course, slowing down whenever they appeared). The change in behavior here is not very baffling. The student was frustrated by being humiliated before his girl; his expectations of favorable response from her diminished. His behavior became aggressive because of his hostility toward the policeman which he could not express directly and which kept bubbling up after the arrest.

24   2. Although frustration as such can occur only to an individual organism, any given frustrating condition may occur to several individuals simultaneously. In such a case, a "group" is viewed distributively rather than as a collective thing. If all or most of the individuals in a group are hungry, the "group" may be said, after this distributive fashion, to be hungry. A group of laborers, for example, had gathered around a boarding-house table at six o'clock for dinner, as was their practice at the end of the day. On ordinary days they ate without much conversation but with a fair approximation of dignity and good manners. On the day in question, the group sat down at the usual hour but no waiters appeared. There were soon murmurs of protest to the general effect that, if the landlady were to stay home, dinner could be served on time; and threats were made that they might stop boarding at that house. Gradually the self-restraints usually governing behavior at the table disappeared and there was a rhythmic stamping of feet. Someone shouted, "We want food"—the rest took up the cry and produced a tremendous uproar. Hard rolls were seized from the table and thrown at the kitchen door, presumably in the direction of the landlady. Soon the object of their aggression appeared and explained the reason for the delay. Dinner was eventually served and the unusual behavior gradually died down, but with many threats and mutterings. Frustration was induced by the inability to continue those responses habitually connected with sitting down at a table and aggressive acts assumed the form of the breaches of etiquette, vociferous demands, shouted threats, and bread-throwing.

25   3. A youngster, aged three, showed a markedly greater tendency to naughty behavior on Monday than on any other day of the week. This child was accustomed to see her parents daily and to receive much of their personal attention, to talk with them, to ask innumerable ques-

tions, to be taken into arms, to be cuddled and swung by her father, to be instructed and noticed. Since her parents played the actual role of caretakers in her life, this smooth routine was inevitably disrupted when she was turned over to the maid. On Mondays she would say that she did not like her parents, quarrel with her little sister, wet her bed, and would cry protestingly if her parents attempted to leave her at all. The question of why Monday elicited this behavior most extensively seemed answered when the parents noticed that they were much more often away from the house on Saturday and Sunday than on any other days of the week. Their absence undoubtedly was experienced by the child as a deprivation, and her bad behavior on Monday appeared to be a reaction to the Sunday frustrations. . . .

4. Deviant as well as normal persons occasionally make the princi- 26
ples in this discussion quite visible. A man was admitted to a mental hospital because of his overpowering fear that be would kill his wife and children. He had first been informed of the existence of such tendencies in himself by dreams; later, what had at first shocked him in dreams became a matter of conscious wishes against which he had to defend himself. He finally fled into the mental hospital rather than be subjected to this temptation to injure those so near to him. In such a case the principles here advanced would require an examination of the man's life to ascertain what, if any, privations he experienced through the existence of his family. It did not require much interrogation to ascertain the truth. The problem centered around having, or not having, children. The skill-level of this individual was so low that he had no chance to increase his income, if, indeed, he were able to maintain it indefinitely at the same level. Additional children meant that the available income would have to be further subdivided, that education of the existing children would be definitely limited, that the food and shelter standards for all members of the family would be lowered, and that the risks which all were running of being truly poverty-stricken would be increased. But this man was not able, for religious reasons, to utilize contraceptive measures. His wife, therefore, was a constant sex temptation to him; he was faced with the necessity of inhibiting his repeatedly instigated sex response. As a result of his own frustrations, he came to hate those who seemed to be pressing this conflict on him, namely his wife and children, and his eventual solution was flight from the whole dilemma to a mental hospital.

5. A young man who was very fond of music was attending a con- 27
cert by a famous violinist. The program was a brilliant one and the young man settled down to what he anticipated would be a thoroughly enjoyable evening. In spite of his interest in the music, however, he soon

became aware of the squirming and wriggling of a man sitting in front of him. For a few minutes the young man tried to ignore this distraction. When the wriggling and the consequent creaking of the seat continued unabated, however, he became very angry and finally spoke sharply to the disturber, suggesting sarcastically that the rest of the audience would appreciate his using the lobby in which to do his scratching if he had to scratch and wiggle. The young man's on-going listening responses had been blocked and he reacted with an overt aggressive kind of behavior. The phrase "on-going listening responses" expresses the conception that the organism does not merely experience a "feeling of esthetic appreciation" but is actually *behaving*. The behavior is comprised of goal responses eventuating from instigation to listen to good music. . . .

28   In defining the various basic concepts and exemplifying them with the above case material it becomes evident that not only do these concepts stretch across from one scientific discipline to another but that they also have a relationship to other concepts basic to a complete systematic theory of behavior. But while every effort will be made to push the frustration-aggression hypothesis as far as it will go with reference either to individual or to social facts that are relevant to it, present knowledge does not permit a detailed linking of these concepts to others within the science of behavior.

Aggression: A Social Learning Analysis

ALBERT BANDURA

For all its usefulness, frustration-aggression theory was gradually replaced by greater emphasis on external environmental cues as psychologists came to search for the precise situations and circumstances that elicit aggression and violence. Frustration-aggression theory looks primarily at forces emerging from within the individual, which, when denied satisfaction, generate aggression. By contrast, attention eventually shifted to the role of learning, defined as the modification of behavior as a result of experience.

Psychological research on aggression thus became increasingly focussed on integrating aggression and violence into general learning theory. The underlying idea was—and for many psychologists, still is— that aggressive behavior is both acquired and maintained by the same fundamental principles governing the acquisition and maintenance of any other behavior; namely, the *contingencies of reinforcement,* or, in common usage, whether individuals are rewarded or punished for certain actions. Contrary to frustration theory, which holds that aggressive behavior is *reduced* when an individual behaves aggressively, learning theory maintains that aggression and violence is made *more likely* when it is experienced. Chief among proponents of this viewpoint has been Albert Bandura, whose pioneering work applying *social learning theory* to aggression is fundamental to psychological insights in this field.

A complete theory of aggression, whatever its orientation, must explain how aggressive patterns of behavior are developed, what provokes people to behave aggressively, and what maintains their aggressive actions. . . . 1

Development of new modes of behavior. Patterns of behavior can be acquired through direct experience or by observing the behavior of others. The more rudimentary form of learning, rooted in direct experience, is largely governed by the rewarding and punishing consequences that follow any given action. People are repeatedly confronted with situations with which they must deal in one way or another. Some of the responses they try prove unsuccessful, while others produce more favorable effects. Through this process of differential reinforcement, successful modes of behavior are eventually selected from exploratory activities, while ineffectual ones are discarded. 2

Although behavior can be shaped into new patterns to some extent by rewarding and punishing consequences, learning would be exceedingly laborious and hazardous if it proceeded solely on this basis. Most of the intricate responses people display are learned, either deliberately or inadvertently, through the influence of example. Indeed, virtually all learning phenomena resulting from direct experiences can occur on a vicarious basis through observation of other people's behavior and its consequences for them. Man's capacity to learn by observation enables him to acquire complex patterns of behavior by watching the performances of exemplary models. Emotional responses toward certain places, persons, or things can also be developed by witnessing the affective reactions of others punished for their actions. And, finally, the expression of previously learned responses can be socially regulated through the actions of influential models. 3

The preceding remarks are not meant to imply that new modes of behavior are fashioned solely through experience, either of a direct or observational sort. Biological structure obviously sets limits on the types of aggressive responses that can be successfully perfected, and genetic endowment influences the rate at which learning progresses. 4

5   *Regulatory functions.*   A comprehensive theory of behavior must explain not only how response patterns are acquired, but how their expression is regulated and maintained. In social learning theory, human functioning relies on three regulatory systems. They include antecedent inducements, response feedback influences, and cognitive processes that guide and regulate action. Human aggression is a learned conduct that, like other forms of social behavior, is under stimulus, reinforcement, and cognitive control. These control functions will be discussed separately for explanatory purposes, although in reality they are closely interrelated.

6   *Stimulus control.*   To function effectively a person must be able to anticipate the probable consequences of different events and courses of action and regulate his behavior accordingly. Without a capacity for anticipatory or foresighted behavior, man could not profit much from experience. Information about probable consequences is conveyed by environmental stimuli, such as verbal communications; pictorial cues; distinctive places, persons, or things; or the actions of others.

7   In the earliest years of development, environmental events, except those that are inherently painful, exert little or no influence on infants and young children. As a result of paired experiences, direct, symbolic, or vicarious, formerly neutral stimuli begin to acquire motivating and response-directive properties. Environmental stimuli gain the capacity to activate physiological reactions and emotional behavior through association with evocative events. Such learning often occurs on the basis of direct experience. People come to fear and to avoid individuals who are commonly associated in their experience with pain or distress. Through a similar learning process they become easily angered by the sight or thought of individuals with whom they have had hostile encounters.

8   Social characteristics generally acquire evocative power through processes that are more subtle and complex than is commonly believed. Emotional responses are frequently acquired on the basis of vicarious rather than direct experiences. The emotional responses exhibited by others toward certain people tend to arouse in observers strong emotional reactions that can become conditioned to the same targets. It is not uncommon for unpopular minority groups or nationalities to become endowed with anger-evoking potency in the absence of personal contact through exposure to modeled animosity. Emotion-arousing words and pictures that conjure up hostile reactions likewise often function as the vehicle for symbolic conditioning of hatreds.

9   The emotional responses that become established to paired events can be evoked by not only direct experience, observation of another's affective expression, and symbolic stimuli, but also by provocative

thoughts. People can easily make themselves nauseous by imagining revolting experiences. They can become sexually aroused by generating erotic fantasies. They can frighten themselves by fear-provoking thoughts. And they can work themselves up into a state of anger by ruminating about mistreatment from offensive provocateurs. The cognitive capacities of humans thus enable them to invest things with positive or negative valence by pairing them repeatedly with thought-produced emotions. This self-arousal process is illustrated in a husband's slaying of a friend who kissed his wife at a New Year's Eve party. The husband had brooded almost incessantly about the kiss over a period of two years. As Thanksgiving approached he further intensified his anger by imagining his foe enjoying a family Thanksgiving dinner while his own family life was irreparably ruined. Shortly after observing how easy it was to kill a man from seeing Oswald shot on television, the brooding husband sought and shot his former friend. . . .

Reinforcement control.   A second control system involves behavior feed-   10
back influences, mainly in the form of reinforcing consequences. An organism that responded foresightedly on the basis of informative environmental cues but remained unaffected by the results of its actions would be too obtuse to survive for long. In fact, behavior is extensively controlled by its consequences. Responses that cause unrewarding or punishing effects tend to be discarded, whereas those that produce rewarding outcomes are retained and strengthened. Human behavior therefore cannot be fully understood without examining the regulatory influence of reinforcement.

Reinforcement control of behavior is most convincingly demon-   11
strated by intrasubject replication. In these types of studies interpersonal modes of response, many of long standing, are successively eliminated and reinstated by altering the effects they produce. The susceptibility of behavior to reinforcement control is further shown by the fact that even subtle variations in the frequency and patterning of outcomes result in different types of performances. Those who have been rewarded each time they respond are likely to become easily discouraged and to give up quickly when their efforts fail. On the other hand, individuals whose behavior has been reinforced intermittently tend to persist for a considerable time despite setbacks and only occasional success. . . .

Vicarious reinforcement.   Human functioning would be exceedingly in-   12
efficient, not to say dangerous, if behavior were influenced only by directly experienced consequences. Fortunately, one can profit greatly from the experiences of others. People repeatedly observe the actions of others and the occasions on which they are rewarded, ignored, or

punished. Observed reinforcement influences behavior in much the same way as outcomes that are directly experienced. . . .

13 *Self-reinforcement.* At the highest level of psychological functioning, individuals regulate their own behavior by self-evaluative and other self-produced consequences. . . . In this process people set themselves certain standards of conduct and respond to their own behavior in self-satisfied or self-critical ways in accordance with their self-imposed demands. Comparative studies show that people can manage their own behavior by self-reinforcement as well as or better than through consequences arising from external sources.

14 After a self-monitored reinforcement system has been established, a given action produces two sets of consequences—a self-evaluative reaction as well as some external outcome. These two sources of reinforcement can occur in several different patterns. Sometimes people are rewarded socially or materially for behavior that they devalue. Anticipation of self-reproach for personally repudiated actions provides an important motivating influence to keep behavior in line with adopted standards in the face of opposing influences. There is no more devastating punishment than self-contempt. . . .

15 Some of the most drastic changes in behavior are achieved in large part by modifying a person's basis for self-evaluation. By legitimizing aggression and dehumanizing potential victims, individuals who have been strictly socialized against brutalizing and slaying people can be led to do so in military situations without experiencing tormenting self-devaluative consequences. . . . Among those who fully adopt the new standards of conduct, skillfully executed carnage may even serve as a basis for self-commendation.

16 *Cognitive control.* If human behavior could be fully explained in terms of external inducements and response consequences, there would be no need to postulate any additional regulatory mechanisms. However, actions are not always predictable from these external sources of influence. Man's cognitive capacities tremendously increase the information he can derive from his experiences, and thus partly determine how he will be affected by them. There are several ways in which cognitive functioning enters into the regulation of human behavior. These are discussed next.

17 *Cognitive representation of reinforcement contingencies.* Popular portrayals of behavioral approaches would lead one to believe that people can be easily conditioned and manipulated without their awareness. This melodramatic sketch receives little support in numerous studies of

how awareness of reinforcement contingencies affects the process of behavior change. In fact, repeated paired stimulation generally fails to produce conditioned emotional responses as long as the connection between stimulus events goes unnoticed. The responses that get conditioned are to a large extent cognitively induced rather than directly elicited by external stimuli. Response consequences similarly have weak effects on behavior when the relationship between one's actions and outcomes is not recognized. On the other hand, awareness of conditions of reinforcement typically results in rapid changes in behavior, which is indicative of insightful functioning. People who are aware of what is wanted and who value the contingent rewards change their behavior in the reinforced direction; those who are equally aware of the reinforcement contingencies but who devalue the required behavior or the reinforcers show little change; those who remain unaware achieve, at best, small increments in performance even though the appropriate responses are reinforced whenever they occur.

Human behavior is regulated to a large extent by anticipated conse- 18 quences of prospective actions. Individuals may accurately assess the customary effects of given activities but fail to act in accordance with existing conditions or reinforcement because of hope that their actions may eventually bring favorable results. Many a social reformer has sustained his efforts in the face of repeated failures by the belief that the rightness of his cause will ultimately produce desired changes. Sometimes people lead themselves astray by inaccurate expectations when they wrongly assume that certain changes in their behavior will alter future consequences. The deterrent value of threatened punishment, for example, is weakened when lawbreakers misjudge their chances of escaping apprehension for antisocial acts. . . .

The notion that behavior is controlled by its immediate consequences 19 holds up better under close scrutiny for anticipated consequences than for those that actually impinge upon the organism. In most instances customary outcomes are reasonably good predictors of behavior because the consequences that people anticipate for their actions are accurately derived from, and therefore correspond closely to, prevailing conditions of reinforcement. However, belief and actuality do not always coincide because anticipated consequences are also partly inferred from observed response consequences of others, from what one reads or is told, and from a variety of other cues that, on the basis of past experiences, are considered reliable forecasters of likely outcomes. When actions are guided by anticipated consequences derived from predictors that do not accurately reflect existing contingencies of reinforcement, behavior is weakly controlled by its actual consequences until cumulative experiences produce more realistic expectations. . . .

20   *Cognitive guidance of behavior.*   Cognitive processes play a prominent role in the acquisition and retention of response patterns as well as in their expression. The memory trace of momentary influences is short-lived, but such experiences often have lasting behavioral effects. This is made possible by the fact transitory external events are coded and stored in symbolic form for memory representation. Patterns of behavior that have been observed and other experiences long past can thus be reinstated by visualizing them or by representing them verbally. These internal models of the outside world can serve as guides to overt action on later occasions. It will be recalled from the earlier discussion of learning processes that internal representations of patterned behavior are constructed from observed examples and from informative feedback to one's trial-and-error performances.

21   Cognitive functioning is especially important in observational learning in which a person reads about or observes a pattern of behavior, but does not perform it overtly until appropriate circumstances arise. Evidence will be cited later to illustrate how modeled activities are acquired in symbolic form without behavioral enactment, how they can be strengthened by mental rehearsal, and how they provide the basis for action on later occasions given suitable inducements.

22   *Thought control of action through mental problem-solving.*   Man's efforts to understand and to manage his environment would be exceedingly wearisome if optimal solutions to problems could be arrived at only by performing alternative actions and suffering the consequences. Actually, most problem-solving occurs in thought rather than in action. Man's higher mental capacities, for example, enable him to design sturdy dwellings and bridges without having to build them until he hits upon a structure that does not collapse. Alternative courses of action are generally tested in symbolic exploration and either discarded or retained on the basis of calculated consequences. The best symbolic solution is then executed in action.

23   The three major systems by which behavior is regulated do not operate independently; most actions are simultaneously controlled by two or more of the component influences. Moreover, the various systems are closely interdependent in acquiring and retaining their power to determine behavior. In order to establish and to maintain effective stimulus control, for example, the same actions must produce different consequences depending on the cues that are present. Stimulus and cognitive influences, in turn, can alter the impact of prevailing conditions of reinforcement. Certain stimuli can acquire such powerful control over defensive behavior that people avoid renewed encounters with feared or hated persons, places, or things. In instances in which

the original threats no longer exist, their self-protective behavior is in-sulated from realistic reinforcement influences.

Even when the things one dislikes or fears are not completely avoided, cues having strong emotion-arousing potential provoke defensive be-haviors that predictably create adverse reinforcement contingencies where they may not ordinarily exist. To the extent that an individual's distrust of certain people leads him to behave in ways that provoke hos-tile counterreactions from them, their negative valence is further strengthened and it, in turn, prompts actions that produce reciprocal neg-ative reinforcement. Both processes thus support each other. . . .

Differential Implications of Drive and Social Learning Theories

A number of predictions that follow from the social learning formulation differ from the traditional frustration-aggression hypothesis. It will be recalled that drive theories of aggression assume that frustration arouses an aggressive drive that can be reduced only through some form of ag-gressive behavior. Frustration, in this view, is a necessary and sufficient condition for aggression. The diverse events subsumed under the om-nibus term frustration have one feature in common—they are all aver-sive in varying degrees. In social learning theory, rather than frustration generating in aggressive drive, aversive treatment produces a general state of emotional arousal that can facilitate a variety of behaviors, depending on the types of responses the person has learned for coping with stress and their relative effectiveness. When distressed, some people seek help and support; others increase achievement strivings; others show withdrawal and resignation; some aggress; others experi-ence heightened somatic activity; still others anesthetize themselves against a miserable existence with drugs or alcohol; and most intensify constructive efforts to overcome their adversities. The major differences among the instinctual, reactive drive, and social learning theories in the ways they conceptualize the motivational component of aggression are depicted schematically in Figure 2.1.

There are several lines of evidence that lend support to the social learning formulation. Psychophysiological studies have been conducted in which people undergo fear- and anger-provoking experiences while changes in their physiological reactions are simultaneously recorded. . . .

It would appear from the available evidence that fear and anger have similar physiological correlates. Looking at the physiological records alone, one could not distinguish whether the individuals had been frightened or angered. The varied array of emotions experienced phenomenologically apparently stem from a common diffuse state of

24

25

26

27

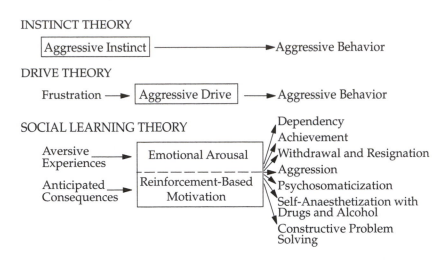

INSTINCT THEORY

Aggressive Instinct ──────────────→ Aggressive Behavior

DRIVE THEORY

Frustration ──→ Aggressive Drive ──→ Aggressive Behavior

SOCIAL LEARNING THEORY

Aversive Experiences ──→ Emotional Arousal

Anticipated Consequences ──→ Reinforcement-Based Motivation

Dependency
Achievement
Withdrawal and Resignation
Aggression
Psychosomaticization
Self-Anaesthetization with Drugs and Alcohol
Constructive Problem Solving

FIGURE 2.1 Diagrammatic representation of motivational determinants of aggression in instinct, reactive drive, and social learning theories.

emotional arousal rather than from distinct drive states. It seems unlikely that small differences in an otherwise identical pattern of physiological arousal are sufficiently distinguishable, if at all, to serve as the cues for differentiating among diverse emotional states. Whether people experience their emotional arousal as fear, anger, euphoria, or some other state depends not on particular somatic cues, but on a number of external defining influences.

28   People judge their emotions partly from the nature of the instigating conditions. Visceral arousal generated by threat is experienced as fear, arousal produced by thwarting is experienced as anger, and that resulting from irretrievable loss of valued objects as sorrow. . . .

29   Evidence that the same physiological arousal can be experienced subjectively as different kinds of emotion has several implications for a theory of aggression. First, it calls into question the validity of invoking an inborn aggressive drive from observations that infants display diffuse emotional upset to physical restraints and painful stimulation. Second, the general arousal model predicts that under conditions in which individuals are prone to behave aggressively, any source of emotional arousal may enhance aggressive behavior.

30   The role of emotional arousal in aggression is magnified when aggression is studied as a function of arousal-producing conditions within a permissive context only. It was previously noted that theories generally give disproportionate attention to aversively motivated aggression.

In the social learning analysis of motivation, incentives also constitute important impellers of action. A great deal of aggression is prompted by its anticipated benefits. Here, the instigator is the pull of expected success, rather than the push of aversive treatment. As depicted in Figure 2.1, anticipatory functions provide a mechanism of response selection from among a variety of alternatives.

Under circumstances in which arousal facilitates aggression, the so- 31 cial learning formulation predicts that arousal decreased through non-injurious means will reduce aggression as well as, or even better than, acting aggressively. In drive theories the actuated aggressive drive presumably endures until discharged by some form of aggressive activity. From the social learning perspective, anger arousal dissipates, but it can be repeatedly regenerated on later occasions by ruminating on anger-provoking incidents. By thinking about past insulting treatment, a person can work himself into a rage long after the initial emotional reactions have subsided. Given this cognitive capacity, it is not necessary to invoke a drive to explain arousal that outlasts its original instigators. Persistence of elevated anger arousal, in this view, reflects self-generated arousal rather than the existence of an undischarged reservoir of aggressive energy. To illustrate the different views, let us consider the example of a person who becomes angered by an apparent social slight only to discover that the invitation to the social function has arrived in the next mail. He is likely to show an immediate drop in anger arousal and aggressiveness without having to assault or denounce someone so as to reduce a lingering aggressive drive.

Research reveals that ventilative therapies aimed at draining aggres- 32 sive drives by having people behave aggressively may be inadvertently reinforcing their aggressive tendencies. By contrast, social learning treatments, which have proved successful . . . help people from the outset to acquire better ways of dealing with social problems so that they have less to get angry about. Aggressive behavior of long standing is reliably reduced by a variety of approaches, including modeling of alternative coping responses; selective reinforcement in which aggressive actions are nonrewarded while better solutions are actively supported; eliminating fantasied instigators of violent outbursts; developing competencies that provide new sources of reward; and reducing aversive social conditions.

There is a third implication of social learning theory that differs from 33 traditional views. Frustration or anger arousal is a facilitative but not a necessary condition for aggression. Frustration is most likely to provoke aggression in people who have learned to respond to aversive treatment with aggressive attitudes and actions. In an early study bearing on this issue following arbitrarily insulting treatment, aggressively trained children behaved more aggressively, whereas cooperatively trained children behaved more cooperatively. Responses to aversive treatment are also frequently patterned on the characteristic actions of salient models.

34   In writings on the causes of aggression, factors such as broken homes, parental rejection, adverse socioeconomic conditions, thwarted strivings, and intrapsychic conflicts are usually identified as important determinants. If one examines the antecedents that have been invoked for other types of behavior disorders, such as drug addiction, alcoholism, and schizophrenia, essentially the same adverse conditions appear in roughly comparable rates. Nor are adversity and familial discord necessarily rare in the backgrounds of people who develop patterns of behavior that are valued in the larger society. Findings of these etiological studies suggest that aversive conditions increase the probability that deviant patterns will arise, but they do not determine what form the behavior will take. Ghetto conditions, for example, probably produce more alcoholism, drug addiction, and resignation and withdrawal than aggression. One cannot account for the presence of elaborate modes of behavior on the basis of deficits or frustrative conditions alone. Response patterns that are socially labeled as deviant, like emulative conduct, require the presence of appropriate social learning influences for their acquisition and maintenance.

35   One can distinguish among aggressive acts, emotional arousal experienced as anger, and aggressive attitudes exemplified in negative evaluations. No evidence is available that behavioral, affective, and cognitive responses are inherently linked in one way or another. They can be coupled through common consequences and dissociated by differential consequences. When people are free to voice aggressive attitudes but injurious acts are strictly prohibited, correspondence between word and deed will be low. It was previously shown how emotional arousal can either facilitate or inhibit aggressive acts depending upon its contingent outcomes. Thus, people often experience anger without taking any aggressive action; conversely, they can be induced to perform injurious acts without accompanying anger. Even the physiological manifestations that are subjectively experienced as anger arousal can be dissociated through selective reinforcement. If individuals are rewarded only when they increase both their heart rate and blood pressure, these two autonomic functions become linked, but if rewards are given only when one response goes up and the other goes down, these physiological reactions become differentiated. . . . Consonance between affect and attitudes will likewise be reduced should emotionally charged attitudes produce negative results while calmly expressed ones are well received.

36   In short, people do not have to be angered or emotionally aroused to behave aggressively. A culture can produce highly aggressive people,

while keeping frustration at a low level, by valuing aggressive accomplishments, furnishing successful aggressive models, and ensuring that aggressive actions secure rewarding effects. Since aggression does not originate internally and its social determinants are alterable, social learning theory holds a more optimistic view of man's capacity to reduce the level of human destructiveness. . . .

Like so many other problems confronting man, there is no single   37
grand design for lowering the level of destructiveness within a society. It requires both individual corrective effort and group action aimed at changing the practices of social systems. Since aggression is not an inevitable or unchangeable aspect of man but a product of aggression promoting conditions operating within a society, man has the power to reduce his level of aggressiveness. Whether this capability is used wisely or destructively is another matter.

On the Formation and Regulation
of Anger and Aggression

LEONARD BERKOWITZ

Further refinement of social learning theory has occurred in several different directions. Of these, one of the most prominent is known as *social cognition,* which—as the phrase implies—involves a synthesis of social learning theory and basic principles of cognitive psychology. In brief, it posits that people use their experiences to develop internal mental maps (sometimes called *cognitive scripts*) that they consult to determine how to behave in the future. Social cognition of this sort is widely thought to influence a wide range of human behavior, including aggression and tendencies for violence.

One of the simplest and most powerful examples of this approach was pioneered by psychologist Leonard Berkowitz, who emphasized the importance of "unpleasant sensations" in predisposing toward aggression and violence. In a sense, anger is identified as a crucial variable that intervenes between negative experiences (including but not limited to frustration) and the occurrence of aggression or violence.

Most people, psychologists and nonpsychologists alike, are fairly confi-   1
dent about when people will be prompted to become angry and attack an available target. Anger arises and aggression occurs, it is widely assumed, as a result of a perceived threat or the belief that one has been

intentionally mistreated or even because of some frustration. However, there may well be more to the origin of aggression than is commonly supposed. Mounting evidence indicates that aggression can also be produced by a remarkably broad range of unpleasant occurrences that are not intentionally or unfairly produced by a human agent. Foul odors, high temperatures, exposure to painfully cold water, and even disgusting scenes can also heighten the hostility displayed, or the aggression that is directed toward another person, even when that individual cannot possibly be blamed for the unpleasantness and the aggression cannot alleviate the negative state of affairs. It is not especially profound to maintain that these aversive events can also create considerable irritation, annoyance, and even anger. Not infrequently, people say that they feel irritated or annoyed, and sometimes even that they are angry, when they are not feeling well or have been afflicted by some unpleasant occurrence.

2   These observations will serve as the starting point for the present analysis. The core notion in this model is that negative affect is the basic source of anger and angry aggression. It is clear, of course, that cognitions can also influence the formation of angry feelings. However, cognitive processes need not operate only in the ways specified by conventional cognitive/appraisal/attributional formulations of emotion. In this article, I suggest how anger can also be affected by both the associative linkages connecting negative affect with aggression-related ideas, memories, and expressive-motor reactions and also by people's schemas regarding the nature of anger. . . .

Are Cognitions Necessary?

3   I noted earlier that a wide variety of unpleasant occurrences can instigate aggressive reactions: immersion in cold water, exposure to high temperatures, foul odors, the sight of morally repugnant scenes, and so on. All of these conditions are aversive, and all generate negative affect. It is this unpleasant feeling that presumably produces the aggressive inclinations and the accompanying angry feelings. A major question, however, is whether these reactions are due to the negative affect alone. More specifically, one might ask, does the suffering person also have to have certain types of beliefs about the aversive event or its consequences before she or he will experience anger?

4   Nearly every cognitive account of the origin of anger maintains that certain kinds of beliefs are necessary if this feeling is to arise (although the theorists taking this stance are not agreed as to whether these beliefs should be called appraisals or attributions). To take only two examples. Weiner has held that people will not be angered by unpleasant conditions unless these events are attributed to someone's intentional and

controllable misdeed, whereas Lazarus has maintained that individuals must view the negative occurrences as threats to their well-being. The present model accepts a weak version of this thesis: Certain kinds of appraisal or attributional beliefs can intensify or weaken the anger experience. A frustration is especially bothersome when it blocks the attainment of personally significant goals and is attributed to another person's deliberate misbehavior, but it is less disturbing when unimportant strivings are thwarted and the interference is viewed as only an accidental occurrence. What the model questions is the strong version of the cognitive analysis maintaining that these beliefs are necessary if the aversive occurrence is to generate anger. . . .

I have advanced a theoretical model that attempts to spell out the relation between the initial negative affect and the resulting angry feelings. Along with several other recent formulations this conception assumes that associative networks link specific types of feelings with particular thoughts and memories and also with certain kinds of expressive-motor and physiological reactions. Also with these other analyses, the model maintains that the activation of any one of the components in the network tends to activate the other parts as well. But this formulation also has some relatively unique features. [5]

Most notably, according to this model, there is an associative connection between negative affect and anger-related feelings, ideas, and memories, and also with aggressive inclinations. It is because of these associations that persons who feel bad for one reason or another—whether they have a toothache, are very hot, are exposed to foul smells or an unpleasant noise, or are just very sad or depressed—are likely to be angry, have hostile ideas and memories, and to be aggressively disposed. More specifically, according to this formulation, the negative affect generated by the aversive occurrence automatically gives rise to at least two sets of reactions at the same time: bodily changes, feelings, ideas, and memories associated with escape from the unpleasant stimulation *and also* bodily reactions, feelings, thoughts, and memories associated with aggression. A variety of factors—genetic, learned, and situational—supposedly determine the relative strengths of these two response classes. [6]

The basic fear experience presumably develops from the person's conscious and preconscious awareness of the initial escape-associated reactions, whereas awareness of the first aggression-associated feelings, thoughts, memories, and expressive-motor responses theoretically produces a rudimentary anger experience. In other words, from this perspective the rudimentary fear and anger experiences do not in themselves produce fearful and aggressive behavior but only parallel the escape and aggressive motor tendencies evoked by the negative affect. [7]

8   But people do not always report being angry or afraid when an unpleasant event takes place. They might describe themselves as anxious, depressed, envious, guilty, or something else, but frequently they say little about being angry. I do not claim that this absence of reported anger is necessarily due only to a denial of these feelings. The negatively afflicted persons may actually not be consciously aware of any anger soon after they encounter the aversive stimulus because other emotional states have arisen and command their attention. The model contends that these other relatively complicated emotional experiences usually develop after the basic, primary reactions to the negative event. Positing a series of stages in the formation of emotions, the model assumes that relatively automatic associative processes are dominant at first and govern the initial primitive reactions. Complicated thoughts of the type postulated by cognitive theorists theoretically play only a small role at this early stage, except for the fairly simple initial appraisal of the incident as unpleasant. A fraction of time afterward, however, other higher-order cognitive processes begin to operate, particularly as thought is given to what has happened and its possible consequences.

9   It is in these later stages that the affected person makes appraisals and causal attributions and considers what feelings and actions are appropriate under the particular circumstances. This additional thought leads to the differentiation, intensification, suppression, or elaboration of the early rudimentary experiences. If the afflicted persons' arousal level is weak, for example, they may decide at this time that they are irritated or annoyed rather than angry. Or as cognitive/attributional theorizing proposes, afflicted persons may come to believe that they are, for example, sad and not angry, because they believe that one does not feel anger in this particular situation. They may even develop relatively complicated emotional experiences such as anxiety, contempt, envy, guilt, and even depression. The present formulation maintains that these later, more developed emotional experiences are essentially constructed as the mind brings together various sensory, ideational, and memorial inputs from all of those available, guided by the individual's prototypic conception of what the specific emotion is like.

10   Another important assumption in this model is that the higher order cognitive processing governing the full development of the anger experience does not necessarily always go into operation. The aversively stimulated persons may have to be motivated to think more extensively and deeper about the various kinds of information they have received. Once they engage in this higher order processing, however, they consider the perceived causes of their arousal, the possible consequences of

any action they might undertake, the goals they would like to attain, and also what sensations they are feeling and what ideas and memories have just occurred to them.

Research Support for the Model

The key proposition in my analysis, then, is that negative affect of any   11 kind will first activate anger-related feelings, action tendencies, and thoughts and memories. Several published studies can be cited in support of this contention. In one, Baron showed that deliberately provoked subjects became less hostile toward their tormentor after they had an irrelevant pleasant experience. It is as if the pleasant feelings had lessened the negative affect-generated aggressive inclinations. In another experiment, Rule, Taylor, and Dobbs demonstrated that aversive events tend to heighten the accessibility of anger-related thoughts, even when the unpleasant stimulation is delivered to the subjects in keeping with approved social rules. In this investigation those participants who were exposed to scientifically legitimate but highly uncomfortable heat used more hostile ideas in constructing emotion-related stories than did the control subjects under a more comfortable temperature.

Findings from Recent Research

Research carried out at the University of Wisconsin has also yielded re-   12 sults in accord with my conception of an associative network linking negative affect, anger-related feelings, and anger-related thoughts. The first experiment along these lines explored whether both physical discomfort and thoughts of unpleasant occurrences would activate anger-related feelings and ideas. Some of the subjects were asked to imagine themselves being frustrated in a certain way (being caught in a traffic jam while driving to an important appointment), others were to think of themselves in a particular anxiety-provoking situation (being alone in an elevator stopped between floors in a deserted office building at night), and the last group had to imagine being in a neutral situation (doing grocery shopping). We assumed here that the thought of either of the aversive incidents would prime negative affect-related ideas and memories and that these, in turn, would activate the anger-related feelings and thoughts. However, we also believed that the people imagining themselves being frustrated would have more of these anger-related feelings and ideas because frustrating events are often associated with anger and aggression. Finally we also expected that the negative affect produced by physical discomfort would heighten these effects.

13   The experiment designed to test this reasoning first established differences in physical discomfort. The individual male and female subjects
extended their nondominant arm throughout the six-minute experimental procedure, either resting the arm on the table (in the low discomfort group) or holding it outward and unsupported (in the high
discomfort condition). After the subjects' arms had been in the specified
position for about three minutes, the experimenter asked the participants to think of themselves in one of the previously described situations
and then relate how they would feel on that occasion. Three minutes
later, at the completion of this task, and with their arm still in this position, they rated their present feelings on a series of mood items. . . .

14   The findings in the low discomfort condition demonstrated that the incidents had the desired effects on the subjects' emotional thoughts. The
people telling the anxiety story expressed the greatest number of fear-
related ideas, whereas those talking about the frustrating the greatest
number of anger-related ideas. . . . The high discomfort group had the
highest number of anger-related thoughts in the frustration situation, significantly greater than the number of such ideas in the high discomfort
group for the anxiety and neutral situations (although the mean for the
frustration situation was not significantly greater than the mean for the
frustration situation under low discomfort). Also as we had expected,
those in the high discomfort group imagining the anxiety-provoking
event mentioned anger-related ideas reliably more often than did their
counterparts thinking of the neutral situation. What is especially noteworthy is the effect of the high physical discomfort on the expression of
anger versus fear in response to the anxiety-provoking incident. The
number of fear-related thoughts dropped significantly from low to high
discomfort, whereas there was a corresponding significant increase in
anger-related thoughts from the low to the high discomfort condition.

15   Putting all of the findings together, the results indicated that physical
discomfort tends to activate both ideas and feelings related to anger.
Moreover, consistent with the associative network model presented in
this article, even thoughts of being in an unpleasant situation served to
heighten the availability of these anger-related ideas. Finally, as expected,
the subjects exposed to both discomfort and unpleasant thoughts—
especially those in the high discomfort group exposed to frustration—
reported the highest level of angry feelings and made the greatest
number of references to anger-related ideas. . . .

16   The emphasis on associative processes up to this point does not
mean that cognitive processes do not intervene to influence the anger
experience. According to my analysis, the feeling of anger is shaped by
relatively high level information processing as well as by lower level as-

sociations, especially after the initial, rudimentary emotional reactions. At this higher level, cognitive processing has to do with more than the introduction of attributions and expectations into the developing experience. Cognitions can also affect the way bodily reactions contribute to the forming experience.

The Regulation of Emotional Effects

The cognitive-neoassociationistic model offered here goes beyond the development of the emotional experience and also deals with the behavioral effects of the emotion arousal. In general, what people say and do when they are emotionally aroused can also be influenced by both associative and cognitive processes. This observation is especially pertinent to the behavioral consequences of negative affect. Even though we are usually inclined to be hostile and even aggressive toward others when we are feeling bad, the hostility and aggression are not always apparent. Rather than lashing out at someone, we often act in a nonaggressive manner because we are more concerned with improving our mood or escaping from the unpleasant situation than with attacking an available target, and, of course, sometimes we do not want to do anything. The angry feelings and aggressive tendencies generated by the negative affect are not necessarily stronger than the other feelings and inclinations that also arise and are frequently masked by these other reactions. 17

Conscious anticipations of punishment obviously can suppress the aversively stimulated aggression. But what is more interesting is that we sometimes also hold back and do not display the hostility or aggression we are inclined to show because of the operation of a self-regulatory mechanism operating at a preconscious level. It is not altogether clear just what is involved in this self-regulation and exactly what activates it. However, five separate experiments conducted in my laboratory leave me with little doubt that this self-regulation of the effects of a bad mood is a fairly reliable phenomenon and that it seems to occur when attention is focused on the unpleasant feelings. 18

My theory is that when people become aware of their moderately negative feelings as a consequence of this attention, they are somewhat surprised or disturbed, and this prompts a relatively high level of cognitive activity. They think about the possible causes of their feelings and even consider what may be the best way to act. These considerations then steer their behavior. Otherwise, in the absence of this awareness-produced high level of cognitive activity, the hostile and aggressive tendencies created by the negative mood are less likely to be restrained and are likely to be expressed openly in a harsh treatment of the available target. . . . 19

Does Television Violence
Cause Aggression?

LEONARD D. ERON, L. ROWELL HUESMANN,
MONROE M. LEFKOWITZ, AND
LEOPOLD O. WALDER

Academic research does have practical implications for social policy . . . although for various reasons, such implications are not always acted upon. One of the most actively debated questions concerns the role of televised and movie violence, augmented of late by concern over the lyrics in popular music (notably gangsta rap). Controversy also swirls around video games: compared to World War II, Vietnam War soldiers were 4.5 times more likely to shoot at their enemy, quite possibly because of extensive training with "first person shooter" devices not unlike violent video games such as Quake, Doom, or Mortal Kombat.

Americans represent violence incessantly, from movies such as *Natural Born Killers* to television cartoons, such that the average eighteen-year-old will have seen 18,000 media murders. In the aftermath of a notorious series of school shootings by young students—most dramatically, a homicidal rampage in Littleton, Colorado that resulted in the death of fifteen persons—serious questions were raised about the long-term effect of such exposure. For some, it is a matter of First Amendment freedom; for others, a question of whether people become more violence prone after such media exposure, or if their entertainment preferences result from preexisting inclinations, or even if such experiences serve to "release" violent fantasies in a harmless manner. An immense amount of research has explored the matter of vicariously experienced violence, and although final answers remain elusive, the basic phenomenon is increasingly clear. The following excerpt is from one of the classic and most convincing research efforts in this difficult field.

1   With the increasing prominence of violence in our society, social scientists have been turning their attention to the antecedents of aggressive behavior in children and adults. Television programming with its heavy emphasis on interpersonal violence and acquisitive lawlessness has been assigned a role both in inciting aggression and teaching viewers specific techniques of aggressive behavior. The relation between overt aggression and television habits has been demonstrated in a few survey studies which, however, because of the nature of surveys have not been able to discriminate cause and effect.

2   One possible way of utilizing survey procedures to demonstrate cause and effect is to use a longitudinal context. By contrasting the mag-

nitude of contemporaneous and longitudinal correlations between two sets of variables, it is possible to account more clearly for which of the variables is antecedent and which consequent. The authors have now accumulated data on both aggressive behavior and television viewing habits over a 10-year period in a large group of subjects first seen when they were 8–9 years of age. Thus, we can implement such an analysis.

The hypotheses of this research are that a young adult's aggressiveness is positively related to his preference for violent television when he was 8–9 years old and, furthermore, that his preference for violent television during this critical period is one cause of his aggressiveness. 3

Method

Longitudinal data were collected on 427 teenagers of an original group of 875 children who had participated in a study of third-grade children in 1960. The original 875 constituted the entire third-grade population of a semirural county in New York's Hudson River Valley, while the 427 subjects were those who could be located and interviewed 10 years later. 4

The information collected about these subjects in both time periods falls into two classes: (*a*) measures of aggression and (*b*) potential predictors of aggression. During the third-grade interviews, four different data sources had been used: the subject, his peers, his mother, and his father. Ten years later, the data sources were the subject and his peers. For convenience, this later time period will be designated as the thirteenth grade. 5

Two variables are of particular importance: peer-rated aggression and preference for violent television programs. In the third grade, peer-rated aggression scores were obtained by asking each child to nominate any of his classmates on 10 "guess who" items describing aggressive behavior; for example, "Who pushes and shoves other children?" "Who takes other children's things without asking ?" "Who starts a fight over nothing?" "Who says mean things?" These aggression items were interspersed among a series of other peer nomination questions. The validity and reliability of the aggression measure have been discussed elsewhere. . . . 6

In the third grade, the children's preferences for violent television were obtained by asking each mother for her child's three favorite television programs. All programs mentioned were then categorized as violent or nonviolent by two independent raters with 94% agreement in their ratings. Differences in the remaining 6% of the programs were resolved by mutual discussion between the raters. Each subject received a score according to the number of violent television programs he was reported by his mother as favoring. Scores ranged from 1 (for no violent programs) to 4 (for three violent programs). 7

8   In the 10-year follow-up study, each subject *himself* was asked for his four current favorite television programs. All programs were then categorized for presence or absence of violence by two independent raters who were only a few years older than the subjects themselves. Scores were assigned to each program on the basis of agreement between the raters. If they both agreed a program was nonviolent, the program received a score of 0; if they both agreed it was violent, the score was 2; if they disagreed in categorization, the program was assigned a score of 1. Here again there was good agreement between the two raters. They agreed on 81% of 125 programs mentioned by the subjects. The score for each subject was the sum of the violence ratings of the four programs mentioned. . . .

9   There is a highly significant relation between boys' preferences for violent television programs in the third grade (TVVL3) and their peer-rated aggression in the thirteenth grade (AGG13). Similarly, there is a significant contemporaneous relation between the boys' television preferences in the third grade and peer-rated aggression in the third grade (AGG3). Neither of these effects was apparent for females. While the correlation between third-grade preferences and thirteenth-grade peer-rated aggression explains only 10% of the variance in aggression, 10% is impressive when one considers the probable limitations on the size of the correlation imposed by the skewed distributions of the variable, the large number of variables affecting aggression, the comparatively small explanatory power of these other variables (see below), and the 10-year lag between measurement times. The extremely low likelihood of achieving such a correlation by chance is a good indicator of the strength of the relation between preference for violent television at age 8 years and peer-rated aggression at age 19. . . .

Discussion

10   The above results indicate that television habits established by age 8–9 years influence boys' aggressive behavior at that time and at least through late adolescence. The more violent are the programs preferred by boys in the third grade, the more aggressive is their behavior both at that time and 10 years later. This relation between early television habits and later aggression prevails both for peer-rated aggression and for self-ratings of aggression. Actually, these early television habits seem to be more influential than current viewing patterns since a preference for violent television in the thirteenth grade is not at all related to concurrent aggressive behavior, nor are early television habits related to later television habits. . . .

The laboratory studies of Bandura furnish a theoretical model to account for these results. Bandura and his associates have demonstrated that aggressive behaviors new to the subject's repertoire of responses, as well as those already well established in his repertoire, can be evoked by observation of models performing such aggressive behaviors. The fact that the model does not get punished for the aggressive behaviors he develops serves to lower whatever inhibitions subjects have against the expression of similar behaviors. The likelihood of performance of the observed aggressive behaviors is stronger when the model is rewarded for his aggressive behavior. It is not unusual on the more violent television programs for central characters to obtain desirable goals by violent tactics. Continued exposure to such models probably strengthens the conviction that these behaviors are permissible, and observation of acquisition of desired goals by aggressive behaviors increases the probability of performance of these behaviors by the observer. It is interesting in this regard that the more the subjects watch television at age 19 and the more violent the programs they prefer, the more likely are they to believe that situations depicted on television crime stories and westerns are realistic representations of life ($r = .28$ between judged realism of television programs and number of hours television is watched; and .36 between judged realism and television violence). Thus, subjects who watch television for many hours and prefer violent programs do not consider these aggressive behaviors as deviant but as appropriate ways of solving real-life problems.

The lack of an effect of television violence on girls also corroborates the Bandura laboratory studies which have consistently found that boys perform significantly more imitative aggression than girls. Why this is so probably has to do with the differential socialization of boys and girls in regard to aggression. Very early in life, girls learn that physical aggression is an undesirable behavior for girls, and so they acquire other behaviors more suitable to expectations for girls. Since they do not learn physical aggression as a response to instigation, they are rarely either rewarded or punished for such behavior and thus are not responsive to aggressive cues in the environment. Bandura has shown that when girls are positively reinforced for imitating aggressive behavior, they significantly increase such behavior and respond in a manner more similar to boys who are reinforced for the same behaviors. . . .

The effect of television violence on aggression is relatively independent of . . . other factors and explains a larger portion of the variance than does any other single factor which we studied, including IQ, social status, mobility aspirations, religious practice, ethnicity, and parental disharmony.

Obedience to Authority

STANLEY MILGRAM

Among the primary virtues taught to young children—as well as adults, under many circumstances—is obedience. Indeed, in the Western religious tradition, disobedience is widely seen as *the* primal sin: Adam and Eve disobediently eating the apple in the Garden of Eden, not to mention Satan's disobedience toward God. It is widely assumed, especially among political conservatives, that a permissive attitude, fostering social disobedience, is largely responsible for society's ills, notably violence. And yet, ironically, it may be that throughout human history, more harm has been caused by obedience than by disobedience! In a sense, violence is a profound disregard for the "authority" of another—notably, the victim. But at the same time, perpetrators of violence are often being obedient to the authority—whether real or imagined—of others who insist upon their violent actions.

In a now-famous experiment, psychologist Stanley Milgram revealed the surprising tendency of normal people to engage in potentially violent acts . . . in the name of obedience to authority. In the following selection, from a book by that name, Milgram describes the phenomenon and suggests its broader applicability, especially to conditions of war. (It remains to be seen whether Milgram's approach sheds light on episodes of interpersonal violence as well.)

1   Obedience is as basic an element in the structure of social life as one can point to. Some system of authority is a requirement of all communal living, and it is only the man dwelling in isolation who is not forced to respond, through defiance or submission, to the commands of others. Obedience, as a determinant of behavior, is of particular relevance to our time. It has been reliably established that from 1933 to 1945 millions of innocent people were systemically slaughtered on command. Gas chambers were built, death camps were guarded, daily quotas of corpses were produced with the same efficiency as the manufacture of appliances. These inhumane policies may have originated in the mind of a single person, but they could only have been carried out on a massive scale if a very large number of people obeyed orders.

2   Obedience is the psychological mechanism that links individual action to political purpose. It is the dispositional cement that binds men to systems of authority. Facts of recent history and observation in daily life suggest that for many people obedience may be a deeply ingrained behavior tendency, indeed, a prepotent impulse overriding training in

ethics, sympathy, and moral conduct. C. P. Snow points to its importance when he writes:

> When you think of the long and gloomy history of man, you will find more hideous crimes have been committed in the name of obedience than have ever been committed in the name of rebellion. If you doubt that, read William Shirer's 'Rise and Fall of the Third Reich.' The German Officer Corps were brought up in the most rigorous code of obedience . . . in the name of obedience they were party to, and assisted in, the most wicked large scale actions in the history of the world.

The Nazi extermination of European Jews is the most extreme instance of abhorrent immoral acts carried out by thousands of people in the name of obedience. Yet in lesser degree this type of thing is constantly recurring: ordinary citizens are ordered to destroy other people, and they do so because they consider it their duty to obey orders. Thus, obedience to authority, long praised as a virtue, takes on a new aspect when it serves a malevolent cause; far from appearing as a virtue, it is transformed into a heinous sin. Or is it? 3

The moral question of whether one should obey when commands conflict with conscience was argued by Plato, dramatized in *Antigone*, and treated to philosophic analysis in every historical epoch. Conservative philosophers argue that the very fabric of society is threatened by disobedience, and even when the act prescribed by an authority is an evil one, it is better to carry out the act than to wrench at the structure of authority. Hobbes stated further that an act so executed is in no sense the responsibility of the person who carries it out but only of the authority that orders it. But humanists argue for the primacy of individual conscience in such matters, insisting that the moral judgments of the individual must override authority when the two are in conflict. 4

The legal and philosophic aspects of obedience are of enormous import, but an empirically grounded scientist eventually comes to the point where he wishes to move from abstract discourse to the careful observation of concrete instances. In order to take a close look at the act of obeying, I set up a simple experiment at Yale University. Eventually, the experiment was to involve more than a thousand participants and would be repeated at several universities, but at the beginning, the conception was simple. A person comes to a psychological laboratory and is told to carry out a series of acts that come increasingly into conflict with conscience. The main question is how far the participant will comply with the experimenter's instructions before refusing to carry out the actions required of him. 5

But the reader needs to know a little more detail about the experiment. Two people come to a psychology laboratory to take part in a 6 study of memory and learning. One of them is designated as a "teacher" and the other a "learner." The experimenter explains that the study is concerned with the effects of punishment on learning. The learner is conducted into a room, seated in a chair, his arms strapped to prevent excessive movement, and an electrode attached to his wrist. He is told that he is to learn a list of word pairs; whenever he makes an error, he will receive electric shocks of increasing intensity.

7   The real focus of the experiment is the teacher. After watching the learner being strapped into place, he is taken into the main experimental room and seated before an impressive shock generator. Its main feature is a horizontal line of thirty switches, ranging from 15 volts to 450 volts, in 15-volt increments. There are also verbal designations which range from SLIGHT SHOCK to DANGER—SEVERE SHOCK. The teacher is told that he is to administer the learning test to the man in the other room. When the learner responds correctly, the teacher moves on to the next item; when the other man gives an incorrect answer, the teacher is to give him an electric shock. He is to start at the lowest shock level (15 volts) and to increase the level each time the man makes an error, going through 30 volts, 45 volts, and so on.

8   The "teacher" is a genuinely naïve subject who has come to the laboratory to participate in an experiment. The learner, or victim, is an actor who actually receives no shock at all. The point of the experiment is to see how far a person will proceed in a concrete and measurable situation in which he is ordered to inflict increasing pain on a protesting victim. At what point will the subject refuse to obey the experimenter?

9   Conflict arises when the man receiving the shock begins to indicate that he is experiencing discomfort. At 75 volts, the "learner" grunts. At 120 volts he complains verbally; at 150 he demands to be released from the experiment. His protests continue as the shocks escalate, growing increasingly vehement and emotional. At 285 volts his response can only be described as an agonized scream.

10   Observers of the experiment agree that its gripping quality is somewhat obscured in print. For the subject, the situation is not a game; conflict is intense and obvious. On one hand, the manifest suffering of the learner presses him to quit. On the other, the experimenter, a legitimate authority to whom the subject feels some commitment, enjoins him to continue. Each time the subject hesitates to administer shock, the experimenter orders him to continue. To extricate himself from the situation, the subject must make a clear break with authority. The aim of this investigation was to find when and how people would defy authority in the face of a clear moral imperative.

11   There are, of course, enormous differences between carrying out the orders of a commanding officer during times of war and carrying out

the orders of an experimenter. Yet the essence of certain relationships remain, for one may ask in a general way: How does a man behave when he is told by a legitimate authority to act against a third individual? If anything, we may expect the experimenter's power to be considerably less than that of the general, since he has no power to enforce his imperative, and participation in a psychological experiment scarcely evokes the sense of urgency and dedication engendered by participation in war. Despite the limitations, I thought it worthwhile to start careful observation of obedience even in this modest situation, in the hope that it would stimulate insights and yield general propositions applicable to a variety of circumstances.

A reader's initial reaction to the experiment may be to wonder why   12
anyone in his right mind would administer even the first shocks. Would he not simply refuse and walk out of the laboratory? But the fact is that no one ever does. Since the subject has come to the laboratory to aid the experimenter, he is quite willing to start off with the procedure. There is nothing very extraordinary in this, particularly since the person who is to receive the shocks seems initially cooperative, if somewhat apprehensive. What is surprising is how far ordinary individuals will go in complying with the experimenter's instructions. Indeed, the results of the experiment are both surprising and dismaying. Despite the fact that many subjects experience stress, despite the fact that many protest to the experimenter, a substantial proportion continue to the last shock on the generator.

Many subjects will obey the experimenter no matter how vehement   13
the pleading of the person being shocked, no matter how painful the shocks seem to be, and no matter how much the victim pleads to be let out. This was seen time and again in our studies and has been observed in several universities where the experiment was repeated. It is the extreme willingness of adults to go to almost any lengths on the command of an authority that constitutes the chief finding of the study and the fact most urgently demanding explanation.

A commonly offered explanation is that those who shocked the vic-   14
tim at the most severe level were monsters, the sadistic fringe of society. But if one considers that almost two-thirds of the participants fall into the category of "obedient" subjects, and that they represented ordinary people drawn from working, managerial, and professional classes, the argument becomes very shaky. Indeed, it is highly reminiscent of the issue that arose in connection with Hannah Arendt's 1963 book, *Eichmann in Jerusalem*. Arendt contended that the prosecution's effort to depict Eichmann as a sadistic monster was fundamentally wrong, that he came closer to being an uninspired bureaucrat who simply sat at his desk and did his job. For asserting these views, Arendt became the

object of considerable scorn, even calumny. Somehow, it was felt that the monstrous deeds carried out by Eichmann required a brutal, twisted, and sadistic personality, evil incarnate. After witnessing hundreds of ordinary people submit to the authority in our own experiments, I must conclude that Arendt's conception of the *banality of evil* comes closer to the truth than one might dare imagine. The ordinary person who shocked the victim did so out of a sense of obligation—a conception of his duties as a subject—and not from any peculiarly aggressive tendencies.

15   This is, perhaps, the most fundamental lesson of our study: ordinary people, simply doing their jobs, and without any particular hostility on their part, can become agents in a terrible destructive process. Moreover, even when the destructive effects of their work become patently clear, and they are asked to carry out actions incompatible with fundamental standards of morality, relatively few people have the resources needed to resist authority. A variety of inhibitions against disobeying authority come into play and successfully keep the person in his place.

16   Sitting back in one's armchair, it is easy to condemn the actions of the obedient subjects. But those who condemn the subjects measure them against the standard of their own ability to formulate high-minded moral prescriptions. That is hardly a fair standard. Many of the subjects, at the level of stated opinion, feel quite as strongly as any of us about the moral requirement of refraining from action against a helpless victim. They, too, in general terms know what ought to be done and can state their values when the occasion arises. This has little, if anything, to do with their actual behavior under the pressure of circumstances.

17   If people are asked to render a moral judgment on what constitutes appropriate behavior in this situation, they unfailingly see disobedience as proper. But values are not the only forces at work in an actual, ongoing situation. They are but one narrow band of causes in the total spectrum of forces impinging on a person. Many people were unable to realize their values in action and found themselves continuing in the experiment even though they disagreed with what they were doing.

18   The force exerted by the moral sense of the individual is less effective than social myth would have us believe. Though such prescriptions as "Thou shalt not kill" occupy a pre-eminent place in the moral order, they do not occupy a correspondingly intractable position in human psychic structure. A few changes in newspaper headlines, a call from the draft board, orders from a man with epaulets, and men are led to kill with little difficulty. Even the forces mustered in a psychology experiment will go a long way toward removing the individual from moral controls. Moral factors can be shunted aside with relative ease by a calculated restructuring of the informational and social field.

What, then, keeps the person obeying the experimenter? First, there   19
is a set of "binding factors" that lock the subject into the situation. They
include such factors as politeness on his part, his desire to uphold his
initial promise of aid to the experimenter, and the awkwardness of
withdrawal. Second, a number of adjustments in the subject's thinking
occur that undermine his resolve to break with the authority. The adjustments help the subject maintain his relationship with the experimenter, while at the same time reducing the strain brought about by the
experimental conflict. They are typical of thinking that comes about in
obedient persons when they are instructed by authority to act against
helpless individuals.

One such mechanism is the tendency of the individual to become so   20
absorbed in the narrow technical aspects of the task that he loses sight
of its broader consequences. The film *Dr. Strangelove* brilliantly satirized
the absorption of a bomber crew in the exacting technical procedure of
dropping nuclear weapons on a country. Similarly, in this experiment,
subjects become immersed in the procedures, reading the word pairs
with exquisite articulation and pressing the switches with great care.
They want to put on a competent performance, but they show an accompanying narrowing of moral concern. The subject entrusts the
broader tasks of setting goals and assessing morality to the experimental authority he is serving.

The most common adjustment of thought in the obedient subject is   21
for him to see himself as not responsible for his own actions. He divests
himself of responsibility by attributing all initiative to the experimenter,
a legitimate authority. He sees himself not as a person acting in a
morally accountable way but as the agent of external authority. In the
postexperimental interview, when subjects were asked why they had
gone on, a typical reply was: "I wouldn't have done it by myself. I was
just doing what I was told." Unable to defy the authority of the experimenter, they attribute all responsibility to him. It is the old story of "just
doing one's duty" that was heard time and time again in the defense
statements of those accused at Nuremberg. But it would be wrong to
think of it as a thin alibi concocted for the occasion. Rather, it is a fundamental mode of thinking for a great many people once they are
locked into a subordinate position in a structure of authority. The disappearance of a sense of responsibility is the most far-reaching consequence of submission to authority.

Although a person acting under authority performs actions that   22
seem to violate standards of conscience, it would not be true to say that
he loses his moral sense. Instead, it acquires a radically different focus.
He does not respond with a moral sentiment to the actions he performs.
Rather, his moral concern now shifts to a consideration of how well he

is living up to the expectations that the authority has of him. In wartime, a soldier does not ask whether it is good or bad to bomb a hamlet; he does not experience shame or guilt in the destruction of a village: rather he feels pride or shame depending on how well he has performed the mission assigned to him.

23   Another psychological force at work in this situation may be termed "counteranthropomorphism." For decades psychologists have discussed the primitive tendency among men to attribute to inanimate objects and forces the qualities of the human species. A countervailing tendency, however, is that of attributing an impersonal quality to forces that are essentially human in origin as if they existed above and beyond any human agent, beyond the control of whim or human feeling. The human element behind agencies and institutions is denied. Thus, when the experimenter says, "The experiment *requires* that you continue," the subject feels this to be an imperative that goes beyond any merely human command. He does not ask the seemingly obvious question, "Whose experiment? Why should the designer be served while the victim suffers?" The wishes of a man—the designer of the experiment—have become part of a schema which exerts on the subject's mind a force that transcends the personal. "It's *got* to go on. It's *got* to go on," repeated one subject. He failed to realize that a man like himself wanted it to go on. For him the human agent had faded from the picture, and "The Experiment" had acquired an impersonal momentum of its own.

24   No action of itself has an unchangeable psychological quality. Its meaning can be altered by placing it in particular contexts. An American newspaper recently quoted a pilot who conceded that Americans were bombing Vietnamese men, women, and children but felt that the bombing was for a "noble cause" and thus was justified. Similarly, most subjects in the experiment see their behavior in a larger context that is benevolent and useful to society—the pursuit of scientific truth. The psychological laboratory has a strong claim to legitimacy and evokes trust and confidence in those who come to perform there. An action such as shocking a victim, which in isolation appears evil, acquires a totally different meaning when placed in this setting. But allowing an act to be dominated by its context, while neglecting it human consequences, can be dangerous in the extreme.

25   At least one essential feature of the situation in Germany was not studied here—namely, the intense devaluation of the victim prior to action against him. For a decade and more, vehement anti-Jewish propaganda systemically prepared the German population to accept the destruction of the Jews. Step by step the Jews were excluded from the category of citizen and national, and finally were denied the status of human beings. Systemic devaluation of the victim provides a measure of psychological

justification for brutal treatment of the victim and has been the constant accompaniment of massacres, pogroms, and wars. In all likelihood, our subjects would have experienced greater ease in shocking the victim had he been convincingly portrayed as a brutal criminal or a pervert.

Of considerable interest, however, is the fact that many subjects 26 harshly devalue the victim *as a consequence* of acting against him. Such comments as, "He was so stupid and stubborn he deserved to get shocked," were common. Once having acted against the victim, these subjects found it necessary to view him as an unworthy individual, whose punishment was made inevitable by his own deficiencies of intellect and character.

Many of the people studied in the experiment were in some sense 27 against what they did to the learner, and many protested even while they obeyed. But between thoughts, words, and the critical step of disobeying a malevolent authority lies another ingredient, the capacity for transforming beliefs and values into action. Some subjects were totally convinced of the wrongness of what they were doing but could not bring themselves to make an open break with authority. Some derived satisfaction from their thoughts and felt that—within themselves, at least—they had been on the side of the angels. What they failed to realize is that subjective feelings are largely irrelevant to the moral issue at hand so long so they are not transformed into action. Political control is effected through action. The attitudes of the guards at a concentration camp are of no consequence when in fact they are allowing the slaughter of innocent men to take place before them. Similarly, so-called "intellectual resistance" in occupied Europe—in which persons by a twist of thought felt that they had defied the invader—was merely indulgence in a consoling psychological mechanism. Tyrannies are perpetuated by diffident men who do not possess the courage to act out their beliefs. Time and again in the experiment people disvalued what they were doing but could not muster the inner resources to translate their values into action.

A variation of the basic experiment depicts a dilemma more com- 28 mon than the one outlined above: the subject was not ordered to push the trigger that shocked the victim, but merely to perform a subsidiary act (administering the word-pair test) before another subject actually delivered the shock. In this situation, 37 of 40 adults from the New Haven area continued to the highest shock level on the generator. Predictably, subjects excused their behavior by saying that the responsibility belonged to the man who actually pulled the switch. This may illustrate a dangerously typical situation in complex society: it is psychologically easy to ignore responsibility when one is only an intermediate link in a chain of evil action but is far from the final consequences of the action. Even Eichmann was sickened when he toured the concentration camps, but to participate in mass murder he had only to sit at a desk and shuffle papers. At the same time the man in the camp who actually dropped Cyclon-B into the gas chambers was able to justify *his* behavior on the grounds that he was only following orders from above. Thus there is a fragmentation of the total human act; no one man decides to carry out the evil act and is confronted with its consequences. The person who assumes full responsibility for the act has evaporated. Perhaps this is the most common characteristic of socially organized evil in modern society.

29   The problem of obedience, therefore, is not wholly psychological. The form and shape of society and the way it is developing have much to do with it. There was a time, perhaps, when men were able to give a fully human response to any situation because they were fully absorbed in it as human beings. But as soon as there was a division of labor among men, things changed. Beyond a certain point, the breaking up of society into people carrying out narrow and very special jobs takes away from the human quality of work and life. A person does not get to see the whole situation but only a small part of it, and is thus unable to act without some kind of over-all direction. He yields to authority but in doing so is alienated from his own actions.

30   George Orwell caught the essence of the situation when he wrote:

> As I write, highly civilized human beings are flying overhead, trying to kill me. They do not feel any enmity against me as an individual, nor I against them. They are only "doing their duty," as the saying goes. Most of them, I have no doubt, are kind-hearted law abiding men who would never dream of committing murder in private life. On the other hand, if one of them succeeds in blowing me to pieces with a well-placed bomb, he will never sleep any the worse for it. . . .

31   Now let us return to the experiments and try to underscore their meaning. The behavior revealed in the experiments reported here is normal human behavior but revealed under conditions that show with particular clarity the danger to human survival inherent in our make-up. And what is it we have seen? Not aggression, for there is no anger, vindictiveness, or hatred in those who shocked the victim. Men do become angry; they do act hatefully and explode in rage against others. But not here. Something far more dangerous is revealed: the capacity for man to abandon his humanity, indeed, the inevitability that he does so, as he merges his unique personality into larger institutional structures.

32   This is a fatal flaw nature has designed into us, and which in the long run gives our species only a modest chance of survival.

It is ironic that the virtues of loyalty, discipline, and self-sacrifice that 33 we value so highly in the individual are the very properties that create destructive organizational engines of war and bind men to malevolent systems of authority.

Each individual possesses a conscience which to a greater or lesser 34 degree serves to restrain the unimpeded flow of impulses destructive to others. But when he merges his person into an organizational structure, a new creature replaces autonomous man, unhindered by the limitations of individual morality, freed of humane inhibition, mindful only of the sanctions of authority.

What is the limit of such obedience? At many points we attempted to 35 establish a boundary. Cries from the victim were inserted; they were not good enough. The victim claimed heart trouble; subjects still shocked him on command. The victim pleaded to be let free, and his answers no longer registered on the signal box; subjects continued to shock him. At the outset we had not conceived that such drastic procedures would be needed to generate disobedience, and each step was added only as the ineffectiveness of the earlier techniques became clear. The final effort to establish a limit was the Touch-Proximity condition. But the very first subject in this condition subdued the victim on command, and proceeded to the highest shock level. A quarter of the subjects in this condition performed similarly.

The results, as seen and felt in the laboratory, are to this author 36 disturbing. They raise the possibility that human nature, or—more specifically—the kind of character produced in American democratic society, cannot be counted on to insulate its citizens from brutality and inhumane treatment at the direction of malevolent authority. A substantial proportion of people do what they are told to do, irrespective of the content of the act and without limitations of conscience, so long as they perceive that the command comes from a legitimate authority.

In an article entitled "The Dangers of Obedience," Harold J. Laski 37 wrote:

> . . . civilization means, above all, an unwillingness to inflict unnecessary pain. Within the ambit of that definition, those of us who heedlessly accept the commands of authority cannot yet claim to be civilized men.
>
> . . . Our business, if we desire to live a life not utterly devoid of meaning and significance, is to accept nothing which contradicts our basic experience merely because it comes to us from tradition or convention or authority. It may well be that we shall be wrong; but our self-expression is thwarted at the root unless the certainties we are asked to accept coincide with the certainties we experience. That is why the condition of freedom in any state is always a widespread and consistent skepticism of the canons upon which power insists.

SUGGESTIONS FOR FURTHER READING

Baumeister., Roy F. *Evil: Inside Human Violence and Cruelty.* New York: W. H. Freeman, 1997. A social psychologist presents a refreshingly candid appraisal of human evil, emphasizing the roles of material gain, threatened egoism, idealism, and sadistic pleasure.

Black, Donald. *Bad Boys, Bad Men: Confronting Antisocial Personality Disorder.* New York: Oxford University Press, 1999. A psychiatrist demystifies one of the more troublesome behavior pathologies, which shows a regrettably bad prognosis in certain cases.

Bok, Sissela. *Mayhem: Violence as Public Entertainment.* Reading, MA: Addison-Wesley, 1998. A readable, sensible, timely assessment of the impact of violence as entertainment on violence as public problem.

Gilligan, James. *Violence: Our Deadly Epidemic and Its Causes.* New York: Putnam, 1996. A psychiatrist with substantial experience dealing with violent prisoners presents a hard-headed yet human perspective, sympathetic to psychoanalysis, yet emphasizing society's responsibilities and practical prospects.

Huesmann, L. Rowell, ed. *Aggressive Behavior: Current Perspectives.* New York: Plenum Press, 1994. A psychologist has assembled a collection of technical yet readable accounts of factors responsible for aggression and violence, strongly emphasizing the "social cognition" school of research and explanation.

STUDY QUESTIONS

1. What are some significant differences between biological and psychological approaches to understanding violence? Some similarities?

2. To what extent are the different psychological approaches presented in this chapter mutually compatible? Incompatible?

3. The Roman playwright Plautus announced that *Homo homini lupus* ("Man is a wolf to man"). Putting aside the question of whether this is a calumny against wolves, draw up a list of some psychologically oriented reasons for violence, commenting on whether these factors are likely to be unique to human beings or shared with animals.

4. Devise some specific examples of "social cognition" (that is, internal mental maps) that might help determine whether someone responds violently to a given social situation.

5. In August 1998, a terrorist bombing in Omagh, Northern Ireland, killed twenty-eight people—most of them women and children—by way of protesting peace agreements established and voted for overwhelmingly a few months before. In an article in the *New York Times* shortly thereafter, titled "When Violence Becomes a Habit," Irish poet and Nobel Laureate Seamus Heaney wrote:

   The violence of the system and the violence directed against the system had a dynamism that derived from violence itself. People ask how and why human beings could do such things as explode bombs in a crowded thoroughfare on a Saturday? Such questions look for proportionality in the answer; they seek for a political intelligence in the ruthlessness. But the truth is darker than such questions can address. Violence grows in pathogenic conditions, and it attracts psychopathic people, but its worst feature is its addictiveness. It becomes habit.

   Use psychological insights from Chapter 2 of this book to help explain and interpret Heaney's observation.

6. Develop some implications for social policy suggested by one or more of the readings in this chapter. Do the same for implications for your personal life.

7. St. Augustine, describing a friend attending the Roman spectacles of gladiatorial violence, wrote: "He opened his eyes, and his soul was stabbed with a wound more deadly than any which the gladiator, whom he was so anxious to see, had received in his body." Explain.

8. In a sense, the selections in this chapter proceeded from the intensely personal to increasingly social (culminating in the next chapter, on sociology). Describe and discuss this progression.

9. Which of the perspectives set out in this chapter did you find the most persuasive, and why? The least?

10. Develop a psychological approach to violence that was not represented in this chapter but perhaps should have been.

3

Sociology

"Everyone alters and is altered by everyone else," wrote Gerald Brenan in *Thoughts in a Dry Season*. "We are all the time taking in portions of one another or else reacting against them, and by these involuntary acquisitions and repulsions modifying our natures." This is a good definition and explanation of sociology, a discipline that concerns itself with the nature and impact of social forces on human lives. Not surprisingly, it has much to say about violence.

Our review of biological approaches was concerned with what might be called "skin-in" considerations, factors operating inside each human being. Then we considered a few of the major psychological approaches, examining some of the issues arising *between* people (rather than *within* them), but still primarily concerned with individuals. In the current chapter, we move our lens to a focus that is wider yet, emphasizing social practices and institutions.

People, after all, are social creatures. Although there is the occasional hermit, a solitary human being is as unnatural as a solitary ant. It is virtually impossible to identify the extent to which human life is constructed around a social dimension, for much the same reason that a hypothetical intelligent fish, asked to describe its environment, would be unlikely to mention that it was "wet." Our lives are immersed in a complex social matrix, so dense and yet so taken for granted that much of it goes unrecognized. Like our imaginary fish, we all swim in an unacknowledged ocean.

There can be little doubt that most of the time our sociality serves us well; indeed, it is an inextricable part of our humanity. Shared enterprise and mutual interaction are at the heart of the creative, constructive projects that help define civilization. This includes not only obvious achievements of technology and construction, but also the less obvious—but probably more important—everyday structures of social life and collaboration, unspoken expectations and assumptions.

At the same time, however, there is the specter of conflict. No matter how important society may be to the ultimate well-being (material no less than psychological) of individuals, and no matter how "well socialized" such individuals may be, the fact remains that the interests of each is unlikely to be identical to the interest of the group to which he or she belongs. And even in those extraordinary cases when group and individual concerns coincide, the interests of different groups are almost certain to diverge. Furthermore, even when fundamental interests are in fact shared—as in the case of the safety and well-being of close family members, or defending the earth itself against environmental destruction or nuclear war—it is often difficult to persuade people to recognize the existence of overarching shared interests.

Not surprisingly, the *sociology of conflict* plays a particularly important role in efforts to understand violence from the perspective of society and group processes. Emile Durkheim (1858–1917) is considered one of the founders of sociology because of his emphasis on the importance of groups as opposed to the behavior of individuals. Durkheim gave special attention to social unity and its two major sources: *mechanical solidarity*, because of shared similarities such as political or religious values as well as ethnic identity, and *organic solidarity*, or the mutual dependence generated by division of labor and responsibilities. In his classic book *Rules of the Sociological Method*, Durkheim used the example of criminal behavior to show the inevitability of "deviant behavior," and also the paradox that "societies are knit together by their contradictions."

Nonetheless, such contradictions remain troublesome even as they are stubbornly persistent.

Many crucial practical questions seem—at least in theory—susceptible to analysis from a broad societal perspective, but in practice they remain unanswered. For instance, political liberals and radicals point to the role of social injustice and economic inequality in generating interpersonal violence. Progressive activist Ralph Nader testified before Congress in 1999 that young people are being "conscripted into violence by methodical, calculating efforts on the part of big business." The same day, conservative members of Congress countered by declaring that youth violence in particular is the "inevitable consequence of having banished God from the classroom" and of "parents failing to live up to their responsibilities." Can both these perspectives be correct? Is either one?

Here are some additional unknowns. Are there causal connections between social structure and interpersonal violence? Between political systems—democratic, authoritarian, left leaning or right leaning—and proneness to war? What about linkages between economic system, as well as one's place within such a system, and violence? How important are such things as role modeling, social stress, boredom, frustration, competition, self-esteem, prejudice, educational and early experience in predisposing to depression, riot, violent personal crime, gang-related violence, war, and so forth? Is it possible to retain the positive components of patriotism while reducing the destructive aspects of nationalism? Are such group identifications as rooting for sports teams and membership in local community groups as well as vocational and service organizations examples of nationalism writ small? Can their benefits be retained and encouraged without leading to sectarianism, intolerance, and violence? (These and numerous other questions are challenges to the next generation of sociologists concerned with violence.)

In any event, it seems beyond doubt that part of being human is to alter and be altered by everyone else . . . although exactly how, and why, and to what end remains uncertain.

Some Social Functions of Violence

LEWIS COSER

Social conflict was a primary organizing principle for most nineteenth-century European social theorists and early sociologists. Thus, economic conflict of interest (between workers and the owners of capital) was fundamental to the ideas of Karl Marx, while social competition loomed large in the thinking of Social Darwinists such as Herbert Spencer and Walter Bagehot and a number of central European theorists such as Gustav Ratsenhofer, Ludwik Gumplowicz, and especially Georg Simmel, who emphasized the creative, constructive aspects of conflict and competition . . . all the while acknowledging its potential for war and violence.

Within the United States, by contrast, sociology—at least in the first half of the twentieth century—was dominated by a *structural-functional* model of social consensus, especially under the influence of Talcott Parsons. In this view, a shared "value orientation" is believed to be institutionalized, resulting in fundamental conformity and leading in turn to a smoothly functioning system. By the second half of the twentieth century, however, cracks began to form in this model, with growing inquiry into conflicts based on race, employment, and educational and life experiences— indeed, an array of differing values that are *not* shared. Prominent in the new inquiry was sociologist Lewis Coser; in the next selection, Coser identifies what he sees as three important social functions of violence.

1   The folklore of psychology has it that animals in experimental studies display systematically different behavioral characteristics depending on the investigator. Rats described by American observers are seen as frenetically active, given to a great deal of motor activity, forever dashing in and out of mazes, always trying to get somewhere—though not always certain exactly where. In contrast, experimental animals seen through the

lens of German investigators, apes, for example, seem given to long and intense periods of pensive deliberation and musing cogitation.

This just highlights an important truth. There *are* systematic differences in the ways a particular scholarly community at a given moment in time chooses to approach the manifold data with which it is confronted. In sociology, for example, even if most American social theorists would readily agree in the abstract that conflict as well as order, tension as well as harmony, violence as well as peaceful adjustment characterize all social systems in varying degrees, social theory actually has settled mainly for a remarkably tame and domesticated view of the social world. This is so despite the fact that European social thinkers such as Marx, Weber, and Simmel, upon whose works so much of American theorizing depends for its inspiration, had an entirely different orientation. 2

It seems as if American social science, developing in a society which, its birth through revolution notwithstanding, has only known one major internal upheaval throughout its history, has failed to be sensitized to the pervasive effects of violence, conflict, and disorder which to the European thinker were facts that they could not but be acquainted with intimately. While to the European thinker the fragility of the social fabric and the brittleness of social bonds seemed self-evident experiences, American social science proceeded from a world view in which social violence was at best seen as a pathological phenomenon. . . . 3

As long as American sociology confined its attention mainly to a limited view of the contemporary American scene, its neglect of conflict and violence was, perhaps, none too disabling, at least until recently. But at present, when sociology has happily awakened to the need of doing comparative studies of social structures in both geographical space and historical time, this domesticated vision of the social world can be severely hampering. In addition, it seems that even the proper study of American society can no longer profit from exclusive emphasis on models and constructs in which conflict and violence are deliberately or unwittingly minimized. Just as analyses of, say, contemporary South Africa, Latin America, or Southeast Asia, or of seventeenth-century England or nineteenth-century France, would be patently unrealistic if they ignored the functions of political violence, so it has become increasingly evident that such ignoring would be just as unrealistic in the study of the current racial scene in the United States. . . . 4

I shall focus selectively on but a few functions of social violence: violence as a form of achievement, violence as a danger signal, and violence as a catalyst. It is to be understood that this is by no means an exhaustive list of the functions of violence, nor will its dysfunctions be dealt with. . . . 5

Violence as Achievement

6 Certain categories of individuals are so located in the social structure that they are barred from legitimate access to the ladder of achievement. Moreover certain categories of persons may find themselves in structural positions which effectively prevent them from utilizing not only legitimate channels of opportunity but criminal and illegitimate channels as well. I shall argue that when all such channels are barred, violence may offer alternate roads to achievement.

7 Cloward and Ohlin take as a case in point adolescents in disorganized urban areas who are oriented toward achieving higher positions and yet lack access to either conventional or criminal opportunity structures. "These adolescents," they argue,

> seize upon the manipulation of violence as a route to status not only because it provides a way of expressing pent-up angers and frustrations but also because they are not cut off from access to violent means by vicissitudes of birth. In the world of violence, such attributes as race, socioeconomic position, age, and the like are irrelevant; personal worth is judged on the basis of qualities that are available to all who would cultivate them. The acquisition of status is not simply a consequence of skill in the use of violence or of physical strength but depends, rather, on one's willingness to risk injury or death in the search for "rep."

8 In the area of violence, then, ascriptive status considerations become irrelevant. Here, the vaunted equal opportunity, which had been experienced as a sham and a lure everywhere else, turns out to be effective. In the wilderness of cities, just as in the wilderness of the frontier, the gun becomes an effective equalizer. Within the status structure of the gang, through a true transvaluation of middle-class values, success in defense of the "turf" brings deference and "rep" which are unavailable anywhere else. Here the successful exercise of violence is a road to achievement. . . .

9 One can make the more general assertion that in all those situations in which both legitimate and illegitimate socioeconomic achievement seems blocked, recourse to aggressive and violent behavior may be perceived as a significant area of "achievement." This may help to explain the ideal of *machismo* in the lower classes of Latin America. Here, as in the otherwise very different violence in disorganized urban areas of American cities, men tend to feel that only prowess in interpersonal violence or in aggressive sexual encounters allows the achievement of personal identity and permits gaining otherwise unavailable deference. Where no social status can be achieved through socioeconomic channels

it may yet be achieved in the show of violence among equally deprived peers.

Somewhat similar mechanisms may be at work in the intrafamilial aggression and violence of American lower-class fathers. These men tend to compensate for inadequate rewards in the occupational world at large by an aggressive assertion of male superiority within the little world of the family. . . . The disproportionately high rate of interpersonal violence among Negro males may yield to a similar explanation. Since Negroes are assigned lowest position in all three major dimensions of the American status system—ethnicity, class, and education—and since their mobility chances are nil in the first and minimal in the second and third, it stands to reason that achievement in the area of interpersonal violence might be seen as a channel leading to self-regard and self-enhancement—at least as long as conflict with the dominant white majority seems socially unavailable as a means of collective action. This does not preclude that violent acting out may not also at the same time call forth a feeling of self-hatred for acting in the stereotypical manner in which the Negro is accused of acting by the dominant white. . . .   10

Violence as a Danger Signal

The late Norbert Wiener once remarked that cancer is so peculiarly dangerous a disease because it typically develops through its early stages without causing pain. Most other diseases, by eliciting painful sensations in the body, bring forth bodily signals which allow early detection of the illness and its subsequent treatment. Pain serves as an important mechanism of defense, permitting the medical readjustment of bodily balance which has been attacked by disease. It seems hardly far fetched to apply this reasoning to the body social as well.   11

A social dysfunction can, of course, be attended to only if it becomes visible, if not to the total community, at least to certain more sensitive and more powerful sectors of it. But the sensitive usually lack power, and the powerful often lack sensitivity. As Merton has phrased the issue, there are latent social problems, "conditions which are . . . at odds with values of the group but are not recognized as being so," which can become manifest, and hence subject to treatment, only when particular groups or individuals choose to take cognizance of them. Merton urges that it is the task of the sociologist to make latent social problems manifest; at the same time he stresses that "those occupying strategic positions of authority and power of course carry more weight than others in deciding social policy and so . . . in identifying for the rest what are to be taken as significant departures from social standards." Granted that the social perceptions of those in power and authority may be   12 influenced by social scientists calling attention to previously neglected problems, it would be an indulgence in unwarranted Comtean optimism to assume that such enlightenment will at all times be sufficient to alert them. It is at this point that the signaling functions of social violence assume importance.

13   Although there are individual, subcultural, and class variations in the internalized management and control of anger in response to frustration, I take it to be axiomatic that human beings—other than those systematically trained to use legitimate or illegitimate violence—will resort to violent action only under extremely frustrating, ego-damaging, and anxiety-producing conditions. It follows that if the incidence of violence increases rapidly, be it in the society at large or within specific sectors of it, this can be taken as a signal of severe maladjustment. I would further suggest that this signal is so drastic, so extremely loud, that it cannot fail to be perceived by men in power and authority otherwise not noted for peculiar sensitivity to social ills. This is not to say, of course, that they will necessarily respond with types of social therapy that will effectively remove the sources of infection. But I suggest that outbreaks of social violence are more apt than other less visible or sensitive indicators at least to lead them to perceive the problem. . . .

14   Much as one might deplore the often senseless violence displayed in such racial riots as those in Los Angeles, one cannot help feeling that they, too, constituted quite effective signaling devices, perhaps desperate cries for help after other appeals had been unavailing. They indicated a sickness in the body social which demands immediate remedy if it is not to undermine social order altogether.

Violence as a Catalyst

15   Marx once remarked: "The criminal produces an impression now moral, now tragic, and hence renders a 'service' by arousing the moral and aesthetic sentiments of the public." Marx here anticipated by many years similar formulations by Durkheim and Mead stressing the unanticipated functions of crime in creating a sense of solidarity within the community. Here I shall argue a related idea, namely, that not only criminals, but law-enforcing agents also, may call forth a sense of solidarity against their behavior. More particularly, the use of extralegal violence by these officers may, under certain circumstances, lead to the arousal of the community and to a revulsion from societal arrangements that rest upon such enforcement methods.

16   It is common knowledge that the violence used by sheriffs and other Southern officers of the law against Southern Negroes engaged

in protest activities and voting-registration drives has had a major impact upon public opinion and federal legislation. The fact is that such methods had been relied upon by Southern police for a very long time without any marked reaction against them. Why, then, did they suddenly become counterproductive? Two major factors seem to account for this reversal. First, modes of control involving the extralegal uses of violence worked well as long as the acts in question could be committed with a minimum of publicity and visibility. They became suicidal when they were performed under the glare of television cameras and under the observation of reporters for national newspapers and magazines. . . .

The matter of publicity, powerfully aided by the recent "communication revolution," though crucially important, is not the only one to be considered here. It is equally relevant to observe that violent tactics of suppression tend to be much less successful when used against people who are publicly committed to the principle of nonviolence. Violence by the police, even extralegal violence, may be approved, or at least condoned, when it can be justified by reference to the supposed actual or potential violence of the offending criminal. That is, such behavior seems to be justified or condoned when there exists, or seems to exist, a rough equivalence between the means used by both sides. A tooth for a tooth tends to be a maxim popularly applicable in these cases. But the matter is very different when the presumed offender is committed in principle to a politics of nonviolence. The nonviolent resisters in the South, as distinct from other cases where nonviolence was not based on principle, had consciously assumed the burden of nonviolence. That is, they had made a commitment to the public not to have recourse to violence. When violence was used against them, this hence came to be seen as a breach of a tacit reciprocal commitment on the part of those they opposed. What is ordinarily perceived as a multilateral relationship in which both sides actually or potentially use violence came now to be perceived as unilateral violence. This impression was still accentuated when acts of official or semiofficial violence were being directed against ministers, that is, against men who enjoy specific mandates and immunities as men of peace.

For these reasons, extralegal violence habitually used in the South to maintain the caste system turned out to be a most effective triggering device for measures to abolish it. One need, perhaps, not go so far as to argue, that the very effectiveness of the nonviolent methods used depended on the assumption or expectation that it would encounter violent reactions that would arouse the public conscience. The violent reactions did not have to be anticipated. But it was nevertheless one of the latent functions of Southern violent response to the nonviolent

17

18

tactics used to lead to the arousal of a previously lethargic community to a sense of indignation and revulsion.

19   Nor is the Southern case unique. Even in earlier periods extralegal violence on the part of law-enforcement agencies has often been suicidal. The Peterloo Massacre of 1819 in Manchester, when a crowd of listeners to speeches on parliamentary reform and the repeal of the Corn Laws was charged by soldiers who killed ten and injured hundreds, became a rallying cry for the reformers and radicals. The wholesale massacre of participants in the French Commune of 1871 created a sense of intimate solidarity, but also of alienation from society at large, among large sectors of the French working class. In these latter cases the impact was not on the total society but only on particular sectors of it, but in all of them the show of violence on the part of officialdom was suicidal in so far as it transformed victims into martyrs who became symbols of the iniquity and callousness of the rulers.

20   Lest it be understood that I argue that unanticipated and suicidal uses of violence are limited to cases involving law-enforcement agents alone, let me remark, even if only in passing, that there are clearly other groups within society whose resort to violence may under specifiable circumstances bring forth similar suicidal consequences. In particular, when minority groups appeal to the public conscience and attempt to dramatize the fact that they are treated with less than justice and equity, their resort to violence may effectively hamper their cause. They must depend on their appeal on winning to their side previously indifferent and unconcerned sectors of the public. Resort to violence, however, even though it may serve as a danger signal, is also likely to alienate precisely those who are potential recruits for their cause. Hence groups such as the Black Muslims and other extremist Negro organizations may, if they resort to violence, bring about suicidal results by turning previously indifferent or potentially sympathetic bystanders into hostile antagonists.

Conclusion

21   The preceding discussion has identified and examined a series of cases in which violence may perform latent or manifest functions. The approach was meant to be exploratory and tentative rather than exhaustive and systematic. It is hoped, however, that enough has been said to show that the curiously tender-minded view of the social structure which has generally predominated in American social theory is seriously deficient and needs to be complemented by a more tough-minded approach.

Intergroup Conflict and Cooperation: The Robbers Cave Experiment

MUZAFER SHERIF, O. J. HARVEY, B. JACK WHITE, WILLIAM HOOD, AND CAROLYN W. SHERIF

In-group amity, out-group enmity: this is a well-known sociological principle. It speaks to several important aspects of human social behavior. First, people tend to associate themselves in groups rather than to be solitary. Second, relationships among members of a given group tend to be amicable, whereas those between different groups are more likely to be antagonistic. And from this antagonism, violence is liable to develop.

In a now-classic study conducted in the 1950s, social psychologist Muzafer Sherif and colleagues arbitrarily divided their 11- and 12-year-old subjects—attending a Boy Scout summer camp near Robbers Cave, Oklahoma—into two groups, called the Rattlers and the Eagles. The researchers generated competitive situations among the boys (tug-of-war, a baseball game, etc.) and recorded the startling rapidity with which the Rattlers and the Eagles became united within each group and antagonistic toward each other. Attempts to bridge the growing—and increasingly aggressive—social chasm failed, until a "superordinate goal" was introduced, requiring members of the two groups to cooperate toward a common end. This study may well apply not only to small group processes, but also to nationalism and war. It is important in showing the potency of "in-group amity, out-group enmity" as well as suggesting a way of transcending it.

1. When individuals having no established relationships are brought together to interact in group activities with common goals, they produce a group structure with hierarchical statuses and roles within it.
2. If two in-groups thus formed are brought into functional relationship under conditions of competition and group frustration, attitudes and appropriate hostile actions in relation to the out-group and its members will arise and will be standardized and shared in varying degrees by group members.

As sociologists will readily recognize, testing of these hypotheses is not so much concerned with the discovery of new facts as getting a clearer picture of the formative process under experimentally controlled conditions. It aims rather at singling out the factors involved in the rise of group structure, group code or norms, and in-group–out-group delineations which will make possible their intensive study with appropriate laboratory methods on the psychological level.

2   To test these hypotheses, 24 boys of about 12 years of age from similar lower middle-class, Protestant backgrounds were brought to an isolated camp site wholly available for the experiment. The early phase (Stage 1) of the study consisted of a variety of activities permitting contact between all the boys and observation of budding friendship groupings. After being divided into two groups of 12 boys each, in order to split the budding friendship groupings and at the same time constitute two similar units, the two groups lived, worked and played separately (Stage 2). All activities introduced embodied a common goal (with appeal value to all), the attainment of which necessitated cooperative participation within the group.

3   At the end of this stage, there developed unmistakable group structures, each with a leader and hierarchical statuses within it, and also names and appropriate group norms, including sanctions for deviant behavior. Friendship preferences were shifted and reversed away from previously budding relationships toward in-group preferences. Thus our first hypothesis concerning in-group formation was substantiated.

4   In the final phase (Stage 3) of the 1949 experiment, the two experimentally formed in-groups were brought together in situations which were competitive and led to some mutual frustration, as a consequence of the behavior of the groups in relation to each other. The result of intergroup contact in these conditions was enhancement of in-group solidarity, democratic interaction within groups, and in-group friendship, on the one hand. On the other hand, out-group hostility, name calling and even fights between the groups developed, indicating that in-group democracy need not lead to democratic relations with outsiders when intergroup relations are fraught with conditions conducive to tension. The resistance which developed to post-experimental efforts at breaking down the in-groups and encouraging friendly interaction indicates the unmistakable effect of group products on individual members. Thus the results substantiated the second hypothesis concerning determination of norms toward out-groups by the nature of relations between groups and demonstrated some effects of intergroup relations upon in-group functioning.

5   One of the main methodological considerations of this experiment was that subjects were kept unaware of the fact that they were participating in an experiment on group relations. The view that subjects cease to be mindful that their words and deeds are being recorded is not in harmony with what we have learned about the structuring of experience. The presence of a personage ever observing, ever recording our words and deeds in a situation in which our status and role concerns

are at stake cannot help coming in as an important factor in the total frame of reference. Therefore, in our work, the aim is to establish definite trends as they develop in natural, life-like situations and to introduce precision at choice points when this can be done without sacrificing the life-like character which gives greatest hope for validity of these trends. . . .

Right after [a] treasure hunt, the two groups were brought together, each on one side of the exhibit of prizes, and results were announced. The scores received by each group for every event were specified, making the outcome hinge on the treasure hunt. The tournament was declared to have been won by the Eagles through their completion of the treasure hunt in 8 minutes 38 seconds versus 10 minutes 15 seconds for the Rattlers. The Eagles were jubilant at their victory, jumping up and down, hugging each other, making sure in loud tones that everyone present was aware of their victory. On the other hand, the Rattlers were glum, dejected, and remained silently seated on the ground.   6

The series of contests was the main focus of attention for both groups, manifested in actual physical encounters and practice sessions in preparation for them, in group discussion, in self-justifying and self-glorifying words used in relation to themselves, and invectives and derogatory terms hurled at the out-group in actual encounters and in reference to the out-group in the privacy of the in-group circle. Various contests had differential effects in producing the above attitudinal and behavioral consequences. At least for these 11-year-old boys, the activities which were not too prolonged and which involved direct physical contact were most effective, with tug-of-war heading the list. The build-up of negative attitudes was cumulative with rapid spurts at times, as determined by the nature of the encounter. Even though the boys hurled invectives starting with the first contest of the tournament, the norms internalized from the larger social setting concerning "good sportsmanship" were clearly evident for the first two days, as revealed through the custom of giving three cheers for the losers.   7

After the second day of the tournament, the "good sportsmanship" stated in specific words during the initial period and exhibited after the first contests in this series (especially by the Eagles) gave away, as event followed event, to increased name-calling, hurling invectives, and derogation of the out-group to the point that the groups became more and more reluctant to have anything to do with one another. This attitude of not having anything to do with each other was intensified owing to the impact of events taking place after the tournament was over, as we shall see presently.   8

The first physical encounter of the two groups, their immediate "sizing up" of each other, the explicit expressions of their rapidly developing   9 attitudes toward each other may have significant implications for the systematic study of the rise of rather sharp in-group and out-group delineation and rapid crystallization of attitudes toward an out-group when the functional relation involved is one of rivalry. Therefore, a description of this very first contact between the two in-groups, which were formed independently of each other, follows:

10   The Rattlers were first at the ballfield (which they considered "ours") as befits the "home team." The Eagles approached with their flag on a pole singing the menacing notes of the "Dragnet" theme. For a time the two groups looked each other over. Than an Eagle used a derogatory word, a catcall from a Rattler answered him, and the razzing was on. Before the game started, Mason gave a little lecture to the Eagles on not getting rattled. As the game got underway, the Rattlers sang "The first Eagle hit the deck, parley-voo . . . The second Eagle hit the deck, parley-voo . . . etc." Eagles called back at them: "Our pitcher is better than yours;" "Our catcher is better than yours." As the game progressed the Rattlers referred to Wilson (E) as Fatty, Tubby, "Little Black Sambo." Myers, the Eagle of such good-will prior to the game, was especially active in calling out at the Rattlers, though Craig tried to hush him. . . .

11   As the game continued, the Rattlers called, "You're not Eagles, you're pigeons!" When the game ended with a Rattler victory, the Rattlers put on a display of "good sportsmanship" for the losers. In the Eagle group, Mason threatened to beat up some Eagles if they didn't try harder, but praised Lane (low status) for his improved performance. Craig, who had not made a good showing, carried a Rattler glove left at the field and dropped it in the water near the Eagle cabin.

12   The two competing groups were together in the mess hall for the first time at lunch on Day 2, after the baseball game. There was considerable name-calling, razzing back and forth, and singing of derogatory songs by each group in turn. Before supper that evening, some Eagles expressed a desire not to eat with the Rattlers.

13   In saying grace at these first meals together, the members of each group expressed their desire for victory. Myers (E) asked that God help them win the tournament and that He keep them together and not let anyone else get homesick and go home. Allen (R) prayed: "Dear Lord, we thank Thee for the food and for the cooks that cooked it, and for the ball game we won today." In the Eagle group, prayers were said for victory at night, and it became standard practice for that group to huddle in prayer before games. Mason (E) attributed their victory in baseball on the following day to this practice. . . .

14   At the first baseball game on the occasion of first contact between the groups, Everett (R), who had been chosen as one nonplayer, was the

loudest of the Rattlers in haranguing the Eagles, cursing them roundly and making up a song about Eagles which was supposed to be very insulting. Harrison, the other non-player (because of an injury), arrived after the exchange of insults between groups had already started. Although he had not witnessed the events leading to friction between the groups, and, in fact, before he had exchanged a single word with any camper, he started yelling insults at the Eagles. . . .

Finally someone suggested the Eagles go back to their cabin. Lane (low status) started off first and noticed the Rattlers' flag on the ballfield backstop. He yelled that they could take it down. The Eagles all ran for the backstop, Craig trying to knock down the flag and then climbing up to take it down. Mason grabbed it and tried, with the help of others, to tear it up. Someone suggested: "Let's burn it." So Mason, Craig, and McGraw (who found matches) set the flag on fire. Mason held it while it burned, then they decided to hang the scorched remnant back up. Craig did so, and the boys sang "Taps." Mason said. "You can tell those guys *I* did it if they say anything. I'll fight 'em!" . . .

This flag-burning episode started a chain of events which made it unnecessary for the experimenters to introduce special situations of mutual frustration for the two groups. The only manipulation necessary to insure that the actions of one group were frustrating to the other was careful timing of arrivals and departures of the groups on certain occasions. For this reason, it was arranged that the Rattlers would complete breakfast and proceed to the athletic field before the Eagles on the next morning, in order that the Rattlers would discover the damage inflicted to their flag.

At breakfast the next morning the Eagles were relatively quiet, not being elated over their progress thus far and perhaps wondering how the Rattlers would act when they found their flag. Later the Rattlers agreed that the Eagles had looked happy at breakfast, but this judgment was made only after they had found their flag.

As arranged, the Rattlers finished breakfast first and went to the ballfield. When they arrived and discovered their burnt flag, their reaction was noisy and resentful. All sorts of suggestions for retaliation were made in a disorganized fashion. Mills climbed the backstop to bring down the burnt remnant, leaving a portion there for "evidence" at the suggestion of Barton and Harrison. Simpson, the baseball captain, suggested that he ask the Eagles if they did it. The Rattlers then made a plan of action to follow when the Eagles arrived. Simpson was to go and ask the Eagles if they burned the flag. If the Eagles said that they did (and there was little doubt in the Rattlers' minds that this would be the reply), Simpson was to start fighting and others were to come to his help. Martin (a mild boy who had earlier espoused sportsmanship) volunteered to grab the Eagles' flag and burn it. When the Eagles arrived, this plan was put in effect. Simpson went to the Eagles and asked if they burned the flag, which they admitted. The Rattlers followed up Simpson, calling invectives; Martin worked his way close to the Eagle flag, grabbed it and ran down the road with some other Rattlers and with Mason (E) in hot pursuit.

19   In the meantime, on the field, the Eagles ran for the Rattlers' second flag which they had left on the field. The remaining Rattlers tried to get it, but the Eagles tore it up. Swift (R) grabbed Craig and held him in a wrestling hold, asking which Eagle had burned the flag. Craig said they all had. Simpson (R) had gotten Cutler (E) down in a fist fight, and the physical encounters had to be stopped.

20   The Rattlers who burned the Eagle flag returned with Mason (E), who was crying mad. He yelled for someone "my size" to whip and Mills, the Rattler leader, said: "Here I am!" Staff prevented further fighting and started the game over the Rattlers' violent objections to the Eagles being "home team" that day, since the diamond was "ours" and "we built everything but the backstop." The game finally got underway, with continued razzing and name-calling from both sides. . . .

21   All afternoon Simpson (R) made suggestions that the Rattlers raid the Eagles' cabin. Now, as a result of the tug-of-war, in which the Rattlers believed the Eagles had used decidedly unfair tactics, the Rattlers' mood was definitely favorable to a raid. Mills, their leader, set the time for 10:30, after the event of skits which each group put on separately that night. Enthusiasm for a raid was high, and the Rattlers decked themselves out for it in true commando style (darkening faces, arms, etc.). The Eagles had gone to bed by this time, and all were asleep but Mason, who jumped up to arouse others when the banging and noise began. Some of the Rattlers entered the cabin to turn beds over and rip mosquito netting on the windows, while others stood outside and challenged the Eagles to come out and fight. Some of the Eagles slept through the raid but those who were awake sat on their beds as though stunned. After the Rattlers left, Mason shouted to the Eagles that they were "yellow," especially Craig who had pretended to be asleep. Mason said the Rattlers had tried to blind them with a light (in reality a flashbulb from a staff camera). Most Eagles were aroused enough to want to retaliate that night; but staff prevented this when it was mentioned that rocks would be used.

22   Back in the Rattlers' cabin, many wild tales of the raid were being repeated over and over. Mills was considered especially heroic because he jumped in a window and secured comic books and a pair of blue jeans which, much to the Rattlers' delight, turned out to be Mason's (E leader). Mills painted these jeans the next day with orange paint, the

legend "The Last of the Eagles" being inscribed on each leg, and carried them like a flag. . . .

After breakfast on Day 4, which the Eagles ate first, the Eagles pre- 23 pared for the retaliatory raid which they had planned the previous night. After making sure that the Rattlers were in the mess hall, they started off, armed with sticks and bats, and led by Cutler who had balked at participating in a raid the previous night. The Eagles messed up the Rattlers' cabin, turning over beds, scattering dirt and posses- sions, and then returned to their cabin where they entrenched and pre- pared weapons (socks filled with rocks) for a possible return raid by the Rattlers.

The Rattlers were furious at the Eagles for the mess created in their 24 cabin, but were stopped from rushing to "get" the Eagles when their counselor suggested that the raid might have been planned so that they would lose cabin inspection. The Rattlers returned to clean up, cursing the Eagles to a man. Simpson (baseball captain) called them "commu- nists," and this was echoed by Everett (low status). . . .

While both groups were swimming, trucks [were] moved to the main 25 camp area. The gear, tents, etc. were dumped in two piles about 50–60 yards apart, the water pump being approximately half-way between the Eagle pile and the Rattler pile. Beside each pile of belongings there were separate picnic tables and fireplaces, in case the Eagles and Rat- tlers chose to have their meals separately. Only one truck was left at this main camp area, and this was the older-looking of the two. The tug-of- war rope was thrown on the ground about 20 feet from the truck, which was parked at a central point. The newer truck and a station wagon were removed and hidden behind trees on side paths away from the main camping area. The food was left in the station wagon; however eating utensils (paper plates, cups, flatware) and jars of pickles and mustard were stacked on a table centrally located and near the lake.

After swimming, the counselor of each group took his group to its re- 26 spective tent and picnic table location. The boys were getting hungry after the early breakfast, trip, and swim. Members of both groups went to inspect the centrally located table on which utensils and accessories were piled. This set the stage for the introduction of a superordinate goal.

Tug-of-War against the Truck: The staff member who drove the truck 27 announced, so that everyone could hear, that he would go down the road a piece to get the food. Both groups (about 15 yards apart now) watched with interest as the driver got into the truck. The driver strug- gled and perspired, the truck made all sorts of noises, but it just would not start (as planned). The boys became more and more interested.

Several Rattlers suggested, "Let's push it," but they abandoned the idea because the truck was parked facing up-hill. The tug-of-war rope was in plain sight of both groups. Mills (R) said, "Let's get 'our' tug-of-war rope and have a tug-of-war against the truck." Someone said, "Yeah, we can't push it." Swift (R) said, "Twenty of us can." Several boys agreed loudly with this, Mills adding, "Twenty of us can pull it for sure." The idea of having a tug-of-war against the truck was repeated by several boys in both groups. Mills (R) ran over to get the rope and started to tie it to the front bumper of the truck. An Eagle said it would be too long, and suggested pulling it halfway through the bumper, thus making two pulling ropes. Clark (E) fed it through the bumper while Mills (R) stretched it out. Harrison (R) suggested that the Eagles pull one rope and the Rattlers the other. Barton (R) said, "It doesn't make any difference."

28   The line-up pulling on the two ends of the rope was Eagles on one side and Rattlers on the other, with the exception that Swift (big R) joined the Eagle side as anchor-man and Craig (E) was next to Brown (R), the anchor-man on the Rattler side.

29   The first pull did not "start" the truck, and it was allowed to roll back down the hill for another pull. (The truck was, of course in running order, but the performance was completely convincing.) On the second pull, the members of both groups were thoroughly intermixed on both ropes. Some members of both groups began chanting "Heave, heave" in rhythm, something the Eagles had started during the tug-of-wars in Stage 2. Finally, the truck started, and the boys all jumped and cheered. Allen (R) shouted: "We won the tug-of-war against the truck!" Bryan (E) repeated, "Yeah! We won the tug-of-war against the truck." This cry was echoed with satisfaction by others from both groups.

30   Immediately following this success, there was much intermingling of groups, friendly talk, and backslapping. Four boys went to the pump and pumped water for each other: Mills (R), Hill (R), Craig (E), and Bryan (E). Thus the successful, interdependent efforts of both groups in pulling the truck, which was to get their food, had an immediate effect similar to that of superordinate goals introduced on previous days at the camp—intermingling of members of the two groups and friendly interaction between them.

31   *Separate vs. Integrated Meal Preparation:*   The driver went to get the food in the truck. While waiting for it to arrive, the participant observer of each group brought up the problem of whether his group wanted to alternate preparing meals with the other group or prepare them separately for themselves. In the Rattler group, Mills (leader) suggested that

the Rattlers prepare one meal that day and the Eagles the other. This was discussed at some length and agreed upon by the Rattlers. There were no derisive comments about the Eagles during this discussion, and no objections made to eating with them, although prior to the trip several Rattlers had objected to the idea of coming to the same place the Eagles were. . . .

When the truck arrived with the food, both groups rushed from their respective camp areas and started carrying the food to the centrally located picnic table. At the table, they gathered around discussing across group lines whether they would alternate in meal preparation, the Rattlers favoring it and the Eagles opposing it. But in the midst of this discussion, food preparation together actually began. McGraw, the customary meat-cutter in the Eagle group, began cutting the meat. He received much advice from everyone, and Mills (R) stood at his elbow for a time and helped him. In the meantime, Simpson (R) and Craig (E) poured Kool Aid into a bucket, Harrison (R) went for water to mix it, and Myers (E) poured in what he thought was sugar. Unfortunately, it turned out to be salt; but Myers was not berated by either Eagles or Rattlers for his mistake, even though the only immediately available Kool Aid was ruined. Harrison (R) pointed out that it wasn't really Myers' fault since the salt was in a sugar sack. Low status members on both sides were particularly active after this in preparing and distributing food. At one point, Mason (E leader) and Simpson (R) were talking and Simpson said, "You never thought we'd be eating together?" The reply was laughter.

The first Eagles through the line went to a centrally located picnic shed nearby and sat down at the tables. The first five or six Rattlers went to tables near their own camp area. Allen (R) asked a staff member where he should sit, and was told to sit any place he wanted. He then went to the shed and sat down with the Eagles. Neither at this time nor later was he criticized for his action. After eating, Mills (R) and Barton (R) also drifted over to the Eagle table for a short time. Shortly both groups went to their respective camp areas for a rest period.

After separate rests, the two groups were taken to swim, one shortly after the other. This time the Rattlers were in first, but got out of the water on seeing a water moccasin darting about. When the Eagles arrived, the Rattlers told them in excited tones of a snake moving around in the vicinity, describing it in detail. For about 15 minutes, all of the boys stood together at the pier and discussed this common threat coming from nature. Then they swam together at another spot for a short period, both groups mixing together in the water.

Behind Closed Doors: Violence in the American Family

MURRAY A. STRAUS, R. J. GELES, AND S. STEINMETZ

Much of the violence in the United States and, indeed, around the world, takes place within families, behind closed doors. People looking at the problem of violence have historically focused on war, gang-related activities, or eyecatching criminal acts between strangers. Yet by some estimates, the largest proportion of global violence is domestic, taking place among intimates; indeed, among individuals who ostensibly (and sometimes really do) love each other! The sociology of marriage and the family has been an ongoing research enterprise for decades. But until sociologist Murray Straus and colleagues published their aptly titled bombshell book, *Behind Closed Doors*, in 1980, this epidemic had gone largely unnoticed . . . or at least, undocumented and un-responded to.

It seems unlikely that domestic violence will escape attention in the future. The next great challenge, after naming and unmasking it, will be to do something about it, by raising awareness, providing alternatives—both for the perpetrators and the victims—and achieving the kind of socioeconomic reforms likely to improve the situation. (At the same time, it should be pointed out that an important underlying assumption of the following selection—the existence of a consistent "cycle of violence"—has been questioned, notably in an important article[1] that could not be included in the present volume because of space limitations.)

1   Drive down any street in America. More than one household in six has been the scene of a spouse striking his or her partner last year. Three American households in five (which have children living at home), have reverberated with the sounds of parents hitting their children. Where there is more than one child in the home, three in five are the scenes of violence between siblings. Over all, every other house in America is the scene of family violence at least once a year.

2   As high as these figures may seem, they are only national averages. Some neighborhoods are actually more violent than this, while other neighborhoods are somewhat less violent. But whatever the case, *every* American neighborhood has violent families.

[1]C. S. Widom, "Does Violence Beget Violence?" *Psych. Bulletin* 106. (1989): 3–28.

A National Survey

These figures come from the first national study of violence in American homes. We have always known that America is a violent society. A war in Vietnam, a riot in Watts, a gangland slaying, a political assassination, or a rape in an alley are all types of violence familiar to Americans. What is new and surprising is that the American family and the American home are perhaps as or more violent than any other single American institution or setting (with the exception of the military, and only then in time of war). Americans run the greatest risk of assault, physical injury, and even murder in their own homes by members of their own families.

Across the country this is borne out by official crime statistics. Tales of battered babies and beaten wives are widespread enough to be identified as "child abuse" and "wife abuse." And the estimated 2 million women and children battered and beaten by family members each year are only the tip of the iceberg identified as "violence between family members."

Brothers and sisters beat, stab, and shoot each other. There are husbands who are struck and beaten by their wives, and even grandparents are battered by their own children. Violence in one generation affects and encourages violence in another generation. In many families, perhaps a majority of violent families, violence is not even considered taboo or wrong. Rather, it is an accepted and integral part of the way the family functions.

Child abuse reporting laws, research, and efforts of the feminist movement have brought on a new awareness of the high level of aggression in the modern family. But there has never been a systematic study of violence based on a representative sample of even a single state or city, much less one that is representative of the whole country.

Our first goal was to measure the extent of violence in the American family. Knowledge concerning how much violence exists, what kinds of families are violent, and what causes violence has been difficult to come by since most of the research to date is based on small, unrepresentative samples from limited geographic areas. Consequently, even the question "What proportion of American families are violent?" could not be answered with any degree of certainty.

A second goal of this study was to uncover the breadth of family violence. Wife abuse and child abuse have captured public attention because of the terms themselves and because they involve terribly violent acts with damaging consequences for the victim. However, "abuse" is only one extreme end of the continuum of violence. There are many other forms and consequences of violence in the family, which, for many reasons, never are publicly identified as "abuse." Our aim was to study a variety of forms of violence, including some which many people do not consider violent, such as spanking a child. We are concerned with the proportion of families who shoot and stab each other, as well as those who spank and shove, because we think that one cannot be understood without considering the other.

9   A third goal was to find out what violence meant to the participants. Is family violence uniformly condemned and viewed as wrong, or are there instances and families where violence is a normal part of family relationships? Additionally, we wanted to learn about what kinds of families were violent, and which families were not. Much of the early thinking on child and wife abuse ascribed the abuse to psychological problems of the abuser. However, further analysis of abusers and abusive families indicates that psychological factors are not sufficient explanations of the violence. Studies of child abuse and wife abuse have yielded information which indicates certain types of *families* are abuse-prone.

Is Family Violence Increasing?

10   If one were to rely on newspaper and television accounts of the battering of children and wives, and if one were to examine official reports of child abuse and wife abuse over the past ten years, one reasonable conclusion would be that families have suddenly turned violent and this violence is increasing at a massive rate. Are families more violent now than they were in 1950, 1850, 1750? Have the changes which have occurred in the society and in the composition of the average family produced a generation of violent parents and violent spouses? Is the family in danger of being destroyed by its members' unbridled violent tendencies?

11   One could use official police, hospital, and social agency statistics to assess changes in the extent of child abuse and wife abuse, but for several reasons these statistics are not suitable for estimating actual levels of violence in the family. First, official statistics compile only the cases of family violence that come to public attention. These are probably only a fraction of the total cases of family violence.

12   Second, official statistics are compiled by organizations and individuals who work in those organizations. These individuals and the units they work in are often influenced by publicity campaigns, public pressure, political pressure, and changes in state and federal law. It was not until 1968 that all fifty states had laws mandating reports of child abuse. Thus, official statistics compiled by the states before 1968 reflect differences in official legal attitudes toward child abuse and not the true level

of abuse in each of the states. Even today, official statistics vary because each state and each compiler of the statistics in state and local agencies draw on different definitions of child abuse and child neglect. In the area of spouse abuse, few if any agencies have ever bothered to compile statistics on how many wives or husbands batter one another.

Although we cannot say definitely whether violence in the American   13
family is on the increase, historical facts argue that family violence certainly is not new and that, probably, we are no more violent and perhaps a little less violent toward our own families than were our ancestors.

Violence toward Children

Although parents' use of violence on children certainly is not new, the   14
addition of the term "child abuse" to our vocabulary has come about only recently. Child abuse typically refers to acts committed by parents on their children which other members of the society view as inappropriate and harmful. Thus, child abuse depends on historically and culturally relative judgments for its meaning.

The historical record demonstrates a use of extensive and often lethal   15
forms of violence by parents. Those who have examined the history of child abuse . . . document a history violence and infanticide dating back to biblical times. The Bible itself chronicles parental violence beginning when Abraham nearly killed his son as a sacrifice. Jesus's birth coincides with Herod's "Slaughter of the Innocents." The dictum "spare the rod and spoil the child" was stated and supported in the Bible. . . . Infanticide, mutilation, and other forms of violence were legal parental prerogatives from ancient Rome to colonial America. Children were hit with birch rods, switches, and canes. They were whipped, castrated, and destroyed by parents, most often with the consent and mandate of the ruling religious and political forces in the society.

The history of violence toward children in America dates back to the   16
arrival of the Puritans. Laws threatening death to the unruly hung over the children's heads, and parents supported their right to whip and punish with biblical quotations.

Religious ideology dictated that all children were born corrupted by   17
original sin and required salvation by their parents. To "beat the devil" out of a child was not just a passing phrase for the Puritans. It was a mandate to provide salvation for their children through physical punishment.

Thus, historically we have a tradition of physical (and emotional)   18
cruelty to children. As a society we have justified this cruelty through religious dogma, or by maintaining it is in the child's best interests. This societal mandate and tolerance of physical violence toward children

may have been one factor which delayed the identification of child abuse as an important social problem.

19   The Society for the Prevention of Cruelty to Animals was established before a Society for the Prevention of Cruelty to Children. When New York church workers, in 1874, tried to get help for a badly abused foster child, Mary Ellen, they found they could only turn to the Society for the Prevention of Cruelty to Animals. And so, they founded the first chapter for a similar society for children. . . .

20   Child abuse may have been identified as a social problem by concerned church workers, social workers, and private citizens in the nineteenth century, but it took almost 100 years after the case of Mary Ellen for violence toward children to be considered a major national social problem. In 1946, through the use of diagnostic X-ray technology, physicians began to notice patterns of healed fractures in young children that could only have resulted from repeated blows from their caretakers. . . .

21   While pediatric radiologists were able to diagnose child abuse, it was not until C. Henry Kempe and his associates published their classic work on "The Battered Child Syndrome" in the *Journal of the American Medical Association* in 1962 that battering and abuse became a focal point of public attention.

22   In 1968, it was estimated that more children under the age of five died from parentally inflicted injuries than from tuberculosis, whooping cough, polio, measles, diabetes, rheumatic fever, and appendicitis combined. . . .

23   By the end of the 1960s, all fifty states had passed and instituted laws mandating the reporting of child abuse and neglect and had begun to take steps at least to treat abused children and their families. In 1974, the federal government established the National Center on Child Abuse and Neglect in an attempt to provide a mechanism to increase knowledge about the causes of child abuse and neglect and identify steps that could be taken to prevent and treat abuse.

24   Thus, while Americans have probably abused their children since the first families established residence in the colonies, serious attention to the issue of abuse has only been achieved in the last twenty years. The public still asks: How many children are abused each year? What causes people to abuse their children? What can we do to prevent abuse? And most experts still shake their heads and admit they really do not know.

Violence toward Women

25   As with child abuse and violence toward children, there is no evidence which can be used to estimate the incidence of "wife abuse" in America over the last 300 years. However, there are historical and legal data

available which demonstrate that women have been subjected to brutal and often lethal forms of violence in their own homes. . . . Wives in America have been raped, choked, stabbed, shot, beaten, had their jaws and limbs broken, and have been struck with horse whips, pokers, bats, and bicycle chains.

Laws and legal precedents sanctioned, to a degree, the right of a husband to use violence on his wife. The classic "rule of thumb" gave legal justification to common law that sanctioned a husband's striking his wife with a switch, provided the stick was no wider than his thumb.   26

While legal records indicate that courts attended to the problems of many abused wives, wife abuse as a social problem did not receive national attention until the mid-1970s. . . .   27

Recognition of wife abuse as a problematic aspect of family behavior was probably a consequence of two forces. The women's movement has done much to bring the issue of wife abuse into focus. Wife abuse emerged as a problem among groups of women who began to come together to discuss women's issues in the late 1960s. It was almost an "accident" that women discovered the common problem of violence in their families. This "accidental" issue swelled as more and more women, who had believed that they were the only ones being beaten and that they "deserved" or precipitated their own victimization, discovered that there were many others with similar experiences and feelings.   28

It is important that we should not be misdirected by "the politics of social problems," which focus attention on issues such as wife abuse and child abuse. These are indeed of major concern. But the larger problem we are facing is not one of a single class of people, sex, or age group in the family being the most victimized. As the historical data show, and as the statistics we review in the following section bear out, the problem is one of *family violence*. Fathers and mothers hitting children, children hitting one another, and spouses physically battling each other are all part of the same topic—violence in the American family. . . .   29

Wife-beating is found in every class, at every income level. The wife of the president of a midwestern state university recently asked one of us what she could do about the beatings without putting her husband's career in danger. Japan's former Prime Minister Sato, a winner of the Nobel Peace Prize, was accused publicly by his wife of many beatings in their early married life. Ingeborg Dedichen, a former mistress of Aristotle Onassis, describes his beating her till he was forced to quit from exhaustion. "It is what every Greek husband does, it's good for the wife," he told her.   30

What is at the root of such violent attacks? Proverbs such as "A man's home is his castle," go a long way in giving insights into human nature   31 and society. The home belongs to the man. It is the woman who finds herself homeless if she refuses further abuse.

32 The image of the "castle" implies freedom from interference from outsiders. What goes on within the walls of the castle is shielded from prying eyes. And a modern home, like a medieval castle, can contain its own brand of torture chamber. Take the case of Carol, a Boston woman who called the police to complain that her husband had beaten her and then pushed her down the stairs. The policeman on duty answered, "Listen, lady, he pays the bills, doesn't he? What he does inside of his own house is his business." . . .

33 *Violence Rates.* A first approach to getting a picture of the amount of violence between the 2,143 husbands and wives in this study is to find out how many had engaged in any of the eight violent acts we asked about. For the year we studied this works out to be 16 per cent. In other words, every year about one out of every six couples in the United States commits at least one violent act against his or her partner.

34 If the period considered is the entire length of the marriage (rather than just the previous year), the result is 28 per cent, or between one out of four and one out of three American couples. In short, if you are married, the chances are almost one out of three that your husband or wife will hit you.

35 When we began our study of violence in the family, we would have considered such a rate of husbands and wives hitting each other very high. In terms of our values—and probably the values of most other Americans—it is still very high. But in terms of what we have come to expect on the basis of the pilot studies, this is a low figure. *It is very likely a substantial underestimate. . . .*

36 "What that kid needs is a good crack in the teeth."

37 How literally do parents take such phrases? For centuries our society has provided parents with the right and even the mandate to use hitting, slapping, spanking, and other physical force against children.

38 Parents have been "beating the devil" out of junior since colonial times. Jokes about being taken behind the woodshed or having one's backside warmed by father's razor strap have been around almost as long.

39 Early colonists, in fact, developed a most effective method of dealing with the unruly child. Many communities enacted "stubborn child laws," which gave parents the right to kill children who were beyond their ability to control.

40 Our culture is full of reminders of the right of parents to employ violence against their children. Fairy tales, folklore, and nursery rhymes are full of violence against children. Hansel and Gretel's parents, for in-

stance, abandoned their offspring to starve in the forest when money got scarce. The wicked queen told her huntsman to take Snow White into the forest and cut out her heart because the young stepdaughter was so beautiful. Mother Goose's "Old Woman in the Shoe" whipped her children soundly and sent them to bed without any bread.

Today, most parents hit their children at one time or another. Few   41
deny it. And if not proud of it, many honestly believe the slap on the bottom is a just and necessary tool of discipline. . . . There are contradictory rules and attitudes about violence between marriage partners. On the one hand, there are norms which define this kind of violence as wrong. On the other hand, there is a set of attitudes, values, cues, and signals that makes the marriage license a hitting license. Parental violence reveals an equally contradictory set of rules. . . .

Most American parents approve of spanking and slapping their chil-   42
dren, and almost two out of three American parents slap or spank their children in any given year. Nearly all parents slap or spank their children at least once in their lifetimes. We have demonstrated for the first time, with reliable scientific data on a nationally representative sample, that violence toward children goes well beyond ordinary physical punishment. Millions of children each year face parents who are using forms of violence that could grievously injure, maim, or kill them. In many families these episodes of violence are not merely one-shot outbursts. They are regular patterned ways which parents use to deal with conflict with their offspring. We do not mean to imply that the majority of parent-child exchanges are violent; rather we mean that many children periodically experience severe beatings, kicks, and punches in their homes.

A second point concerns the level of severe violence in families. Our fig-   43
ures do offer some solace since they demonstrate that relatively few parents do use beatings and guns and knives on their children. Nevertheless, although the actual percentage of parents who physically beat their children is small, when you extrapolate the figures to the national population it means that millions of children are involved. Consider how we would react if we found that millions of children faced guns and knives and experienced beatings in schools. If we were talking about smallpox, mumps, or flu, these figures could be interpreted to mean that there is an epidemic of these diseases in the United States. Somehow, people tend to focus on the more dramatic instances of child abuse and exhibit less concern over the mundane and undramatic forms of violence children experience. But violence of any kind is important. The consequences are potentially dramatic, since children who experience violence in their home experience it from those who claim love and affection for them.

One wonders why, when so many have expressed concern about   44
violence in television, no one has ever voiced concern about the

consequences of children seeing or being victims of violence in their own homes. The conventional theory is that the more violence a child sees on television, the more he or she tends to be violent, or is at least tolerant of violence. If this is the case, imagine the consequences of millions of children growing up seeing their parents using violence on each other, and on their children. . . .

45 Violence in the streets, violence in the schools, assassinations, murders, assaults, wife abuse, child abuse—are they caused by violence on television, violence in the movies, permissive upbringings? These probably contribute something. But the evidence appears to support the notion that our homes and how we raise our children are the main sources of our violent society. The more violent the couple we interviewed, the more violent their children are to each other, and to their parents. "Violence begets violence," not only against people who are violent to you (in this case, parents), but also against others (brothers and sisters, husbands and wives).

46 Some of the learning about violence in the family occurs by example: Children see their parents hitting each other.

47 Some of the learning occurs as a result of being the victim of violence: The more children are hit by their parents, the more likely they are to hit others.

48 When a child grows up in a home where parents use lots of physical punishment and also hit each other, the chances of becoming a violent husband, wife, or parent are greatest of all: About one out of every four people who grew up in these most violent households use at least some physical force on their spouses in any one year. Some of this is an occasional slap or shove. But one out of ten of the husbands who grew up in violent families are wife-beaters in the sense of serious assault. This is over three times the rate for husbands who did not grow up in such violent homes. The same thing applies to assaults by wives on husbands.

49 The effect of growing up in a violent home is even more predictive of child abuse: Over one out of every four parents who grew up in a violent household were violent enough to risk seriously injuring a child.

50 At the same time, it would be a mistake to put the whole burden of violence on what is learned in the family. To see this one needs only to look at the violence rates for the children of the non-violent parents in each chart (the zero group). This shows that there is lots of violence by people whose parents are *not* particularly violent to them and not violent to each other, even though the rates are a fraction of the rates for those who came from violent homes. The family may be the main training ground for violence, but in a violent society like ours, this role is shared with others. . . .

51 Do social factors have a bearing on violence in the family?

52 Who most likely beats his wife—a man with an eighth-grade education or one who finished college? Do Catholic mothers abuse their children

more than Jewish mothers? Is there apt to be more violence in a black welfare family in Georgia than in a white middle class family in Michigan?

The possibility that social factors such as race, income, education,   53
and regional differences are related to violence in the family was often overlooked in early studies of the problem. People tended to view family violence as a rare occurrence.

When social factors were considered, most people looked on family   54
violence as a lower class problem. There was, in fact, evidence to support the claim that domestic violence was an exclusive problem of poor people. The research on child and wife abuse carried out in the 1960s and early 1970s was based primarily on clinical cases of family violence which came almost exclusively from police or medical records. As in most instances of illegal behavior, the poor, powerless, and defenseless are more likely to get caught and labeled for their illegal acts, and therefore, theirs were the cases recorded.

Middle class families, with the privacy of separate houses and larger   55
house lots of suburbia, are far more insulated from prosecution for illegal behavior than the lower class city dwellers in their three-room tenements. Moreover, middle class families rely most often on private medical and legal agencies for help with their problems. We know, for example, that injured children seen by private physicians are less likely to be reported as victims of child abuse than are children treated in public clinics or emergency rooms. . . .

To sum up this detailed examination of the factors which were and   56
were not related to violence in the family, we can say that social factors do indeed make a difference in a family's inclination to engage in violent behavior. The factors which had a strong bearing on family violence were age, income, having a full-time, part-time, or no job. To a lesser extent, religion, residence in a city or the country, region of the country, and race were related to violence in the home.

We encountered a surprise when we learned that the uneducated   57
were not the most violent, and we saw that some factors were more strongly related to specific types of family violence—for instance race was more strongly related to husband-to-wife violence than the other forms of violence.

There is a very important insight to be gained from our finding that   58
social factors do influence whether or not a child, wife, or husband is physically abused. The majority of all treatment approaches to family violence involve some kind of personal counseling, for violent family member(s). The counseling is proposed because most people assume that there is something "wrong" with a person who uses abusive violence on a family member.

To be sure, our national survey of family violence cannot be used to   59
rule out the theory that personal factors are related to violent behavior.

But because we found social factors are related to violence we can argue with conviction that personal counseling will never be enough to treat or prevent violence in the home. According to our study, psychological health will not prevent family violence if a person is young, poor, and unemployed. Even if we "cured" the presumed psychological malady of violent individuals, the cure would have no effect if we send them back into the same social environment which influenced them to be violent in the first place. . . .

Summing Up

60 The steps . . . to reduce family violence involve extremely long-term changes in the fabric of a society which now tends to tolerate, accept, and even encourage the use of violence in families.

61   Many of the proposals would appear to confront and challenge some of our basic notions about the privacy of the family and the belief that a man's home is his castle. Some proposals appear to be out of the question— Can we ever achieve full employment? Can poverty be eliminated? Can we guarantee health care to all Americans? Clearly, some of the steps we propose are costly and some will seem completely unworkable.

62   However, the alternative to taking steps such as those outlined is a continuation and extension, and perhaps even an escalation, of the deadly tradition of domestic violence which:

1. Creates a cycle of violence.
2. Is one of the causes of all types of assault and homicide outside of the home, including political assassination.
3. Makes the family a source of untold misery for millions of Americans who know only violence and danger from those who should most provide love and security.

63   No meaningful change will take place without some drastic social and familial changes and this means a change in the fundamental way we organize our lives, our families, and our society.

Violence and the Social Control of Women

J. HANMER

A good look at violence needs as many perspectives as possible. One of the most challenging and important such perspectives has been provided by feminist scholars, who—for understandable reasons—have looked especially at the problem of male violence toward women. And they have found plenty.

It is debatable whether men abuse women out of an intentional plan to achieve collective mastery, but it is not debatable that male-female violence is widespread, that it is unacceptable, and that it contributes to the widespread subordination and victimization of women. It is also debatable whether male-female violence is more of a problem than male-male violence, but it is not debatable that men are the primary perpetrators of violence, whoever the victims. It is debatable whether a humane feminist perspective requires one to acknowledge male-female differences in behavioral tendencies (or to argue for similarity if not identity), but it is not debatable that men and women are entitled to equal opportunities and legal protection and that, by and large, they have received neither.

This paper is concerned with the social phenomenon of male violence   1
to women. It is not concerned with explaining variations in the amount and type of violence, in when, where and among whom it occurs, or with explaining why it occurs. Nor is the concern with explanations of individual violence, but rather the focus is on the significance and meaning of violence from the male to the female at the social structural level.

To understand this phenomenon requires a reassessment of the role   2
of violence in male-female relations. The universality of the subordination of women is considered first, and then the definition, forms, and incidence of violence. Sociological explanations of interpersonal violence are criticized, followed by an examination of the role of the state in creating "symmetrical" dependency between the sexes. The relevance of an analysis of violence in male-female relations for an understanding of the relationships between sex and class is raised. And the final question is, can male violence be successfully challenged?

Male Violence and Female Subordination

To the extent that the issue of male versus female power and authority   3
in society is considered cross-culturally, the dominant view today seems to be that women always, everywhere have less power and authority in society than men. Male activities, whatever they are, are always, everywhere more highly esteemed than those of women. Two materially based reasons are usually given to explain this phenomenon. One is that the female reproductive function limits their social participation. Bearing, nursing, and looking after young children is seen as the basis for the exclusion of women from the most highly valued (and violent) activities of many societies, i.e., hunting and warfare. This sexual division of labor

is also a division between the public and private spheres of cultural life, which may be embryonic or highly developed, and the rigidity of the separation further affects the access of women to power and authority. The second material factor is the role of women in economic production, but it has been found that even in societies where their share is in excess of 50 percent women never achieve full equality.

4   The relation of force and its threat to other variables is rarely examined, but a recent paper attempts to assess the relative importance of the institutionalized use of violence, ideology, and economic stage of development in ensuring women's acquiescence in their own subordination. K. Young and O. Harris argue that in societies with the least control over nature the dominant mode of control is the institutionalized use of force, where men collectively punish individual women who have violated social rules, for example, through group rape. At a somewhat higher degree of control over nature ideological mechanisms dominated, "there is a proliferation of lived, repressive institutions," and violence is restricted to the individual use of force. At a still higher level of production, the dominant mode of control becomes the economic. "Women are denied access to the means of production, no longer control even their own household surplus, have no access to labor, etc." Ideological control weakens and violence is further masked.

5   Certainly within our society neither men or women are eager to acknowledge the importance that force or threat play in the daily drama of everyday life. Hostile feelings and behavior towards the opposite sex are often carefully concealed, even from the self, as a matter of everyday routine. Within the family, violence from men to women has the character of a tabooed subject that occasionally surfaces in at least a proportion of public consciousness. For example, in our immediate past in Britain public discussion of marital violence in the late nineteenth century led ultimately to a change in matrimonial law enabling a wife to gain a legal separation from a persistently violent husband. The issue then sank into obscurity to surface again during the time of the struggle for women's suffrage, to sink and resurface again today. Thus women have from time to time become conscious of the use of force against them as a group; but more important sociologically, most of the time the use of force and its threat has not been recognized, except possibly as a problem limited to a few individuals. Thus efforts to reinterpret marital violence, and also rape and other assaults on women in the public area of life as activities carried out by individual men on behalf of all men, may strike one as novel, daring, perhaps ludicrous, so individualized is our consciousness of these important phenomena.

6   Given the difficulties of comparison and lack of data no attempt will be made to argue that the quantity or quality of violence is less or

greater in other societies than in our own. What will be argued, however, is that the use of force and its threat, even though highly masked, is of sufficient importance in our own western industrialized society to be recognized as a major component in the social control of women by men. Further, I will argue that force and its threat is the basis for the extraction of all benefits that men make from women; that is, economic, sexual, and prestige gains. As with subservience based on social class, ethnic group, or third world country, that of sex, too, rests ultimately on force and its threat.

Violence and the fear of violence molds behavior. The phenomenon   7
is preeminently sociological, but in order to further sociological insight the definition must include the perceptions of the recipient as well as that of the aggressor and society at large. . . .

Structural Stress and Socialization

Within sociology the role of violence in structuring and maintaining   8
male-female relations is inadequately considered. In apparently relevant documents the use of force may be completely ignored or underplayed. And when sociological efforts are made to explain some aspect of male violence to women, the social fact that violence usually flows from the male to the female is not taken theoretically into account. The response of the state through its various officials and departments is often ignored, but even if mentioned is not seen as integral to an understanding of the violent act.

But even with these omissions the researcher confronting individual   9
case material still concocts a potpourri of explanations, as no one theory can account for the remaining phenomena. At crucial moments there seems to be a tendency to individualize and psychologize. The use of social structural theory of frustration, stress, and blocked goals to explain individual behavior and the development of categories unconnected with social structure, such as irrational and expressive violence, are examples of this practice. In theories of socialization, at their worst sociologically, norms and values of violence are seen as deviant, affecting either subcultures or some individual families while society as a whole remains unaffected. At best violence is seen as widespread and the family described as a social institution providing basic training in norms, values, and techniques of violence. Subcultures of violence then become the tip of an iceberg arising from an underlying social structure with norms and values that approve of violence.

For example, this is the stance adopted by Gelles in the first analysis   10
of marital violence in American families. He combines socialization theory with theories of frustration, stress, and blocked goals to account

for variations in the behavior of his respondents. With socialization theory he attempts to explain present behavior by past events, while present behavior is accounted for by theories of frustration, stress, and blocked goals. A multitude of explanations are necessary as not all the violent adults in the study were exposed to or treated with violence as children (also we know from other sources that not all who are grow up to be violent, while others from apparently nonviolent backgrounds become so in adulthood). The relationship between violent behavior in adulthood and childhood socialization is statistical and an unknown correlation at that, as we do not know what proportion of the population observe or experience violence in childhood, even if we could agree on how it is to be defined. This same point applies to theories of frustration, stress, and blocked goals. Further these theories are used to explain individual behavior, and thus the proposed explanations of social phenomena equal the simple sum of individual characteristics. To change the emphasis to sex role socialization does not resolve these difficulties, even though both past and present socialization (including reinforcement or its lack) can be included in the same concept.

11   Dominant ideology states that female submissiveness and dependency on the male is self-chosen. The liberal challenge to this view does not blame women so obviously for their difficulties, as female submissiveness and dependency, like male aggression, is said to be taught through childhood socialization into sex roles. While these explanations may have some validity in that they potentially expose the role of ideology in human conduct, as well as describe aspects of learned behavior, on their own they are inadequate explanations of social structure and process based on dominance and submission.

Resource Theory

12   W. Goode with resource theory hovers on the edge of a new analysis but safely turns away with the view that violence is used when other resources, which he defines as economic, prestige or respect, and friendship or love, are lacking. Goode, however, recognizes that marriage is a power relationship and that force or its threat is a resource usually held by the husband/father (as, it can be added, is the economic and a general higher status position). Only in the area of friendship or love has the women a good chance of gaining more of a resource, and then only by lifelong devotion to husband and children.

13   Love and sexuality is an aspect of male-female relations that has been widely written about within the women's liberation movement. A common theme is that through love and sexual relations with men, women are oppressed psychologically and materially. Women are turned

against women in their competition for men and alienated from their sexuality; hence the furor in the movement when the biological basis of the female orgasm was finally established. Love is seen as double-edged. It is all a woman can hope for, yet once received and given it confirms a woman's subordinate social position. Through love of husband, home, and children they are inducted into a relationship characterized by dependency on the male. Thus love, too, becomes a mechanism of control of women by men.

Asymmetrical Reciprocity + The State = "Symmetrical" Dependency

But in industrial societies we cannot discuss modes of social control and particularly the use of interpersonal force without considering the role of the state, as the organization, deployment, and control of force and its threat is incorporated within it. The question to be considered is for whose benefit is this force used. This is partly exposed by how the state deploys its force and controlling function and partly by how the state reacts to those outside the state apparatus who use force.   14

E. Marx in a recent study of an Israeli township analyzes a number of violent encounters within the family and community and relates these to the organization of the state. He divides violence against officials of the state as coercive and that against other family members or general public as appealing (for help). When interpersonal assaults are carried out in public they receive the attention of the police, but when carried out in the privacy of the home they may not be treated as offenses even if the participants sustain injury and the matter becomes public knowledge, as " 'public interest' is not at stake, and the law organs tend to apply a more restricted definition of violence to them."   15

For example, in the Ederi family the husband regularly attacks his wife physically, the children accept it matter-of-factly, and no one intervenes. The analysis focuses on Mr. Ederi's blocked goals. He was said to have beaten his wife this time because of the prospect of being unable to provide for his family. There was an unexpected debt and Mrs. Ederi wanted to give up her job. But Mrs. Ederi suffered severe leg pains, was nearly exhausted, finding it difficult to run a large household and keep her part-time job. After the attack Mrs. Ederi "muttered under her breath: 'What he wants is that I should go out (to work) so he can stay at home and attend to the children.' " The author in the following sentence interprets this to mean "She realized, then, that her husband's concern was not this particular debt, but the prospect of being unable to provide the family's minimum requirement in the near future."   16

17   Another interpretation is that Mrs. Ederi is imputing an instrumental motive to the attack, which if taken seriously would do more than call into question the acceptability of so-called noninstrumental categories of violence. If the action was coercive, designed to keep Mrs. Ederi in paid employment against her will and to reduce her spending, does she not have blocked goals as well? . . .

18   To be able to fulfill or not fulfill social expectations is the language of power and dominance. It is the actions of the state that both give Mr. Ederi this power and deny it to Mrs. Ederi, *and thus public interest is defined and served*. That the state can be treated as irrelevant to an understanding of domestic violence is a measure of the power of men to define social reality. In this . . . example, state power takes the form of restraining force, what Backrach and Baratz call nondecision-making.

Male Power and the State

19   The view that the purpose of male violence to women is to control them parsimoniously explains both acts of public and private violence. It also accounts for what might appear to be an excessive use of force. It may be, or seem to be, necessary to kill, mutilate, maim, or temporarily reduce a woman's ability to carry out services, etc., in order to be in control. Prestige, self-esteem, a sense of personal worth is gained, expressed, and made public by the acquiescence of others.

20   In this perspective the state represents the interests of the dominant group, i.e., men, in confrontations with the subordinate group, i.e., women. Thus it is consistent that in domestic disputes the status of the victim determines the response of that section of the state given the task of controlling violence. That men unknown to the woman (the policemen) would back up the man known to her (the husband) in pursuit of their joint state-defined interest is to impartially enforce the law, for in practice the state defines women as less equal. This knowledge, however, comes as a shock to most women when they seek protection from the police for the first time. Women lack consciousness of the rights they surrender on marriage or cohabitation, but once in a violent domestic dispute the contradiction between their interests and that of their husband and men in general begins to become apparent.

21   The preeminent interests of men are expressed through explicit policies; for example, in Britain a major plank of the welfare state is to maintain the family, and within this unit the woman is defined as the dependent of the male. To create "symmetrical" dependence between the sexes the state aids the man by making it difficult for a woman to leave marriage. Law and law enforcement, housing policies, income maintenance, employment, and earnings interlock to trap the woman in

dependency. For a woman and her children to leave a violent husband she must have protection from violence, and in common with all other women she must have somewhere to go and an income. The Select Committee raised the issue of state induced dependency by asking rhetorically, "Why should it be the wife and children who have to leave and not the husband? . . . Why should we not create hostels to receive the battering husband? . . . "

On both and ideological and practical level the problem is the victim's. Women passing through women's aid refuges provide examples of how their husband's violence becomes "their problem," i.e., is turned back upon them, by all the relevant departments of the state (health workers, social workers, voluntary and statutory, as well as the police and legal services). In turning the problem back upon the woman it is individualized, the direction of violence is ignored, and the ideology supporting male dominance is confirmed. . . . 22

The violent act that has received the most public attention is rape. There is a growing exposure of police and court procedures and reactions. As the National Council for Civil Liberties explains, rapists are more likely to be acquitted if the rape is socially possible and if the victim's life style, even if unknown to the rapist, expresses autonomy. Thus to live alone, to walk alone, to hitchhike, or wear "indecent clothing," to have talked or drunk with a rapist are acts likely to make rape possible. To be celibate, a divorcée, an adulteress, to have an illegitimate child, a lover, to have had an abortion, all irrelevant to the act of rape, may absolve the rapist of guilt. As Féministes Révolutionaires explain, "only a married woman, locked in her home, in company, and fully clothed can be recognized as a victim. Then rape is not only physically impossible, but, above all, socially unjustified from the point of view of the patriarchy." Thus men apparently unconnected with the organization of state force and its control can be seen as fulfilling that function. Men who pester, attack, or rape women in the streets of the city can be described as "these inquisitors, the cops, the warders, of the patriarchal system," and not demented, ill-socialized, or sex-crazed, "for woman-hunting season is 24 hours a day all the year around." 23

The pervasive fear of violence, and violence itself, has the effect of driving women to seek protection from men, the very people who commit violence against them. Husbands and boyfriends are seen as protectors of women from the potential violence of unknown men. Women often feel safer in the company of a man in public, and the home and marriage is portrayed, and often feels, the safest place of all, even though statistically speaking women are more likely to be violently assaulted in marriage and from men known to them. Fear created by violence in public places is another factor underwriting female dependency on the male. 24

The fact that many husbands do not beat their wives, and many men do not attack women in the streets, either regularly or ever, is not proof that wife-beating and other assaults are irregular, unsystematic practices limited to a few unfortunates either of birth, or training, or low economic resources, but merely that it is not necessary to do so in order to maintain the privileges of the superior group.

25   The main argument of this article is that force and its threat is never a residual or secondary mode of influence; rather it is the structural underpinning of hierarchical relations, the ultimate sanction buttressing other forms of control. While this is not a unique view, it is rarely applied to male-female relations, possibly in part because to do so is to raise the issue of the relation between sex and class exploitation.

Sex and Class

26   The black analogy is useful in making explicit the role of force in maintaining a particular social structure and process. J. Dollard's analysis of black-white relations in a southern American town and the economic, sexual, and prestige gains whites make at the expense of blacks parallels that of the women's liberation movement in the sense that movement writers focus on the areas of sexuality, waged and unwaged work, and status or prestige to describe exploitative relations between men and women. But Dollard goes on to show how these gains to whites are maintained by ideology backed up by force and its threat. Deference is continuously exacted from blacks, and infractions of social rules are punished primarily by force, although economic sanctions may be used.

27   While the analysis of exploitative relations between men and women is not as developed as that between blacks and whites, marriage and family life has been identified as the primary form of control. Love and "a woman's nature" have been explored as ideologies of oppression. There is also a growing body of literature on the domestic economy of women that examines the economic value of the unpaid labor of the wife, but who benefits is disputed: the husband, the capitalist, or both.

28   The role that male violence plays in economic exploitation, which includes lower incomes for women in paid employment, is discussed tangentially, if at all. One argument is that capitalism, not men, benefit from male aggression to women. For example, R. Frankenburg in his reinterpretation of relations between miners and their wives in "Coal is Our Life" argues that there is an economic gain, but not to men. Capitalism is the beneficiary because men take out their frustrations on their wives and not their bosses. Although the emphasis differs, this is also the position taken by the Wages for Housework campaign. Every act of servicing the male worker is seen as work for which wages are due, not

from the man, the wage slave, but from the capitalist. Men are never held accountable for the gains they make by virtue of their wives' unpaid work. Sociologically these views ignore the reality of marriage as a power relationship and the meaning that control over finances and the ability and will to use force has for the marital pair. D. Barker's analysis of marriage as a labor relation does not make this mistake.

But the relation between the use of force and the economic output in the marital situation is not direct. If the purpose were to extract maximum labor from women, then force and its threat should be finely administered to ensure it, much as it needs to be in industry in order to maintain profit. For example, Harris in describing the generality of wife beating among the Peruvian villagers she was studying noted that the degree of beating did not relate to the skill of women in fulfilling their marital role, which included agricultural production, but rather appeared to be random. The "best" wives were among the most beaten, while the lazy and incompetent might well escape. Closer to home in the experience of women's aid, physical violence by husbands and cohabitees does not seem to be related to competence in domestic work. The force is too often counterproductive; not only may the woman be seriously injured, but she may suffer nervous disturbance that makes it even more difficult for her to look after the children, prepare the meals, manage on the housekeeping allowance, etc., and she may end up in the hospital, medical or psychiatric, thus depriving the man of her services at least for a time.

Peruvian males said they beat their women in order to control them, as do British men, and, in my view, this rather than the economic stage of development of society, or economic relations between the sexes in society, or between individual pairs should be accepted as the reason. But to do so is to view force and its threat as more fundamental to the inferior position of women in society than the role women play in economic life. Economic exploitation becomes only one benefit men gain at the expense of women. As the control men exercise over women is more extensive, there are also benefits to them in the areas of sexuality, reproduction, status, and internalized feelings, for example, of superiority. . . . Anthropological findings are that male violence to women predates monogamy, and thus this behavior is not an unfortunate vagary of human nature called forth by class society. However, to the extent that women have lost social power over time, male use of force should be considered at least as part of the explanation of how this occurred, as a better reason is needed to explain why women accepted that the surplus belonged solely to the male and male progeny.

Unfortunately we do not have the information which would permit an informed discussion of whether male violence to women became

29

30

31

greater once monogamy had been instituted among the bourgeoisie, but Delmar reminds us that in Engels' view the most oppressed women in the society of his day were the wives of this class. A century later the experience of women's aid in providing refuges for battered women has established that violence continues to occur in all social classes. Public violence, too, is not class specific.

32   For these reasons I argue that violence operates independently (if not totally, then substantially) from the economic organization of society.

Exclusion and Compulsion

33   The male use of force or its threat towards women has two currents: one is to exclude participation or restrict behavior, while the second is to compel particular responses. The two interact, so that achieving one is an aid in achieving the other.

34   Women are excluded from, or have restricted access to, male social, economic, and political groups. Men have the power to define social reality because they can exclude women, while women cannot exclude men without appearing unreasonable or deviant (witness the difficulties Women's Aid has "explaining" why there are so few men in their organizations and their difficulties in excluding them totally). The power to exclude is the language of dominance; and thus men's groups become public groups, while those of women are on the whole private or seem less permanent as they lack the social validation that flows from a supraordinate position. Because men's groups are public, women are excluded from, or have restricted access to, certain buildings, or parts of the city. Exclusion carries with it the threat of retaliation (i.e., use of force) should women become "uppity" and attempt to gain admission to forbidden areas.

35   The second current in the male use of force or its threat to women is to compel them to behave in given ways or to undertake certain tasks, particularly nurturing and housekeeping work. The more women are excluded from social, economic, and political areas the easier it is to enforce domesticity. But even if there is little exclusion from the public sphere, deferential servant-like roles for women can be enforced through ideology and material control, both economic and violent, and state policies that favor this type of family organization. In its harshest form there is isolation from other adults and total economic dependency so that the smallest material wants and even conversation depend on male largesse.

36   It is interesting to note that the women's movement at the end of the nineteenth and early twentieth century was largely concerned with the power of men to exclude women (from education, employment, politi-

cal process), while that of today is largely concerned with the power of men to compel a particular kind of domesticity. A focus on violence, the social cement ensuring female dependency, offers an opportunity to unify these two concerns.

Challenging the Use of Force by Males

While from time to time there are examples of men as a group physi-   37
cally attacking women as a group, almost all violence is to individual women carried out by individual men or groups of men. The major point seems to be that it is rarely necessary physically to attack women as a group in order to control them. The only recent British examples that I know of are attacks on lesbian women; for example, a group of men attacked the women who attended the last National Lesbian Conference in 1976. Within the women's liberation movement this group offers the greatest challenge to males, as of all women they are the most independent of men; but it is worth noting that no National Lesbian Conference has been held since then, as the women concerned say no safe venue can be found. That women as a group rarely challenge male dominance may be partly the result of fear and partly that they are too well controlled by other means to make this necessary.

For the individual, challenging male dominance is like running a   38
gauntlet or breaking through a series of barriers, beginning with a consensual acceptance of the sexual social system, moving on to overcoming a fear of deviating, of breaking cultural norms and possibly unleashing a violent response, to an acceptance of possible violence and finding ways of surmounting state supported dependency in the areas of income, housing, and law and its enforcement.

Clearly we are in a period of renewed consciousness of male vio-   39
lence, and in a small way it is being challenged by women. In the early analyses of female subordination during the present wave of the women's liberation movement, violence was one of a number of factors. In the United States help for victims subsequently developed around rape, while in Britain the original focus was on women assaulted in marital relationships, and both have been taken up elsewhere in the Western world. But we cannot know what this will mean for the future. Will consciousness be lost again, the "problem" individualized once more, or will the knowledge of the social meaning of male violence continue to spread and the analysis and the response be extended?

The "problem of men" has yet to be raised theoretically and with it   40
the question of the extent to which men can be reeducated. Psychology, anthropology, sociology have served largely as publicists and apologists for the male view of society, culture, women, and ideal male-female

relations. A new perspective is needed to right the balance: one that focuses on force and its threat as an elemental factor holding together a social structure and social process based on female subordination. An analysis of violence in the maintenance of male power and authority, individually and collectively on varying levels of organization from local informal groups through to the national formal operation of the state, also should clarify, relative to social class, the independent basis and functioning of sexual divisions in the exploitation of women.

War and Religion in a Sociological Perspective

GORDON ZAHN

Sociologists have long been interested in the structure and function of major (and minor) social institutions. There are military sociologists, medical sociologists, sports sociologists, and others who specialize in examining political parties, the "corporate culture" of various businesses, universities, and the like. Sociology of religion is also a vibrant arena for research, one that is especially relevant for our purposes because of the prominent and often paradoxical position of religion with regard to violence. Thus, religions deal with some of humanity's most intense concerns, and virtually every religion has taken a firm stand in opposition to violence; at the same time, virtually every religion has elected to condone violence . . . at least in certain situations, notably war and the punishment or restraint of dangerous criminals.

And so we have the paradox of Christianity, for example—whose defining and perhaps most original concept is the power of redeeming love and the injunction to "turn the other cheek"—having given rise to one of the world's great warrior traditions. Many of today's most violent international situations involve believers from different and competing faiths (Islamic Pakistan versus Hindu India, Protestant England versus Catholic Ireland, Orthodox Serbs versus Islamic Albanians and Bosnians versus Catholic Croats, etc.). It is also not uncommon for members of the same religion to go to war against each other, each claiming the saction of the same God. In our next selection, Gordon Zahn explores the sociological paradox that unites religion and war.

1   The first problem facing one in attempting to write on this topic is the sheer immensity of the task. Religion and war are among man's oldest practices and also among the most universal. Of the two, religion can

claim something of an edge in both respects. War as such could not emerge as a social phenomenon until human society had at least progressed to the tribal level of organization, though it goes without saying that interpersonal lethal conflict was not unknown before that stage of development was attained. So, too, with the universality factor. Anthropologists are pretty much agreed that all known human societies have some form of religion or (as in the more "advanced" societies which have left religion behind) some kind of religious surrogates or substitute whereas some human societies and cultures have been studied which are totally unfamiliar with war either as practice or as concept.

A second and more troubling (sociologically at least) problem has to do with the variety and complexity of relationships that can and do exist between war and religion. Quite apart from the most direct relationship, the "wars of religion" in which societies with different conceptualizations of the Divinity set out to force each other to "see the truth" or, that failing, simply eliminate the offending infidel, there is the question of where and how warfare can fit into any given religious system. There is a certain convenience and simplicity to be found in the polar extremes. Some religions—or sects and cults within broader religious contexts—are war-promoting; the acts of war becoming the sacred worship offered to gods of war and combat, the warriors constituting a select priesthood, and captives or even entire vanquished populations made literal or at least symbolic sacrificial victims. In some instances the waging of the war can become so much a religious ritual that it actually involves little or none of the carnage we take for granted. Instead the valiant participants fulfill their obligations in battles of stylized movement which run their course with a minimum of injury or bloodshed on either side. The only problem for the social scientist with respect to such war-promoting religions is to identify and analyze the various forms and intensities of combat and, if possible, relate them to some cross-cultural indices of religiosity. 2

At the other extreme are the religions which condemn war and forbid the believer to participate in war. The task here must be broadened to study the social arrangements and life styles which make it possible for a people to adhere to the pacific traditions and still maintain a stable human existence. To put the issue in these terms may imply a conceptual bias, an acceptance of the Social Darwinist assumption of a never-ending struggle of all against all which must always be taken into account. A society committed to a religious value system which sees conflict-free life patterns as the natural norm might see no reason to "explain" the absence of war. This author and, sad to say, most of the readers of the article do not live in such a society. Even if we did, it would 3 be reasonable to suggest that religious deviance in the pacific society (i.e. the warlike or violent nonbeliever or "sinner") would provoke more disruptive consequences than would a failure on the part of the believer to give the God of War his due measure of devotion in the society dominated by a war-promoting religion.

4   These simple cases of religions which dogmatically endorse or forbid war probably embrace a small minority of the world's population. The great world religions, forced to come to terms with the fact of war, present a problem of far greater complexity, sometimes incorporating explicit specifications as to when and to what degree war is to be permitted or even required, sometimes making the adjustment by means of broad "interpretations" of ambiguous moral precepts and doctrines. In fact, seemingly unequivocal directives can be and have been "interpreted" into a justification of the behavior they seem to exclude or forbid. Some religious value systems (Islam, Judaism) are or appear to be more compatible than others (Hinduism, Buddhism, Christianity) with the values and the behaviors associated with warfare, but none is completely indifferent to the planned and intended destruction of human life war involves. To the extent that such ambivalence is structured into the belief systems of the major world religions, it offers a distinct challenge to the social scientist and it is the purpose of this paper to develop some of the dimensions of that challenge.

5   The religious dilemmas raised by war and the adjustment mechanisms that have been developed to ease them are best illustrated perhaps by the Christian experience and traditions. Much can be made of the contrast between Old Testament accounts of wars fought and bloody victories won at the command and with the direct assistance of a jealous and vengeful Deity and, on the other hand, the message of the New Testament which stresses the obligations of the true follower of the One God to give himself in self-sacrificial love even to the "enemy" and promises rewards of eternal blessedness to him who pursues the role of peacemaker. Though an occasional note of ambiguity enters in such things as the display of Christ's righteous anger in clearing the Temple of the money-changers, the cryptic instruction to the apostles to buy a sword for their journey, and the favorable mention in various parables of householders who marshall and use superior armed strength, it is impossible to deny that the main thrust of the Gospel teachings and example is toward loving forgiveness and avoidance of actions which would cause injury to others. So, too, with the ambiguity some find in the warning that "they who take the sword shall perish by the sword" (a warning which would seem to authorize wielding the weapon to punish the unrighteous); the circumstances under which it was issued, the rebuke to Peter for daring to strike out in violent defense of the Mas-

ter, lend considerably more weight to the pacifist interpretation of this particular lesson. . . .

The conversion of the Emperor Constantine early in the fourth cen-   6
tury created an essentially new social environment for the Christian community and its members. Elevated now to the status of a state religion, the Church gained new privileges and, along with them, a wide range of mutual interests with the secular authority which until then had been so dedicated to its destruction. A new perspective on war and violence developed which was to culminate in the familiar "just war" formulations which continue to hold a dominant position in Catholic theological thought. In its earliest statement, particularly in the writings of St. Augustine, the new doctrine was not the complete rejection of the pacifism of the primitive church it was to become in its later stages. Indeed, the so-called "law of self-preservation" which is generally advanced today to justify participation in the "just" war would be quite inconsistent with Augustine's teaching. Nevertheless, the right to kill in self-defense which he would deny became a duty obligating that same individual to kill in defense of the state as custodian and preserver of the common good. . . .

One thinks in particular of the scandal of the Crusades and the reli-   7
gious wars of the post-Reformation era in which organized violence, far from being forbidden to the followers of "the Prince of Peace", somehow became a favored instrument for the defense (and spread!) of the Faith. Such a review would find it impossible to ignore the link that often obtained between imperialist conquest and economic exploitation by the secular power and the missionizing activities of the Church— both cooperating in a strange and often brutal partnership in the systematic destruction of entire cultural and societal orders and sometimes of their hapless human populations as well.

Even the advent of modern war, distinguished primarily by the mas-   8
sive scale made possible by universal conscription and "advances" in weaponry and military strategies, was taken in stride. Flexible enough to adjust to each new situation as it arose or, where this proved too much to ask, riddled through with convenient theological loopholes (the "presumption of justice" in favor of the ruler in case of doubt being the most obvious perhaps, the just war tradition made it possible for the Christian on any side of almost every conflict to "do his duty" and still rest secure in his conscience, believing he was performing a virtuous act. . . .

Once the world had witnessed the introduction of nuclear war at Hi-   9
roshima and Nagasaki, it became abundantly clear that henceforward war, the actuality if not the gallant abstractions still to be found in moral guidance handbooks, could no longer be reconciled with the Christian message of peace and love. Nor was this all. The changed nature of the

secular power itself and the moral perspective of the kind of men in whose hands it was placed left little basis for any expectation that moral considerations would carry any weight in war-and-peace decisions. Admired though they might be, there was little in the open and frequently ruthless pragmatism of a Churchill and a Roosevelt to suggest the "Christian Prince" so basic to the underlying rationale of the just war doctrines; and for a Stalin or a Hitler to be made the beneficiary of "the presumption of justice" should have been rejected out of hand as a moral and intellectual enormity. Unfortunately, it was not. No better evidence of the theological bankruptcy of the just war tradition can be found than the shocking fact that German Catholics could find assurance in the writings of well-known theologians and statements issued by their ecclesiastical leaders that service in Hitler's wars was "a Christian duty."

10   Sociologically speaking, another corner has been turned. Like the conversion of the Empire centuries before, the Second World War had created an essentially new situation and this fact, in turn, is forcing another reformulation of the Christian religious teachings on war. The most immediate response took the form of a somewhat limited "nuclear pacifism", a position one might abscribe to such prominents as Cardinals Ottaviani and Alfrink and even Pope John XXIII. This has been broadened considerably under the stimulus of the Second Vatican Council and its call for an "entirely new attitude" on war and has found its most dramatic expression in the American Catholic opposition to the war in Indochina. What the outcome will be—whether, for instance, the Catholic community will return to the full pacifist commitment of its earliest days, though in a more sophisticated form—is not yet certain. What is certain, however, is that the relationship between the Christian religion (and, be it noted, that other Christian denominations are far ahead of the Catholic Church in many respects) and war is undergoing a profound change, one that will (or should) have great behavioral impact for its adherents and for the societies of which they are a part. . . .

11   The very notion that Christian religious values can and do change may seem inconsistent with the claims of immutability that have always been made for Christian truth and belief systems. The fact is, however, that past experience shows that these claims have always allowed for the possibility of development and discovery, two processes which have come into special prominence as the post-conciliar Church divests itself of the lingering remnants of stultifying triumphalism. There is a greater readiness to recognize that revelation and tradition, while they must remain the twin sources of Christian truth and values, have always been subject to the mode in which they are approached and received, and that there is something of a built-in strain between literal and explicit application on the one hand and a more flexible, or "situa-

tionalist", emphasis upon interpretation on the other. Instead of viewing this strain in terms of a forced dichotomy between fundamentalism and relativism, it is increasingly recognized that it provides the internal dynamism which has enabled the Christian religion to survive and surmount the challenges of vastly different times and places. . . .

Religion, for its part, is called upon to validate secular authority, 12 sometimes even to the point of providing sacramental investiture or conducting coronation rituals. More ordinary contributions center upon helping to form the "good" citizen by inculcating patriotic "virtues" and patterns of obedience to "legitimate" authority. The polity, through the instruments of state authority, offers the religious community in return protection and privileges (tax exemption, even in some instances outright tax support) and displays a measure of public support and respect for the "higher" ideals and values it proclaims along with the structures and activities through which they are presumably given expression.

Even in pluralistic societies professing a "separation of Church and 13 State" this pattern of mutual reinforcement generally prevails, and it becomes particularly evident when the polity finds itself in a situation of crisis. It should be unnecessary to add that war represents a crisis of highest order, involving as it does a threat to national survival. The response of the churches takes many forms of direct and indirect support all designed to aid in forming and maintaining military and civilian morale. The "blessing of the cannons" may not be as frequent an occurence as formerly, but in subtler ways the same objective is accomplished. There are special war services, parish honor rolls listing the men who have gone off to war or who have fallen in battle, sermons and pastorals extolling the militant virtues and calling upon the faithful to bear the sacrifices the war may impose. There is, above all, the military chaplaincy, the most direct and visible sign that Church and State are in effect, and often enough in actuality as well, active collaborators in the war effort.

Of course, these positive relationships of mutual reinforcement, nor- 14 mal and important though they are, are not the whole story. Built into the Church-State relationship, as in all inter-institutional relationships, is a negative strain as well; and sometimes this becomes the dominant factor. History provides ample evidence of the potential for conflict between them and the values for which each claims priority. Most obvious are the occasions of outright persecution not to mention lesser interferences with the religious community and its activities on the part of the secular powers. More subtle and much more common are instances in which secular values and practices promoted or protected by the State undermine or otherwise jeopardize those fostered or proclaimed in the name of religion. The reverse of this, though perhaps less frequent in occurence, lies in the extent to which the religious community and its values constitute at least a potential source of dissent and disobedience in the secular order. Old Testament type prophets may be an anachronism or, when they do appear, may be written off as eccentrics, a disruptive embarrassment to all concerned. Still it would be a serious mistake to assume that the spirit of moral dissent they once personified is no longer with us. . . .

15   The techniques and the knowledge provided by the social sciences can be of significant value in . . . the special contexts outlined here. They can identify and describe competing value systems and trace the changes in these value systems or in the strength of their appeal; they can develop and explore the institutional interrelationships in their full complexity; finally, they can test the efficacy of existing controls within the religious institution itself and, where necessary, may even suggest how existing controls can be improved and appropriate new controls devised. The usual tasks assigned to the sociologist of religion tend to be instrumental or operational in nature, providing such services as organizing, compiling, and interpreting religious demographics to assist ecclesiastical authorities in deciding where new parishes are to be established, old parishes consolidated, and the like. The more qualitative services suggested here could have a far more profound impact upon religion and the role it could play in human affairs.

16   War, of course, is but one area in which the influence of religion is important and could be decisive. Poverty, over-population, the promise and perils of modern technology and the technological society are others. If war has been chosen for preferred attention here, it is because it poses the gravest challenge to contemporary religion and religious values. More than that, since it presents an immediate and ever-present threat to continued human existence, it may, in the last analysis, make all the other problems and religion itself irrelevant.

Violence, Peace, and Peace Research

JOHAN GALTUNG

Norwegian-born Johan Galtung is one of the founders of the field of peace studies. He has written a remarkable number of important research articles, theoretical studies, and books. Among his major contributions is the identification of *structural violence* as a component of society that is distinct from, and yet related to, personal violence. It is noteworthy that whereas virtually everyone is opposed to violence, the concept of structural violence has met with substantial resistance, especially from conservative scholars and politicians. Indeed, as Galtung himself has noted, it is tempting for many conservatives to condemn outright violence while condoning social phenomena (injustice, lack of educational opportunities or health care, unemployment, censorship) that are structurally violent; at the same time, many radicals conveniently ignore the horror of outright interpersonal violence or justify it in the interest of eliminating structural violence! (Ironically, the process of abbreviating Professor Galtung's nuanced and sophisticated argument has necessarily subjected it to a kind of structural violence, for which the editor apologizes . . . and urges interested students to consult the original, in its unviolated entirety.)

As a point of departure, let us say that *violence is present when human beings are being influenced so that their actual somatic and mental realizations are below their potential realizations.* This statement may lead to more problems than it solves. However, it will soon be clear why we are rejecting the narrow concept of violence—according to which violence is *somatic* incapacitation, or deprivation of health, alone (with killing as the extreme form), at the hands of an *actor* who *intends* this to be the consequence. . . .   1

The *first distinction* to be made is between *physical* and *psychological* violence. The distinction is trite but important mainly because the narrow concept of violence mentioned above concentrates on physical violence only. Under physical violence human beings are hurt somatically, to the point of killing. It is useful to distinguish further between 'biological violence', which reduces somatic capability (below what is potentially possible), and 'physical violence as such', which increases the constraint on human movements—as when a person is imprisoned or put in chains, but also when access to transportation is very unevenly distributed, keeping large segments of a population at the same place with mobility a monopoly of the selected few. But that distinction is less important than the basic distinction between violence that works on the body, and violence that works on the soul; where the latter would include lies, brainwashing, indoctrination of various kinds, threats, etc. that serve to decrease mental potentialities. . . .   2

Can we talk about violence when no physical or biological object is hurt? This would be a case of what is referred to above as truncated violence, but nevertheless highly meaningful. When a person, a group, a nation is displaying the means of physical violence, whether throwing stones around or testing nuclear arms, there may not be violence in the sense that anyone is hit or hurt, but there is nevertheless the *threat of physical violence* and indirect threat of mental violence that may even be characterized as some type of psychological violence since it constrains   3 human action. Indeed, this is also the intention: the famous balance of power doctrine is based on efforts to obtain precisely this effect. And correspondingly with psychological violence that does not reach any object: a lie does not become more of a truth because nobody believes in the lie. Untruthfulness is violence according to this kind of thinking under any condition which does not mean that it cannot be the least evil under some widely discussed circumstances.

4   Is destruction of things violence? Again, it would not be violence according to the complete definition above, but possibly some 'degenerate' form. But in at least two senses it can be seen as psychological violence: the destruction of things as a foreboding or threat of possible destruction of persons, and the destruction of things as destruction of something very dear to persons referred to as consumers or *owners*. . . . If people are starving when this is objectively avoidable, then violence is committed, regardless of whether there is a clear subject-action-object relation, as during a siege yesterday or no such clear relation, as in the way world economic relations are organized today. . . .

5   In order not to overwork the word violence we shall sometimes refer to the condition of structural violence as *social injustice*. . . .

6   Tradition has been to think about violence as personal violence only, with one important subdivision in terms of 'violence vs. the threat of violence', another in terms of 'physical vs. psychological war', still another (important in ethical and legal thinking) about 'intended vs. unintended', and so on. The choice is here to make the distinction between personal and structural violence the basic one; justification has been presented (1) in terms of a unifying perspective (the cause of the difference between potential and actual realization) and (2) by indicating that there is no reason to assume that structural violence amounts to less suffering than personal violence.

7   On the other hand, it is not strange that attention has been focussed more on personal than on structural violence. Personal violence *shows*. The object of personal violence perceives the violence, usually, and may complain—the object of structural violence may be persuaded not to perceive this at all. Personal violence represents change and dynamism—not only ripples on waves, but waves on otherwise tranquil waters. Structural violence is silent, it does not show—it is essentially static, it *is* the tranquil waters. In a *static* society, personal violence will be registered, whereas structural violence may be seen as about as natural as the air around us. Conversely: in a highly *dynamic* society, personal violence may be seen as wrong and harmful but still somehow congruent with the order of things, whereas structural violence becomes apparent because it stands out like an enormous rock in a

creek, impeding the free flow, creating all kinds of eddies and turbulences. Thus, perhaps it is not so strange that the thinking about personal violence (in the Judaeo–Christian–Roman tradition) took on much of its present form in what we today would regard as essentially static social orders, whereas thinking about structural violence (in the Marxist tradition) was formulated in highly dynamic northwest-European societies. . . .

Inequality shows up in differential morbidity and mortality rates, be-   8
tween individuals in a district, between districts in a nation, and between nations in the international system—in a chain of interlocking feudal relationships. They are deprived because the structure deprives them of chances to organize and bring their power to bear against the topdogs, as voting power, bargaining power, striking power, violent power—partly because they are atomized and disintegrated, partly because they are overawed by all the authority the topdogs present.

Thus, the net result may be bodily harm in both cases. . . . The dis-   9
tinction that . . . remains is between violence that hits human beings as a *direct* result of . . . actions of others, and violence that hits them *indirectly* because repressive structures (as analyzed in preceding section) are upheld by the summated and concerted action of human beings. . . .

One may argue that all cases of structural violence can, by closer   10
scrutiny, be traced back to personal violence in their *pre-history.* An exploitative caste system or race society would be seen as the consequence of a large-scale invasion leaving a thin, but powerful top layer of the victorious group after the noise of fighting is over. A bully would be seen as the inevitable product of socialization into a violent structure: he is the rebel, systematically untrained in other ways of coping with his conflicts and frustrations because the structure leaves him with no alternatives. That structural violence often breeds structural violence, and personal violence often breeds personal violence nobody would dispute—but the point here would be the cross-breeding between the two. . . .

One could now proceed by saying that even if one type of violence   11
does not presuppose the manifest presence of the other . . . there is nevertheless the possibility that manifest structural violence presupposes latent personal violence. When the structure is threatened, those who benefit from structural violence, above all those who are at the top, will try to preserve the status quo so well geared to protect their interests. By observing the activities of various groups and persons when a structure is threatened, and more particularly by noticing who comes to the rescue of the structure, an operational test is introduced that can be used to rank the members of the structure in terms of their interest in maintaining the structure. . . .

12   It does not seem *a priori* unreasonable to state that if the absence of personal violence is combined with a pattern of structural violence, then personal violence is nevertheless around the corner—and correspondingly that if absence of structural violence is combined with personal violence, then structural violence is also around the corner. All we are saying is only that the sum of violence is constant, only that one has to take into account the latent variety of the type of violence 'abolished' to see more clearly how that type is in a standby position, ready to step in once the other type crumbles. Absence of one type of violence is bought at the expense of the threat of the other.

13   But, however insight-stimulating this may be in certain situations we refuse to accept this pessimistic view for two reasons. First, the two propositions seem simply not to be true. It is not at all difficult to imagine a structure so purely structural in its violence that all means of personal violence have been abolished, so that when the structure is threatened there is no second trench defense by mobilizing latent personal violence. Similarly, a structure may be completely unprepared for freezing the released forces stemming from a reduction of personal violence into a hierarchical order. Empirically such cases may be rare, but yet significant.

14   Second, the assumption would be that human beings somehow need violence to be kept in line; if not of the personal type, then of the structural variety. The argument would be that if there is no personal violence or threat of personal violence then a very strong hierarchical order is needed to maintain order and to control conflict; and if there is no structural violence or threat of structural violence, then personal violence will easily serve as a substitute. But even if this may be a reasonable theory to explain possible empirical regularities, that in itself is not sufficient argument for reifying a regularity into a principle supposedly eternally valid. On the contrary, this would be a highly pessimistic view of the human condition, and to accept it fully would even be a capitulationist view.

15   From the problem of whether one type of violence is necessary to *obtain* or *sustain* the other type, whether at the manifest or the latent levels, it is not far to the opposite problem: is one type of violence necessary or sufficient to *abolish* the other type? The question . . . brings us directly into the center of contemporary political debate. . . .

16   *The view that one cannot meaningfully work for both absence of personal violence and for social justice can also be seen as essentially pessimistic, as some sort of intellectual and moral capitulationism.* First of all, there are many forms of social action available today that combine both in a highly meaningful way. We are thinking of the tremendously rapid growth in the field of nonviolent action, both in dissociative nonviolence that serves to keep

parties apart so that the weaker part can establish autonomy and identity of its own, and associative nonviolence that can serve to bring them together when a basis for equal nonexploitative partnership exists. We are thinking of all that is known about the theories of symmetric, egalitarian organization in general. We are thinking of the expanding theory of vertical development, of participation, decentralization, codecision. And we are thinking of the various approaches to arms control and disarmament issues, although they are perhaps of more marginal significance. This is not the place to develop these themes; that will be done in other contexts. But secondly, once the double goal has been stated—that peace research is concerned with the conditions for promoting both aspects of peace—there is no reason to believe that the future will not bring us richer concepts and more forms of social action that combine absence of personal violence with fight against social injustice once sufficient activity is put into research and practice. There are more than enough people willing to sacrifice one for the other—it is by aiming for both that peace research can make a real contribution.

SUGGESTIONS FOR FURTHER READING

Arendt, Hannah. *On Violence*. New York: Harcourt, Brace, 1970. In this short but dense and rewarding book, one of the twentieth century's most notable philosophers examines the roles of bureaucracy and feared loss of power, respectively, in stimulating violence.

Giddens, Anthony. *The Nation-State and Violence*. Berkeley, CA: University of California Press, 1987. A social theorist takes on the interface among sociology, politics, history and violence.

Sharff, J. W. *King Kong on 4th St.: Families and the Violence of Poverty on the Lower East Side*. Boulder, CO: Westview Press, 1998. The subtitle says it well: a powerful review and indictment of the corrosive and violence-generating effects of poverty.

Straub, Ervin. *The Roots of Evil*. Cambridge: Cambridge University Press, 1992. Detailed treatment of the origins of genocide and other group-focused patterns of violence, with good coverage of the role of hate groups.

Turpin, J., and L. Kurtz, eds. *The Web of Violence*. Urbana: University of Illinois Press, 1996. A stimulating collection of essays, approaching the problem of violence from various perspectives, but all emphasizing its social dimension.

STUDY QUESTIONS

1. Agree or disagree with the contention that violence serves one or more functions in society. Distinguish between whether these are unintended or unintended effects; also discuss whether they are— or can be—beneficial.

2. Psychology and sociology are especially likely to merge, almost imperceptibly, into each other in some cases. Explain some of these cases, with examples.

3. In other situations, psychology and sociology are quite distinct. Explain some of these, with examples.

4. The phenomenon of domestic violence is related to the fact of marriage as a social institution. To what extent is this relationship necessary? Avoidable? Predictable? Arbitrary?

5. Can you imagine a society *not* based on violence? How would it differ from our own?

6. "Blaming the victim" is common in cases of violence. Show how this effect might occur in one or more of the readings presented in this chapter.

7. Disagree with Galtung's concept of structural violence by introducing some arguments of your own; or agree with it, adding additional arguments to those he has made.

8. Separate yourself from your own religious faith or lack thereof and attempt to assess, objectively, the contribution of religion to violence in general and/or to war in particular.

9. It has been proposed that human beings have a need for enemies. If so, then perhaps the end of the Cold War has left an unfilled gap in our psyches as well as in our social institutions. Agree or disagree.

10. Biology, psychology, and sociology all have their own take on violent crime; describe some of these differences. Is one of these disciplines especially well positioned to take on the problem of crime and/or of violence generally?

4

Anthropology

Humans are notable for the diversity of their behavior. It has long been the task (and delight) of anthropologists to catalog this diversity, both for its own sake and in the hope of revealing basic principles of wider applicability. In the process, anthropologists no less than the general public have often embraced rather extreme viewpoints when it comes to violence.

Thus, following the early lead of Jean-Jacques Rousseau in the eighteenth century, many have adored the "noble savage" as inherently peace loving and altogether admirable. In 1959, Elizabeth Marshall Thomas published *The Harmless People,* a study of the !Kung people of the Kalahari Desert. "It is not their nature to fight," wrote Thomas. "Bushmen cannot afford to fight with one another and almost never do. . . . The !Kung call themselves *zhu twa si,* the harmless people." At that time, the United States had a homicide rate of just under five per 100,000 (it had more than doubled by 1980). Nonetheless, even when anthropologist Thomas wrote her account, the !Kung had a homicide rate of more than 29 per 100,000, higher than that of New York City or Los Angeles! Moreover, "harmless people" is not even an accurate translation: something like "true" or "real" people is closer.

At the other extreme, we have seemingly endless and breathless accounts of headhunters, cannibalism, massacres, and apparently unending patterns of ambush, hostility, and revenge. When it comes to humanity's alleged penchant for violence—or nonviolence—there has thus long been a tendency to exaggerate accounts of nontechnological people, often depicted as either brutal, bloodthirsty barbarians, or meek and kindly, almost childlike in their innocent simplicity. Who or what, we must ask, are the "true or real people"?

A case can be made that sociology is merely the anthropology of "advanced" (Western) societies, or that anthropology is but the sociology of the dark-skinned (former) colonized. Both disciplines are primarily concerned with describing and understanding the function of cultures; the major difference is whether the subjects are members of the specialists' own society (in which case it is sociology), or from a very foreign group (in which case it is anthropology). Nonetheless, this difference can be significant, especially since it endows anthropology with the potential of stepping outside the homogenizing blinkers of looking only at people like oneself.

This extension, in turn, offers many possible benefits. A traditional practise of cultural anthropology is to accumulate a wealth of descriptive detail, portraying exactly what it is that people *do*, not what they say they do (which is revealed by the use of surveys by many psychologists and sociologists), or what they do in contrived, laboratory settings (typically representing a "cross-section" of college sophomores) . . . but what actually transpires when real people are living real lives. There is also a risk here: the danger of drowning in a sea of description, or—to switch the metaphor—missing the forest for the trees. At the same time, anthropology helps us to appreciate the range of human potential, reminding us that societies can be of many different types, functioning in a remarkable variety of ways. Simultaneously, it can also have the opposite effect, but one that is equally beneficial: helping to reveal "cross-cultural universals" or at least, commonalities; that is, patterns of behavior that remain more or less constant despite the enormous superficial variety in human ways of living, from Greenland to the Galapagos, Siberia to the Sahara. Out of such a heterogeneity of perception there can arise, if nothing else, a deeper understanding of what it means to be human, and some of the pitfalls as well as some of the opportunities.

There is an often unstated assumption that underlies many anthropological studies of war and violence: that nontechnological people can teach us something about the development of such behavior over the course of human history. Of course, no existing human groups are literally ancestral to any others, and yet it seems clear that warfare and violence among, say, the precontact aboriginal population of Australia is likely to have at least some parallels with more widespread ancestral patterns among human beings generally.

(There is also, of course, value in documenting and understanding the behavior of different human societies because they are inherently interesting in themselves, and because knowing about them is worthwhile for the same reason people climb mountains: because they are there. And also because, in a genuine sense, *they* are us.)

Surprisingly, perhaps, anthropologists have said relatively little about violence generally; somewhat more about war. There was a notable spurt of interest in the voices of anthropologists during and just after the Vietnam War, which gave rise to several significant volumes of collected articles. Some anthropologists argue about whether warfare among nontechnological people should even be designated *war*, preferring to apply this term only to armed military encounters between nation-states or entities of comparable size and technological sophistication. But for most, war is the appropriate designation for violent, structured clashes between designated social and cultural units, even though debate also persists over whether nontechnological war carries any important lessons for modern war among—and within—technologically advanced countries.

The majority perspective among anthropologists is aptly captured in the title of a well-known contribution by famed anthropologist Margaret Mead: "War is only an invention—not a biological necessity." The word *only* should not be taken dismissively, however; as many have shown, war is an exceedingly complex and multifaceted "invention," even in ostensibly "primitive" societies.

Especially since the end of the Cold War, a conspicuous trend has been that "traditional" interstate war has become increasingly rare, whereas civil wars and ethnically based armed conflicts have become more frequent. It would appear that an anthropological perspective would be particularly valuable in providing insight into such "tribal" antagonisms as those between Serbs and Kosovars, Hutus and Tutsis, Arabs and Israelis, and so on.

Given its potential, it is disappointing that anthropology has not made a more sustained and substantial contribution to our understanding of violence generally. Perhaps such a contribution can be expected in the future, particularly in the context of greater interdisciplinary dialog. For now, students of human violence can only look ahead to a much-desired but as yet unaccomplished synthesis of the social and natural sciences on this crucially important topic.

Intergroup Hostility and Social Cohesion

ROBERT MURPHY

It is at least possible that violent intergroup hostility—and interpersonal violence as well—has no function, that it is simply a manifestation of human perversity or bad luck. For obvious reasons, however, social scientists generally resist such interpretations, preferring to identify *functions* . . . not necessarily why the behavior occurs, but at least the effect it has, regardless of how it came to be. One potential effect is the generation of social cohesion, a suggestion that, as we have seen, is consistent with the ideas of several influential sociologists.

Anthropologist Robert Murphy's account of violence between groups of the Brazilian Mundurucu of the Amazon rainforest has become a classic. Note that it also assumes several other theoretical perspectives already presented in this book. Note also the distinction between the avowed goals of Mundurucu warfare and its likely function, analogous to Freud's distinction between the *manifest* and *latent* content of dreams: The former are the apparent reasons for war (or violence generally), whereas the latter include the deeper needs that such behavior presumably meets.

1   Georg Simmel noted that warfare is frequently the only mode of social interaction between primitive societies. He saw the social relations of such groups to be characterized by diametric opposition between the norms of behavior applicable to members of the ingroup, on one hand, and toward members of outgroups, on the other. This dichotomy was internally self-consistent to Simmel, and he wrote:

> For this reason, the same drive to expand and to act, which *within* the group requires unconditional peace for the integration of interests and for unfettered interaction, may appear to the outside world as a tendency toward war.

2   Intergroup conflict was viewed by Simmel has having positive functions; it provides the basis for group formation and cohesion, and it accentuates and maintains group boundaries. Conflict, then, is not aberrant or dysfunctional. Rather, it structures social relations both within and between societies.

3   Lewis Coser, writing to Simmel's general thesis, points out that social cohesion does not automatically follow from conflict, for "social systems lacking social solidarity are likely to disintegrate in the face of conflict, although some unity may be despotically enforced." The corollary proposition is offered that:

> . . . if the basic social structure is stable, if basic values are not questioned, cohesion is usually strengthened by war through challenge to, and revitalization of, values and goals which have been taken for granted.

Coser's view by no means contradicts that of Simmel but is an elaboration of the latter's thesis, as cited above, that intergroup hostility and social cohesion are only analytically different aspects of the same social process. Conflict and social solidarity are mutually re-enforcing; conflict promotes social integration, and solidarity is necessary if the group is to take effective common action against the outer world.

4   The present paper will analyze the warfare pattern of a Brazilian Indian group, The Mundurucu, in the light of the propositions given by Simmel and elaborated by Coser. We will go beyond the thesis that warfare contributes to the maintenance of the social structure to consider also how this social structure organized the membership for military

activity. Further, the thesis will be advanced that this type of social structure actually generated the bellicose activities and attitudes that functioned to preserve it, and that this circular relationship allowed Mundurucu society to continue through a period during which it was subjected to severe internal and external threats. Finally, we will conclude with a general hypothesis upon the relation between social structure, social cohesion, and conflict. . . .

The membership of the men's house was eclectic in relation to descent. The Mundurucu were divided into more than forty patrilineal clans, linked by loose and unnamed phratric affiliations, and parcelled almost equally between patrilineal, exogamous moieties. But the matrilocal residence rule and the resultant shift of men from their natal households and, commonly, villages continually blocked the formation of co-resident descent groups.   5

Despite the diversity of their local and lineal origins, the men of a village, and ultimately of the whole tribe, were expected to maintain harmonious and cooperative relations. Cooperation in economic activities transcended the minimal necessities of their ecological adaptation, and any open show of aggression between men was strictly prohibited. The men's house provided the organizational framework within which this unity was expressed, while male values were supernaturally reinforced by their possession of the sacred trumpets, or *karökö*. Each village maintained a set of three of these instruments, and they were absolutely taboo to the eyes of the women, who were thought to have once owned them.   6

Political controls were not elaborate. Each village had a chief, whose position was bolstered by the fact that his sons were generally exempt from the matrilocal residence rule. Although there were no patterns of continuous supravillage leadership, relations between communities were very close and involved intermarriage and joint participation in ceremonies and warfare. Tribal feeling was highly developed and conflict between villages was totally absent.   7

The Conduct of Warfare

Mundurucu warfare was distinguished by a complete lack of any defensive psychology, and the Mundurucu looked upon themselves as aggressors and victors. They have been described as ". . . one of the most valorous and feared [tribes] of all the hinterland of Amazons" while, on the other hand, the French explorer Henri Coudreau wrote in righteous indignation that, "The Mundurucu practice neither justice, nor duel, nor warfare, but only assassination." This harsh judgment seems not to fit the people who extended my wife and me kindness and hospitality, and who were invariably soft-spoken, humorous, and gentle. But these same   8 gentle people spoke at length and with great animation of their former prowess as warriors and of expeditions against other tribes in which the enemy men and women were killed and decapitated and their children stolen. Nothing about their own culture interested the Mundurucu as much as the extinct but still remembered patterns of warfare, and the older men were zealous informants on that subject.

9   The human world was seen by the Mundurucu to consist of two distinct spheres; there were "people" or Mundurucu, and *pariwat*, a term referring to any non-Mundurucu human. With the exception of the neighboring Apiacá Indians and the white men, all pariwat were enemies. An enemy was not merely a person to be guarded against but was a proper object of attack, and the Mundurucu pursued this end with extraordinary vigor and stamina. . . .

10   As among the Indians of the North American Plains, youths sought openly for the excitement of war and looked upon it as a means of self-validation and aggrandizement of prestige. But unlike the Plains Indians, the Mundurucu did openly assert this prestige once it was won; if anything, the person who achieved status became even more self-effacing and less prone to open competitiveness. The young men, however, did not embark upon raids by themselves. They expressed their desire to the chief of the village in words indicative of the martial disposition of the society: "My grandfather, take us to hunt the pariwat. We wish to die in the forest, not in the village." The chief consulted with the older men in order to decide whether the occasion was auspicious. If there was general approval, he proceeded to organize a war party that would include the eager young but would be under the competent direction of experienced elders, for age in Mundurucu society was an important criterion of status. . . .

11   The warriors waited for the cry of a species of bird that breaks into song at dawn. When this signal was heard, the chiefs sounded blasts on their horns and cried the order to attack. Incendiary arrows, made by affixing dried corn-cobs to the end of the arrow shaft, were ignited and loosed at the thatch roofs of the houses. The Mundurucu then broke from cover and dashed into the clearing of the enemy village, emitting wild shouts calculated to terrify the people. Adult males and females were killed and decapitated, and prepubescent children of both sexes were captured by the attackers. The Mundurucu then beat a hasty retreat before the enemy could reorganize his forces and summon additional support.

12   The retiring Mundurucu force drove its captive children ahead hurriedly and stopped at the temporary shelter only long enough to pick up the women and supplies. They then made a day and night forced march until they had reached a safe distance from the enemy. At this

point, the expedition turned toward home or, frequently, to new fields of conquest.

A central object of the raid was the taking of enemy heads, and a strict protocol was observed in the preparation of the trophies. . . .   13

The war party broke up after reaching Mundurucu country, and the participants proceeded to their respective villages. Signals were sounded on horns a short distance outside the villages, and two messengers were sent to inform the people of the results of the raid. The boys of the community went to meet the waiting warriors and received the trophy heads from them. They ran ahead to the men's house and displayed the prizes to the older men and told them who had taken each. The warriors and their accompanying women then entered the village, and each delivered his captive children to the care of his wife and went to the men's house, where the trophy heads were returned to their owners. . . .   14

The most important status was that of a taker of a trophy head, who was referred to as *Dajeboisi*. Literally, the title means "mother of the peccary," an allusion to the Mundurucu view of other tribes as being equivalent to game animals. The "mother" part of the term is derived from the trophy head's power to attract game and to cause their numerical increase, and the headhunter was so titled because of his obvious fertility promoting function; paradoxically for such a seemingly masculine status, he symbolically filled a female role. . . .   15

The Dajeboisi was also responsible for sponsoring a series of ceremonies that took place during three successive rainy seasons following the return of the expedition. During the first, which took place shortly after the return of the war party, feather pendants were attached to the ears of the trophy head. . . .   16

The final phase of the ceremony involved the greatest degree of intervillage participation, for it served as a ceremonial reunion of the *Dareksi* or "mothers of the arrow." The Dareksi was a society devoted to the celebration of Mundurucu arms, and included all adult males. At this time, a great feast was held, martial songs were sung, and the young boys were given instruction in the songs of the Dareksi. At the conclusion of the celebration, the ceremonial cycle terminated and the Dajeboisi and his wife resumed their normal life.   17

Goals of Warfare

George Fathauer maintains in a recent article that the Mohave "conception of war was largely non-instrumental: it was an end in itself." The Mundurucu looked upon warfare in much the same way; war was considered an essential and unquestioned part of their way of life, and foreign tribes were attacked because they were enemies by definition.   18

This basic orientation emerged clearly from interviews with informants. Unless direct, specific questions were asked, the Mundurucu never assigned specific causes to particular wars. The necessity of ever having to defend their home territory was denied, and provocation by other groups was not remembered as a cause of war in Mundurucu tradition. It might be said that enemy tribes caused the Mundurucu to go to war simply by existing, and the word for enemy meant merely any group that was not Mundurucu.

19   Despite the seemingly undirected aggressiveness, it was possible to establish through direct questioning and by analysis of field data that certain individual and social goals were realized through warfare. The more important of these goals will be analyzed and their significance as causes of the institution of warfare will be evaluated in the following section.

20   The Mundurucu were partially motivated to war by the quest for manufactured goods, which, as noted earlier, were obtained from the Brazilians in return for service as mercenary warriors against unpacified tribes. . . .

21   The secondary nature of economic goals in Mundurucu warfare is even more manifest when looting is considered. No objects of significant economic value were taken, and the raiders maintained their mobility by traveling light. Captive children were a far more important class of booty than were material items. Captive-taking was a means of strengthening the group through the addition of new members, but it is not certain whether the increment compensated for the loss of mature warriors and their female followers. If, however, one accepts intense warfare as a given factor, the capture of children was important to its successful continuance. Moreover, the Mundurucu valued and desired children, and the captives were treated as the captor's own.

22   The Mundurucu warrior was strongly motivated by the desire to achieve prestige through the demonstration of valor, especially as signified by the taking of a trophy head. . . . Prestige was not openly asserted among the Mundurucu, and the tone of the society was strongly egalitarian. Decision-making was decentralized and informal and joint activity depended upon the consensus of the participants, but the successful headhunter exerted considerable influence in the attainment of such consensus—albeit through subdued means.

23   Despite the fact that individual wars were undertaken because of the desire of the participants to gain prestige, it would be most dubious to admit this as a fundamental cause of warfare. It seems almost a truism to say that the individual who demonstrates proficiency in the attainment of a socially desirable goal will himself be valued and that this will motivate him to appropriate action, but this still does not answer the question of why the goal and the accompanying activity is valued. . . .

The trophy head was prized as a symbol of Mundurucu prowess and   24
of its owner's status, but it was also sought because it was the center of
a number of magico-religious observances. . . .

However, this aspect of the trophy quest does not cast much light   25
upon Mundurucu headhunting, for alternate ways of pleasing the spirits were known and practiced. The ceremonial and shamanistic techniques of propitiating the spirit protectors of game animals were
complex both in practice and in ideational content. In contrast, the link-
age of the trophy head and the spirits was vague and ephemeral; it is
probable that headhunting developed subsequent to the rites connected
with the animal spirits and had become only loosely integrated with
them. It is to be expected that any important social activity will become
value and belief cathected in this manner, but it would be erroneous to
proceed to explain the activity by its supporting ideology.

Finally, it should be considered that the Mundurucu looked upon   26
fighting as a source of sport and excitement. The enemy was looked
upon as game to be hunted, and the Mundurucu still speak of the pariwat in the same terms that they reserve for peccary and tapir. War was
a relief from boredom, but it is not surprising that peace would be boring to people who consider themselves warriors. One might ask why
they did not relieve boredom in log racing as do some groups, or in
drinking bouts as did many of their neighbors. In short, can we not look
upon activity and play drives as being inherent within the species and
proceed from that vantage to explain the particular way they are manifested in particular cultures?

Functions of Mundurucu Warfare

The manifest goals of warfare provide us with an understanding of the   27
incentives that motivated the Mundurucu warrior. The religious and
sportive aspects of warfare were found to be considerably more
ephemeral than were the economic and prestige goals involved, but
even the latter two depended upon the existence of a social organization that allowed and encouraged intensive military activity by its very
nature. Moreover, the most important single motivation to hostility was
a generalized aggressiveness that recognized no specific aims, and this
factor yields the most important single clue to an understanding of
Mundurucu warfare. If specific goals do not fully explain the extent and
intensity of the pattern, and if the pressure of external circumstances
did not force battle, then the main dynamics of warfare must be sought
within the structure of the society. We must explain the function of warfare, or the social conditions that caused the Mundurucu to direct enormous hostility against an amorphously inimical outside world.

28   As a first step toward answering this question, we turn briefly to a reexamination of Mundurucu military organization. Leaving out of consideration for the moment the bellicosity of the Mundurucu, the single factor that contributed most to the success of their arms was the tribal organization of war parties. The recruitment of men from a number of communities aggrandized their expeditions while leaving unimpaired the economic and defensive functions of the villages. Tribalism was also central to the ceremonies that were held at the conclusion of a war. On these occasions the tribal warrior society, or Dareksi, gathered to celebrate the prowess of Mundurucu arms, and the widely scattered members of certain clans assembled to exercise their prerogative of attaching particular decorations to the trophy heads. . . .

29   The organization of 19th-century Mundurucu society made male solidarity on the village and tribal level not only possible but a functional necessity. Conflict had to be rigorously suppressed, for if men became arrayed in overt violence along lines of residential affinity, it would pit patrilineal kin against each other and destroy the very fabric of the kinship structure. And if the combatants aligned themselves according to kinship affiliations, strife could break out within villages and even within households. . . .

30   The necessity for suppressing overt conflict as the only alternative to serious disruptions of social relations was complemented by the necessity for male cohesion and unity in villages whose hereditary inhabitants were the women. As a result, Mundurucu ethical values enjoined absolute harmony and cooperation upon all the males of the tribe. No such feeling was expected in interfemale relations. The female ingroup was limited to the membership of one or two extended families; beyond these limits, open jealousy and fighting could and did occur. This dichotomy in ethical values is understandable when one considers how different were the male and female social contexts.

31   Interpersonal and intergroup grievances will arise in all human societies as a necessary concomitant of social life, and the Mundurucu are no exception to this rule. Despite the surface tranquility of interpersonal relations among the males, numerous causes of latent antagonism existed. . . .

32   Given the potentially centrifugal nature of leadership, descent, and residence, warfare functioned to preserve, or at least prolong, the cohesiveness of Mundurucu society. The chief was able to maintain his leadership over his lineally eclectic group of followers through his position as war leader and his complementary role as mediator between them and Brazilian society. To the Mundurucu these are the essential functions of chieftainship, and contemporary informants commonly ascribe

the decline of nucleated village life to the disappearance of such attributes of leadership.

Of even greater importance to the integration of Mundurucu society, warfare activated and intensified male unity and values. . . . Finally, the only permissible intrasocietal mechanism for the release of aggression was sorcery and the killing of sorcerers, and . . . they created as many tensions as they resolved. Actually, the only way in which hostility could be unleashed without damage to the society was against the outside world. Paradoxically for a people who considered all the world as an enemy, the true cause of enmity came from within their own society. . . .   33

Conclusion

Our analysis of the functions of Mundurucu warfare has concluded that the institution operated to preserve the integration and solidarity of Mundurucu society. These findings accord closely with Simmel's theory of conflict. . . . The means by which this social end was accomplished can be viewed as a variable of the Mundurucu type of society. The latter was of a unique order; it was structured so as to ramify kinship bonds throughout the tribe, but it was extremely vulnerable to any open display of aggression within the group. This, and the ambivalent position of the men, resulted in the suppression of hostility and the emphasis upon solidarity that characterized male social relations. Such solidarity could be maintained only through the release of latent aggression in a socially valued manner upon surrogate objects. Mundurucu warfare thus corresponds to Coser's formulation of the "safety valve" mechanism in society: 34

> Social systems provide specific institutions which serve to drain off hostile and aggressive sentiments. These safety valve institutions help to maintain the system by preventing otherwise probable conflict or by reducing its disruptive effects. They provide substitute objects upon which to displace hostile sentiments, as well as means of abreaction. Through these safety valves, hostility is prevented from turning against its original object.

The achievement of specific ends or the defeat of a particular enemy were secondary considerations in Mundurucu warfare. They fought any group and they fought for the sake of fighting. The ultimate source of their bellicosity was the repressed hostility generated within the society, and the ultimate source of repression was the potential destructiveness of intrasocietal aggression.   35

36   Safety valve institutions of one kind or another are probably universal in culture. . . .

37   Coser has considered the relationship between conflict and the rigidity of the social structure, which he defines as "the degree to which it disallows direct expression of antagonistic claims," and concludes:

> Our hypothesis, that the need for safety-valve institutions increases with the rigidity of the social system, may be extended to suggest that unrealistic [i.e., cathartic and not oriented toward the frustrating object] conflict may be expected to occur as a consequence of rigidity present in the social structure.

Mundurucu warfare was clearly "unrealistic" and the social structure was rigid in Coser's sense. It is possible to broaden our example to include a larger category of rigid social structures and to consider their functional concomitants. . . .

38   Any conflict involving men therefore becomes a matter of deep community concern. As among the Mundurucu, if the lines of allegiance in a conflict situation are drawn according to kinship, bonds of local contiguity will be sundered; if primary loyalty is given to bonds of residence, the ties of kinship will broken. In short, when the residence and kin groups of the male do not coincide, he acquires multiple commitments that may come into conflict. Also, the individual male will more readily repress his grievances if he cannot rely upon the full support of a solidary group. . . .

39   Turning to North America, we have the classical example of the matrilocal and "Apollonian" Puebloans. Ellis has noted of Pueblo warfare:

> Beyond protection, warfare served to provide legitimate outlet for the frustrations and aggressions arising from unpermitted competition or suspicions thereof among peoples of the same general culture.

The repression of open conflict among the Puebloans accounts for the latent hostility that many ethnologists have seen seething below surface relations. Under modern conditions this often results in community fission, and the same process can be noted among the contemporary, nonwarring Mundurucu. Lacking adequate safety-valves for the release of aggression, the Mundurucu now tend to withdraw from the frustrating situation.

40   Not all matrilocal groups repress aggression to the same extent as do the Mundurucu, nor are they as warlike. . . . But warfare, it can be concluded, is an especially effective means of promoting social cohesion in that it provides an occasion upon which the members of the society

unite and submerge their factional differences in the vigorous pursuit of a common purpose.

Life Histories, Blood Revenge, and Warfare in a Tribal Population

NAPOLEON CHAGNON

The Yanomamo people have become widely known, even outside the circle of professional anthropologists, as among the most violent people on earth. Our next selection, by Napoleon Chagnon, presents a carefully documented summary of Yanomamo violence. It is especially impressive in connecting such interpersonal phenomena as "blood revenge" to the life histories of the participants. This study represents a comparatively recent and minority tradition within anthropology: interpreting behavior, including violence and war, as deriving from evolutionary factors, specifically, a benefit derived from increasing the success of genetic kin, plus enhanced reproductive success associated with being "fierce," especially a killer of other men.

The implications of findings such as these remain unclear; it is not known, for example, whether they imply the literal selection of genes for aggressiveness and violence, or social approval of behavior likely to lead to biological as well as cultural success. In any event, biological interpretations of this sort stand in dramatic contrast to those of Murphy, presented earlier.

In this article I show how several forms of violence in a tribal society 1 are interrelated and describe my theory of violent conflict among primitive peoples in which homicide, blood revenge, and warfare are manifestations of individual conflicts of interest over material and reproductive resources.

Violence is a potent force in human society and may be the principal 2 driving force behind the evolution of culture. For two reasons, anthropologists find it difficult to explain many aspects of human violence. First, although ethnographic reports are numerous, data on how much violence occurs and the variables that relate to it are available from only a few primitive societies. Second, many anthropologists tend to treat warfare as a phenomenon that occurs independently of other forms of violence in the same group. However, duels may lead to deaths which, in turn, may lead to community fissioning and then to retaliatory killings by members of the two now-independent communities. As a result many restrict the search for the causes of the war to issues over which whole groups might contest—such as access to rich land, productive hunting regions, and scarce resources—and, hence, primitive warfare as being reducible solely to contests over scarce or dwindling material resources. Such views fail to take into account the developmental sequences of conflicts and the multiplicity of causes, especially sexual jealousy, accusations of sorcery, and revenge killings, in each step of conflict escalation.

3   My theory synthesizes components drawn from two more general bodies of theory. One is the approach of political anthropology in which conflict development is analyzed in terms of the goals for which individuals strive, individual strategies for achieving these goals, and the developmental histories of specific conflicts. The second draws on several key insights from modern evolutionary thought. Specifically, (i) the mechanisms that constitute organisms were designed by selection to promote survival and reproduction in the environments of evolutionary adaptedness. This implies that organisms living in such environments can be generally expected to act in ways that promote survival and reproduction or, as many biologists now state it, their inclusive fitnesses. For humans, these mechanisms include learning and mimicking successful social strategies. (ii) Because no two organisms are genetically identical (save for identical twins and cloning species) and many of life's resources are finite, conflicts of interest between individuals are inevitable because the nature of some of life's resources ensure that individuals can achieve certain goals only at the expense of other individuals. (iii) Organisms expend two kinds of effort during their lifetimes: somatic effort, relevant to their survival, and reproductive effort in the interests of inclusive fitness. Such life effort often entails competition for both material resources (for example, food, water, and territory) and reproductive resources (for example, mates, alliances with those who can provide mates, and favor of those who can aid one's offspring). (iv) It is to be expected that individuals (or groups of closely related individuals) will attempt to appropriate both material and reproductive resources from neighbors whenever the probable costs are less than the benefits. While conflicts thus initiated need not take violent forms, they might be expected to do so when violence on average advances individual interests. I do not assume that humans consciously strive to increase or maximize their inclusive fitness, but I do assume that humans strive for goals that their cultural traditions deem as valued and esteemed. In many societies, achieving cultural success appears to lead to biological (genetic) success.

In this article I focus on revenge killing, using data collected among 4 the Yanomamo Indians of southern Venezuela and adjacent portions of northern Brazil. Blood revenge is one of the most commonly cited causes of violence and warfare in primitive societies and it has persisted in many state-organized societies as well.

I am using the terms revenge and blood revenge here to mean a re- 5 taliatory killing in which the initial victim's close kinsmen conduct a revenge raid on the members of the current community of the initial killer. Although Yanomamo raiders always hope to dispatch the original killer, almost any member of the attacked community is a suitable target.

Yanomamo Conflicts: Homicide, Revenge, and Warfare

. . . Most fights begin over sexual issues: infidelity and suspicion of in- 6 fidelity, attempts to seduce another man's wife, sexual jealousy, forcible appropriation of women from visiting groups, failure to give a promised girl in marriage, and (rarely) rape.

Yanomamo conflicts constitute a graded sequence of increasing seri- 7 ousness and potential lethality: shooting matches, chest pounding duels, side slapping duels, club fights, fights with axes and machetes, and shooting with bows and arrows, with the intent to kill.

In all but the last case, fights are not intended to and generally do not 8 lead to mortalities. Nevertheless, many fights lead to killings both within and between villages. If killing occurs within the village, the village fissions and the principals of the two new groups then begin raiding each other. The most common explanation given for raids (warfare) is revenge (*no yuwo*) for a previous killing, and the most common explanation for the initial cause of the fighting is "women" (*suwä tä nowä ha*).

At first glance, raids motivated by revenge seem counterproductive. 9 Raiders may inflict deaths on their enemies, but by so doing make themselves and kin prime targets for retaliation. But ethnographic evidence suggests that revenge has an underlying rationality: swift retaliation in kind serves as a deterrent over the long run. War motivated by revenge seems to be a tit-for-tat strategy in which the participants' score might best be measured in terms of minimizing losses rather than in terms of maximizing gains.

If gain (benefit) is associated with revenge killing in the primitive 10 world, what is gained and precisely who gains? Casting these questions into evolutionary terms, where gain (benefit) is discussed in terms of individual differences in inclusive fitness, might shed new light on the problem. Losing a close genetic relative (for example, a parent, sibling, or child) potentially constitutes a significant loss to one's inclusive fitness. Anything that counterbalances these losses would be advantageous. Yanomamo data suggest two possibilities. First, kinship groups that retaliate swiftly and demonstrate their resolve to avenge deaths acquire reputations for ferocity that deter the violent designs of their neighbors. The Yanomamo explain that a group with a reputation for swift retaliation is attacked less frequently and thus suffers a lower rate of mortality. They also note that other forms of predation, such as the abduction of women, are thwarted by adopting an aggressive stance. Aggressive groups coerce nubile females from less aggressive groups whenever the opportunity arises. Many appear to calculate the costs and benefits of forcibly appropriating or coercing females from groups that are perceived to be weak. Second, men who demonstrate their willingness to act violently and to exact revenge for the deaths of kin may have higher marital and reproductive success.

11   Approximately 30% of deaths among adult males in this region of the Yanomamo tribe is due to violence. This level of warfare mortality among adult males is similar to rates from the few other anthropological studies that report such data. Warfare mortality among adult males is reported as 25% for the Mae Enga, 19.5% for the Huli, and 28.5% for the Dugum Dani, all of Highland New Guinea.

Life Histories, Killers, Kinship, and Revenge Motives

12   In order to understand why avenging the death of a kinsman is such a commonly reported cause of warfare in primitive societies, one needs to document the vital events in the lifetimes of all or most individuals, recording marriages, abductions, genealogical connections, births, deaths, and causes of death. These data must then be put into the historical context of specific wars whose origins and development are described by multiple informants. Finally, native views, explanations, and attitudes have to be taken into consideration, particularly on topics such as vengeance, legitimacy of violent actions in particular circumstances, and societal rules and values regarding principles of justice.

13   The Yanomamo are frank about vengeance as a legitimate motive for killing. Their very notion of bereavement implies violence: they describe the feelings of the bereaved as *hushuwo*, a word that can be translated as "anger verging on violence." It is dangerous to provoke a grieving person no matter what the cause of death of the lost kin. It is common to hear statements such as, "If my sick mother dies, I will kill some people."

14   Vengeance motivation persists for many years. In January 1965, for example, the headman of one of the smaller villages (about 75 people)

was killed by raiders in retaliation for an earlier killing. His ashes were carefully stored in several tiny gourds, small quantities being consumed by the women of the village on the eve of each revenge raid against the village that killed him. According to the Yanomamo, women alone drink the ashes of the slain to make raiders *hushuwo* and fill them with resolve. In 1975, 10 years after his death, several gourds of his ashes remained, and the villagers were still raiding the group that killed him, who by then lived nearly 4 days' walk away.

This case is telling in another way as well. When the headman was killed, his death so demoralized the group that for about a year its members refused to conduct revenge raids, thereby acquiring the reputation of cowardice. They sought refuge and protection among several neighboring groups whose men grew bolder in direct proportion to the visitors' cowardice. These neighbors openly seduced the visitors' women and appropriated a number of them by force, predicting, correctly, that the visiting men would not retaliate. The group later regained its dignity and independence after embarking on an ambitious schedule of revenge raids. . . . 15

Unokais: Those who have killed. When a Yanomamo man kills he must perform a ritual purification called *unokaimou*, one purpose of which is to avert any supernatural harm that might be inflicted on him by the soul of his victim, a belief similar to that found among the headhunting Jivaro of Peru. . . . Men who have performed the *unokaimou* ceremony are referred to as *unokai*, and it is widely known within the village and in most neighboring villages who the *unokais* are and who their victims were. Recruitment to the *unokai* status is on a self-selective basis, although boys are encouraged to be valiant and are rewarded for showing aggressive tendencies. 16

Most victims are males killed during revenge raids against enemy groups, but a number of killings were within the groups. Most of the latter have to do with sexual jealousy, an extremely common cause of violence among the Yanomamo, other tribal groups, and our own population. 17

Raiding parties usually include 10 to 20 men, but not all men go on all raids and some men never go on raids. An enemy village might be as far as 4 or 5 days' march away. Many raiding parties turn back before reaching their destination, either because someone has a dream that portends disaster, or because the enemy group is not where it was believed to be. In all but the most determined raiding parties, a few men drop out for reasons such as being "sick" or "stepping on a thorn." Some of these dropouts privately admitted to me that they were simply frightened. Chronic dropouts acquire a reputation for cowardice 18 (*têhe*) and often become the subject of frequent insult and ridicule, and their wives become targets of increased sexual attention from other men.

19   The number of victims per raid is usually small—one or two individuals—but occasionally a "massacre" takes place resulting in the deaths of ten or more people. On the eve of a raid the warriors make an effigy (*no owä*) of the person they most want to kill; but in fact, they usually kill the first man they encounter. When a raiding party strikes, usually at dawn, as many raiders as possible (but almost never all members of the raiding party) shoot the victim or victims from ambush with their arrows and hastily retreat, hoping to put as much distance as possible between themselves and the enemy before the victim is discovered. Everyone who has shot an arrow into the victim must undergo the *unokaimou* ceremony on reaching home. Most victims are shot by just one or two raiders, but one victim was shot by 15 members of the raiding party.

20   The number of (living) *unokais* in the current population is 137, 132 of whom are estimated to be 25 or older, and represent 44% of the men age 25 or older. A retrospective perusal of the data indicates that this has generally been the case in those villages whose *unokais* have not killed someone during the past 5 years. I have recorded 282 violent deaths during 23 years of studies of villages in the region under consideration—deaths that occurred sometime during the past 50 to 60 years. These include victims who were residents of villages in this area or victims from immediately adjacent areas killed by residents or now-deceased former residents of the groups considered here. Of these 282 violent deaths, the number of victims of living *unokais* is 153. These victims were killed during approximately the past 35 years. All the *unokais* come from the villages under discussion, but not all of the victims do; some are from villages in adjacent areas beyond the focus of my field studies.

21   *Individual capacities of* unokais.   Most killers have *unokaied* once. Some, however, have a deserved reputation for being *waiteri* (fierce) and have participated in many killings. One man has *unokaied* 16 times. The village from which he comes is considered to be, by its neighbors, a particularly *waiteri* group: 8 of the 11 men who have *unokaied* ten or more times come from this one village. In this village, 97% of the 164 members are related in at least one way to 75% or more of the other residents of the village. The "village" in this case is almost synonymous with "kinship group." . . .

22   In order to understand why blood revenge is such a powerful motive among the Yanomamo and other tribal groups organized by kinship,

one must first understand how complex and pervasive kinship relationships are in such communities and that the major fount of the individual's political status, economic support, marriage possibilities, and protection from aggressors derives from kinsmen. One of the most important functions of kin groups is to pool resources and reallocate them to needy members. In the context of threats or coercion by others or of potentially violent encounters, group members cooperate for mutual protection and use their collective skills and abilities to this end, including the capacities of group members to act violently if necessary. . . .

Headmen are usually polygynous, and over a lifetime a successful   23
man may have had up to a dozen or more different wives, but rarely more than six wives simultaneously. One result is that some men have many children. In the sample considered here, one man (now deceased) had 43 children by 11 wives. Needless to say, nuclear and extended families cannot only become very large but their respective members, because of repetitive intermarriage, are related to each other in many ways.

The village, then, is composed of large kin groups: people who are   24
related to members of their own lineal descent group through male links and related to members of other lineal descent groups through consanguineal marriages and matrilateral ties. If someone in the village is killed, the probability is very high that he or she will have many bereaved close kin, including the village leader or leaders who have more kin than others; the leaders are the very individuals who decide whether killings are revenged. All headmen in this study are *unokai*. If, as Clauzewitz suggested, (modern) warfare is the conduct of politics by other means in the tribal world warfare is ipso facto the extension of kinship obligations by violence because the political system is organized by kinship.

Kinship density and the will for revenge.   The quantitative dimensions of   25
kinship relatedness in Yanomamo communities can be referred to as kinship density, which is a combination of the numbers of kin each individual has, how closely related the individual is to these kin, and the obligations and expectations that are associated with particular kinds of kinship relatedness.

A kinship density factor appears to be involved in revenge raids. It is   26
difficult for a small or heterogeneous Yanomamo group to put together a raiding party. The risks are high and men are willing to take them in proportion to the amount of mutual support they receive from comrades and where unwillingness to do so is condemned and ridiculed. Lone raiders do not exist. The higher the kinship density in a local community, the greater is the likelihod that a large number of mutually supportive

individuals will take such life-threatening risks and that retaliation will occur if one of the members of the group is killed. Included is the support of the women, who alone consume the ashes of the slain in order to put the raiders in a state of frenzy and strengthen their resolve. The existence of a tradition of revenge killing promotes kinship density by encouraging individuals to remain with close kin when new communities are formed by fissioning. High levels of relatedness also makes it likely that almost every violent death will trigger revenge killing, for most of the members of the victim's community will be close genetic kin.

27   *Measuring levels of societal violence: Numbers and kinds of kinsmen lost by individuals.*   Anthropology has no generally accepted measure for describing and comparing levels of violence and warfare cross culturally. With few exceptions much, if not most, of our knowledge about tribal warfare is based on fragmentary reports by untrained observers or on information collected long after the tribes studied had been decimated by introduced diseases and their political sovereignty taken from them by colonial powers. If the data contain numbers, one never knows the universe from which the sample is taken.

28   This presents a problem in interpreting Yanomamo violence and placing it into a comparative framework. Are the Yanomamo more or less violent than other tribesmen of the past or present? What should be measured or counted to compare levels of violence in different societies? I suspect that the amount of violence in Yanomamo culture would not be atypical if we had comparative measures of precontact violence in other similar tribes while still independent of colonial nation states.

29   One potentially useful measure of the amount or level of violence in tribal societies (or even modern nations) is the fraction of the population that has participated in the deliberate killing of one or more members of his own or some other community. Another useful measure might be the extent to which violence affects the lives of all (or a significant sample) of society's members in terms of the numbers and kinds of close kinsmen each person has lost through violence. As individuals age, more and more of them lose a close genetic kin due to violence. Nearly 70% of all individuals (males and females) age 40 or older have lost at least one close genetic kin due to violence, and most (57%) have lost two or more.

Reproductive Success and *Unokais*

30   The deterrent effect of vengeance killing might not be the only factor driving and maintaining Yanomamo warfare. Men who are killers may gain marital and reproductive benefits.

31   A preliminary analysis of data on reproductive success among *unokais* and non-*unokais* of the same age categories indicates that the former are

more successful. The higher reproductive success of *unokais* is mainly due to their greater success in finding mates either by appropriating them forcibly from others, or by customary marriage alliance arrangements in which they seem to be more attractive as mates than non-*unokais.*

Discussion

A number of problems are presented by these data. First, high repro- 32 ductive success among *unokais* is probably caused by a number of factors, and it is not clear what portion might be due to their motivation to seek violent retribution when a kinsman is killed. I can only speculate about the mechanisms that link a high reproductive success with *unokai* status, but I can cast doubt on some logical possibilities. For example, it is known that high male reproductive success among the Yanomamo correlates with membership in large descent groups. If *unokais* come disproportionately from these groups, that might explain the data: both could be caused by a third variable. But *unokais* do not come disproportionately from larger descent groups. . . .

Second, it is possible that many men strive to be *unokais* but die try- 33 ing and that the apparent higher fertility of those who survive may be achieved at an extraordinarily high mortality rate. In other words, men who do not engage in violence might have a lower risk of mortality due to violence and produce more offspring on average than men who tried to be *unokais.* This explanation would be supported by data indicating that a disproportionate fraction of the victims of violence were *unokais.* The data do not appear to lend support to this possibility. Of 15 recent killings, four of the victims were females: there are no female *unokais.* Nine of the males were under 30 years of age, of whom four were under an estimated 25 years of age. Although I do not have the *unokai* histories of these individuals, their ages at death and the political histories of their respective villages at the time they were killed suggest that few, if any of them, were *unokais.* Also, recent wars in two other regions of the study area resulted in the deaths of approximately 15 additional individuals, many of whom were very young men who were unlikely to have been *unokais.*

Third, additional variables not fully investigated might help account 34 for the correlations. . . . For example, there might be biometric attributes of *unokais* and non-*unokais* not readily apparent to the outside observer, such as differential skills at concealment, agility in moving through dense forest on raids, athletic ability, or other factors.

Fourth, there is the issue of the deterrent effects of swift, lethal, re- 35 taliation and whether or not it can be measured. A logical assumption would be that if *unokais* deter the violence of enemies, they would lose fewer close kin than non-*unokais.*

36   The last problem suggests that the argument that cultural success leads to biological success among the Yanomamo might be the most promising avenue of investigation to account for the high reproductive success of *unokais*. Indeed, the Yanomamo frequently say that some men are "valuable" (*a nowä dodihiwä*) and give, among the several reasons, that they are *unokai*, avenge deaths, or are fierce (*waiteri*) on behalf of kin. In short, military achievements are valued and associated with high esteem, as they are in many other cultures, including our own. Until recently in human history, successful warriors were traditionally rewarded with public offices and political power which, in turn, was used for reproductive advantage. Among the Yanomamo, non-*unokais* might be willing to concede more reproductive opportunities to *unokais* in exchange for a life with fewer mortal risks and fewer reproductive advantages.

37   Some Yanomamo men are in general more responsible, ambitious, economically industrious, aggressive, concerned about the welfare of their kin, and willing to take risks. Becoming an *unokai* is simply one of a number of male characteristics valued by the Yanomamo and an integral component in a more general complex of goals for which ambitious men strive. All the characteristics just mentioned make some males more attractive as mates in arranged marriages and dispose some of them to take the risks involved in appropriating additional females by force. Both paths lead to higher reproductive success.

Yanomami Warfare

R. BRYAN FERGUSON

There is comparatively little debate over the reality of Yanomamo (or "Yanomami") aggressiveness, but much dispute over its extent as well as its cause(s). In deciding to devote two selections to this controversy, the intent is not simply to continue examining violence in just this one group of people, but to exemplify the diversity of interpretations and explanations that often emerge once something so complex is subjected to careful scrutiny (even when the subjects are the same!).

Note that whereas the previous article reflects a sociobiological tradition within anthropology, the present one bears some similarities to Robert Murphy's interpretation of Mundurucu warfare in that it looks toward sociocultural causes. At the same time, R. Bryan Ferguson's approach is consistent with another powerful current in anthropological thinking about "primitive war," namely, a focus on its economic/ecological causes, sometimes called *cultural materialism*, which has been used to explain violent behavior as diverse and far-flung as warfare among New Guinea high-landers, and ritual human sacrifice (and cannibalism) among the ancient Aztecs. To this theme must also be added the possible impact of political and technological developments, specifically the impact of contacts with Western colonial authorities and its possible effect in stimulating violent competition.

The Yanomami people occupy a special place in Western thought. Their ancestral homeland, the mountainous country between Brazil and Venezuela, is the last major region of the New World to be explored and mapped by Europeans. The source of the Orinoco River in the Parima highlands was not reached by outsiders until 1951. For centuries, this rugged frontier has been the stuff of legends, the land of the fabled Lake Parimé and El Dorado. The rapids and waterfalls that defeated Spanish and Portuguese invaders enabled the Yanomami to escape the holocaust that obliterated most Amazonian peoples. To the outside world, the Yanomami have remained shadowy figures, subjects of considerable fantasy. . . .

Much of the credit for raising global consciousness about the Yanomami belongs to Napoleon Chagnon, who has portrayed Yanomami men as embroiled in virtually endless warfare over women, status, and revenge. In his more recent works, Chagnon has invoked a sociobiological or "evolutionary biological" paradigm to explain Yanomami warfare, attributing it to "reproductive striving." For years, Chagnon has debated the causes of Yanomami warfare with Marvin Harris and others, who have explained Yanomami conflict as a culturally evolved adaptive response to the limited availability of nutritionally crucial game resources. . . .

In fact, Western encroachment on Yanomami lands since the 1940s is only the latest of several waves of state expansion to afflict the Yanomami. I believe that only by putting Yanomami society in historical perspective can we understand their warfare, and only by understanding the causes of their warfare can we understand what Western contact has meant to them and how they have acted as agents in shaping their own history.

Although some Yanomami really have been engaged in intensive warfare and other kinds of bloody conflict, this violence is not an expression of Yanomami culture itself. It is, rather, a product of specific historical situations: the Yanomami make war not because Western influence is absent but because it is present, and present in certain specific forms. All Yanomami warfare *that we know about* occurs within what Neil Whitehead and I call a "tribal zone," an extensive area beyond state administrative control, inhabited by nonstate people who must react to the far-flung effects of the state presence.

5   I hope to show that the occurrence of warfare among different Yanomami groups almost invariably follows identifiable changes in the Western presence—including the presence of anthropologists—and that without those changes there is little or no war. I also hope to explain the causality of this temporal connection by showing that the patterning of who attacks whom is primarily a result of antagonistic interests in the acquisition of steel tools and other Western manufactures. . . . Machetes, axes, and knives are in great demand among indigenous Amazonian peoples. The reason is clear. Various studies show that steel edges bring an increase in work efficiency of 300 percent to 1,000 percent, depending on circumstances and method of calculation. . . .

6   Steel tools, however, are only part of the situation. Indigenous people typically come to need, or at least want, a wide variety of Western manufactures, including metal pots and griddles, fishhooks and line, shotguns and ammunition, clothing, matches, medicines, and sometimes foodstuffs. Nor is the demand entirely utilitarian. Combs, mirrors, and glass beads are avidly sought. Frequently, the expanding demand for Western goods is an open-ended process leading to the assimilation of native peoples into the lowest levels of Western society. . . .

7   The Yanomami have long depended on iron and steel tools. All ethnographically described Yanomami had begun using metal tools long before any anthropologist arrived. Except for one deliberate experiment conducted by an anthropologist I have found no outsider's account from any period reportedly witnessing Yanomami using stone axes, although some Yanomami interviewed in the 1960s recall a time when they used stone axes found in ancient gardens. More striking, perhaps, I have never found any report of a Yanomami who knew how to make stone axes or who said that an ancestor had made them. The Yanomami ax usually found at "first contact" is the *haowe,* made not of stone but from a broken piece of machete hafted on wood. . . .

8   In contrast to the widespread overestimation of woman-capture as an incentive to raid, there is an equally great underappreciation of another objective: the plunder of material items, especially Western goods. As will be documented in the historical chapters to come, this incentive is reported frequently from diverse areas and time periods. In its most common form, attacks are aimed at small parties of Westerners, but plunder is also cited as the reason for raids on other Indian populations and among the Yanomami themselves.

9   But in the wars that have received the most ethnographic attention, especially those of the Orinoco-Mavaca area, the routing of a sizeable village, leaving it open to plunder, is unusual and cannot be taken as

an expectable outcome of a raid. In my perspective, the goal of most conflicts is related to the first and third strategic objectives: eliminating a competitor for valuable resources—with "resources" defined broadly to encompass trade—and imposing an exploitative relationship on other independent groups. . . .

One way to assess the reason for a raid on another village is to look   10 at the most likely outcome of such an action. A likely result of a successful raid is that the victims will move away from the attackers. Most wars are resolved when an endangered group moves out of range, and the Yanomami are certainly aware of this regularity. (On the advent of one raid, a Yanomami said, "We'll make them flee far away from us." . . .

When the targets of a raid or of a surprise attack during a trading   11 visit had been, by virtue of their geographic position, monopolizing access to Westerners or controlling trade in Western manufactures, and the attackers had been less able to get goods because of that monopoly, the forcible displacement of the trade controllers can "eliminate the middleman," open better access to the sources of Western goods, and perhaps allow the victors to establish themselves as middlemen with all the benefits that implies. On the other hand, those in a highly beneficial trade position may, rather than move, respond in kind to attacks from more isolated groups, seeking to force them out of striking range. This response reflects the fourth strategic objective of war, to forestall future attacks by others. . . .

In all these situations, the principal benefit of war is to improve access to Western manufactures. The most direct manifestation of this   12 benefit, the simple goal of plunder, applies to only a minority of situations. The other manifestations are attempts to affect intervillage exchange patterns: by making life unlivable for monopolists ensconced in prime locations, thus forcing them to move; by precluding any group from unilaterally improving its position in local trade networks by moving to a better location; and by forcing those who travel for trade to respect the village-to-village organization of commerce. All involve a clear spatial component. In practice, the "state of war" is geopolitical: one's danger of being assaulted by members of an enemy group is directly related to one's location. . . .

I do not maintain that my logic of violence corresponds to Yan-   13 omami conceptions about war in general or to their way of thinking about specific conflicts. With the exception of overt plunder raids directed against outsiders (Westerners or distant, unrelated, native groups), antagonistic interests shaped by the spatial distribution of Western goods will likely be conceptualized and discussed in terms of moral rights, obligations, and offenses—usually invoking revenge and witchcraft—and in terms of concrete, personal relationships. The closer the social ties, the more moralistic and personalistic will be the rationalizations of war. . . .

14   When Western manufactures are in short supply everywhere, or when they are available in abundance from multiple sources—so that in either case there is relative equality in possession of them—no raiding is expected, according to the terms of this model (although other sources of conflict could certainly develop). Raiding is predicted to occur when there is a general scarcity of steel but marked local inequalities in possession. The standard pattern is that more isolated groups raid better connected villages when the latter do not have the political and military advantages provided by a resident, armed Westerner. This direction of raiding is typically reversed as Western outpost villages establish military hegemony; then violence often occurs out beyond the first dependent allies. Other strategic uses of violence are to prevent a group from establishing a new garden in a location that would harm the aggressors' trade interests, and to keep people from more remote groups from attempting to bypass middlemen and approach the sources directly. . . .

15   In the following sections, I contrast my approach to the other major theories that have been offered to explain Yanomami warfare.

The Protein Hypothesis

16   One major line of explanation has come to be known as the protein hypothesis that Yanomami warfare was an adaptive response to the limited availability of nutritionally necessary game animals. . . .

17   The basic structure of the theory begins with the observation that it is the male's role to provide meat. Culturally patterned expectations require that men provide meat to women who provide sex. Game is depleted by hunting, and hunting pressure is a function of village size and the length of time spent in one location. As local game availability declines and hunters experience diminishing returns for their effort, male competition over women intensifies, leading to fighting within groups and raiding between them. Thus—the theory goes—game depletion leads to conflicts over women, which lead to war.

18   The fact that war makes Yanomami groups move apart from each other is interpreted as having two adaptive consequences: the no-man's-land between enemies acts as a kind of game preserve, allowing animal populations to replenish themselves; and people in flight may pioneer new or long-unused territory where game is more abundant. A related hypothesis was first proposed by Divale and elaborated by Divale and Harris: by fostering a male supremacist ideology, war among the

Yanomami leads to a devaluation of females, a preference for male babies, and a pattern of female infanticide. Divale and Harris suggest that female infanticide, so induced by war, is a primary means of population regulation in band and village societies. . . .

All these observations appear to be applicable to Yanomami warfare. [19] It has been documented repeatedly that wars end when one group moves away from another. It seems only common sense that sometimes those in flight will enjoy better hunting in their new location, and that a no-man's-land between blood enemies will witness an increase in local game. But there is no evidence that either of these considerations plays a crucial role in the Yanomami's adaptation to their natural environment. Moreover, long-distance movements into new territory, although often spurred by the "push" of war, are much more often motivated by the "pull" of sources of Western goods. And when people have to put up with a diminished game supply in order to preserve access to Western goods, they learn to cope. In sum, there is only a very tenuous relationship between game depletion, war, and movements that increase game availability.

Regarding the postulated adaptive effect of increased female infan- [20] ticide, the issue is more complicated. Divale attributes his formulation of the model to a reading of Chagnon, and Chagnon's own descriptions repeatedly state that there is a circular relationship among warfare, preference for male children, female infanticide, a scarcity of adult women, conflict over women, and war. What Divale and Harris do is relate the competition over women to game scarcity and extend the argument to postulate consequences of population regulation. . . .

Overall, there is a great deal of evidence that the integrated proposi- [21] tions that make up the "protein hypothesis" deal with genuine relationships. Where it is weakest, however, is precisely as an explanation of the occurrence of warfare.

An Eye for an Eye?

. . . I do not question that Yanomami see war this way. It is part of my [22] model that material interests are converted into moral terms, and always, "they started it." But how can reciprocity explain the change from peace to war and war to peace? How can it explain spatial and temporal variation in the history of conflicts? . . .

Revenge is frequently cited as a cause of "primitive warfare," but its [23] value as an explanation is questionable. I distinguish revenge—a desire to strike back at someone who has wronged you—from retaliation—a counterstrike against an enemy intended to deter future attacks. In some, but not all, political circumstances, retaliation is a sensible tactic.

When a group is retaliating, or even when it is initiating new hostilities, it will use the rhetoric of vengeance to rationalize action and mobilize support. . . .

24 Except where many different members of a local group have similar losses to avenge—such as after the Shamatari's killing of as many as 15 Bisaasi-teri men—a blood debt alone will generally not lead to war. In a great many cases reported in this book, perhaps even a majority, a killing is not followed by any counterraid within the next few years. Chagnon probably would not restrict the time frame that narrowly: "Vengeance motivation persists for many years." . . .

25 In my view, the Yanomami control revenge; they are not controlled by it. For people other than the victim's very closest kin, revenge is a real but highly malleable motivating factor. There are frequently many dormant reasons for seeking revenge, and if none exists, some can be made up. They come to the fore in conflict situations because that is one way to frame materially self-interested actions in moral terms. Vengeance is "good to think" and good to persuade. But a focus on vengeance will not elucidate why wars happen. Nor do I think that those who take revenge are doing themselves a reproductive favor. . . .

Fighting over Women

26 There is no question that Yanomami men on many occasions fight over women; there is no doubt that such fights sometimes lead to war. What is in dispute is the theoretical significance of this fighting and, in particular, its utility in explaining war. Chagnon acknowledges that men will compete and fight over material resources when they are scarce, but he argues that when resources are abundant, men will compete and fight over women and reproductive success. It is the latter situation, he maintains, that applies to the Yanomami. . . .

27 My own position regarding men fighting over women has several components. In an earlier comparative study I noted that regardless of what causes war, the Yanomami stand out among Amazonian societies for the political prominence of their fighting over women, and I suggested several underlying features that may be responsible for that distinction: the unusually limited basis for female cooperation in an economy reliant on plantains rather than bitter manioc; the existence of strong fraternal interest groups in some areas; and the ideological reinforcement associated with unusually intensive warfare. In my article on "warrification" of the Orinoco-Mavaca Yanomami I identified additional factors: the atypical number of marriages between villages, which make women more significant as political symbols and leave them more subject to abuse; and the high number of deaths from disease and

war, which in an otherwise disturbed environment encourage the instrumental use of force to decide marriage arrangements. . . .

I have been concerned with marriage primarily as the capstone of a   28
total relationship between groups. The tone of that relationship is determined in part by each group's ability to apply force, but also and more fundamentally by the distribution of Western goods. From my perspective, it is the total relationship that is at issue in any fight. In a good relationship, many things can be overlooked. In a bad one, any dispute can trigger violence. The detonator may be food, status, or sorcery, but fights will frequently be "over women" because exchanged women are the ultimate medium of alliance.

Striving for Reproduction

A further difference between my position and Chagnon's is that I do not   29
accept the presumption expressed in his sociobiological writings that conflict over women is in itself evidence that male behavior is motivated by "reproductive striving." Men may fight over women for reasons other than maximization of inclusive fitness. Yanomami women may be part of a contract between groups who have definite expectations about trade and political support. Women are laborers, and their value may increase when they have the option of working for missionaries. They are sex partners—a role quite distinct from that of being a mother. Obviously, sex leads to reproduction, but what Chagnon is arguing is that reproductive success in itself is a goal with a direct impact on individual behavior.

The proposition that people deliberately act in ways that maximize   30
their inclusive fitness is the most distinctive and debatable point in human sociobiology. Chagnon holds that "Yanomamö males are tracking their environment with their own fitness interests at stake," and they "manipulate and adapt to [this environment] in striving for reproductive success and maximal inclusive fitness." In earlier work Chagnon held this motivation to be unconscious but strongly determinative—comparable to the effect of gravity on a falling rock or to planetary motion. . . .

I find nothing to argue about in the proposition that individuals   31
tend to their material self-interest and that in evolutionary perspective, such self-interest has a generally favorable impact on reproductive success. But it remains very much in question whether aggressive behavior itself can be seen as a reproductive strategy even among the Yanomami. . . .

Although I have stressed the role of Western contact, it is nevertheless   32
true that the Yanomami have been more isolated from Westerners longer

than any other large group of Native American people. They stand as the end point—the outer limit—of the post-Columbian, New World tribal zone. For others with more history of exposure to Westerners, the impact of Western presence should be even greater than that described here.

33   The Yanomami have also acquired in popular and some anthropological literature a reputation for being the most warlike people on earth. This study shows how misleading such statements can be. Some Yanomami in some places and times have been extremely warlike, but most Yanomami in most places and times have been peaceable. And the violent periods, I have argued, are caused by circumstances introduced by intrusive Westerners. Considering the Yanomami's "most remote" status, analysts should proceed with caution in alleging that any observed warfare among nonstate peoples anywhere is a purely indigenous pattern.

Anthropological Perspectives on Aggression: Sex Differences and Cultural Variation

DOUGLAS P. FRY

One of the particular strengths—perhaps *the* particular strength—of an anthropological perspective is the diversity of subject matter that it conveys. Our next offering, by Douglas P. Fry, does multiple duty. It served as the orienting article in a special anthopology issue of the journal *Aggressive Behavior* (a publication that should be perused by anyone interested in aggressive behavior and violence generally). Fry also capably reviews evidence from anthropology concerning sex differences in aggression, giving balanced treatment to both biological and cultural influences. Finally, Fry considers the question of diversity among human societies, pointing out the immense cross-cultural range of variation as well as the important fact that aggressive, violent cultures can become more peaceful, and vice versa. His article is especially useful in showing that anthropology also provides information on cross-cultural violence more generally, not just "primitive warfare."

1   In recent years, the corpus of anthropological research on aggression and conflict continued to grow and diversify. Various anthropological subfields—psychological, ecological, evolutionary, political-legal, applied anthropology, and others—offer insights about aggression. . . .

First, I discuss anthropological findings related to sex differences in aggression, including the nature of sex differences in cross-cultural perspective, evolutionary considerations, and variation in types of aggression, specifically *direct* and *indirect* approaches. Second, I consider the cross-cultural continuum of peaceful and violent cultures, and, in so doing, highlight certain topical areas and controversies. For example, attention is given to how to assess the level of aggression within a culture, culture change in aggression, the multidimensional nature of aggression, the debate over emic (actor-based) vs. etic (observer-based) interpretations of aggression, and the diversity of conflict management options cross-culturally. . . .

Anthropology and Sex Differences

Several conclusions emerge from a consideration of the anthropological data on sex differences and aggression. First, sex differences in physical aggression clearly exist. Second, females may employ *indirect aggression* more than males, but here more data are necessary before a definitive conclusion can be reached. Third, evolutionary theory offers an ultimate explanation for observed sex differences in aggression, and more proximate cultural influences clearly are important as well.

The cross-cultural evidence shows men to be more *physically* aggressive than women. It is virtually always men who raid, ambush, feud, and meet on the battlefields. Cross-culturally, men also tend to commit more homicides than women. In comparing male-male homicides to female-female homicides, Daly and Wilson conclude from their extensive review of the literature that "intrasexual competition is far more violent among males than among females in every human society for which information exists." Overall, behavioral findings and criminological statistics show that *physical* aggression is both *more frequent* and *more severe* among males than among females. Furthermore, this pattern of sex differences (which is typical of primates and mammals generally) is understandable through evolutionary models of sexual selection and differential male-female parental investment. . . . Drawing on the work of Sherwood Washburn, Symons concludes, "If one focuses on the anatomy that is primarily responsible for sex differences, it becomes clear . . . that human males have evolved roughly *twice* the aggressive apparatus of females" [emphasis in original]. In accordance with parental investment theory, Symons proposes that men fight more than women because men are evolutionarily adapted to compete over women more than vice versa: "Although ethnographic reports may sometimes have an androcentric bias that obscures the subtleties of female-female competition, it is certain that intense competition evidenced by organized fighting and killing—as is common among men—occurs nowhere among women."

5   Based on the findings of a cross-cultural survey of societies, Burbank emphasizes that simply because men are physically more aggressive than women does not mean that women are always nonaggressive. Burbank reports that women do engage in physical aggression in 61% of 137 cultures she examined, and her findings as to why women are aggressive suggest that in the majority of cases women's aggression involves competition over males. Fifty-two percent of all female-female aggression was provoked by a husband's adultery, while another 21% involved competition among rivals for the attention of a man.

6   Cook reports that out of 18 instances of physical aggression she observed on Margarita Island off the coast of Venezuela, 8 (44%) involved women being physically aggressive. Cook writes, "In San Fernando, the use of verbal and physical aggression by women is a frequent and expected occurrence. . . . Upon several occasions I observed women engaged in ferocious verbal fight among themselves which were accompanied by fist waving, insults, and the hurling of pebbles at the feet of their opponents." Various instances of female physical and verbal aggression also have been described among Argentines, Australian Aborigines, Bellonese, Chinese, Zambians, Zapotecs, and other cultures. Hines and Fry write that "women in Argentina do engage in physical aggression. They may push and shove each other in lines or hit their husbands or boyfriends. But women's physical aggression is perceived as less frequent, less severe, and relatively harmless compared with men's aggression." The same is the case among the Zapotec, where women are less often physically aggressive than men and women's attacks are comparatively mild, generally consisting of slapping, pulling, and pushing. Hence, women in some cultural settings obviously engage in physical aggression, although they are generally less physically aggressive than men. Such findings are in accordance with the evolutionary predictions that intermale competition over females will be more pronounced than interfemale competition over males.

7   Aggression can be verbal as well as physical, and indirect as well as direct, and women may express competition differently than men. Bellonese women make considerable use of verbal aggression, as contrasted to Bellonese men's greater use of physical threats and assaults. In Argentina, both sexes are verbally aggressive, and this finding corresponds with several reports that suggest that both men and women use verbal aggression. However, verbal aggression can take many direct and indirect forms, such as gossip, ridicule, criticism delivered in front of others or behind the victim's back, song duels, derogatory poems or

songs composed and shared about someone else, jokes about someone, insults, and so on. The many subtleties of how men and women use various types of verbal aggression in different cultural contexts has barely been explored.

Indirect aggression involves use of social networks, third parties, elements   8 *of the social organization, and/or other covert means to inflict harm on another individual.* By using indirect aggression, the attacker can inflict physical, psychological, and/or social harm on a victim, perhaps without ever being detected. Anthropological studies from different cultures provide illustrations and conceptual elaborations of the indirect aggression construct. Indirect aggression, as expressed within the social context of a given cultural meaning system, might entail, e.g., the spreading of malicious gossip about someone, arranging for the social exclusion of a rival from group activities, blocking social benefits that an individual would otherwise accrue, arranging for a third party to attack the victim (either verbally or physically), practicing witchcraft or sorcery directed at harming the victim, and so on.

Research indicates that at least in several cultural contexts, females   9 may make greater use of indirect aggression than males, although members of both sexes have been found to employ indirect tactics; examples of females employing indirect aggression, perhaps in greater frequency than males, have been noted for Finland and Mexican Zapotec. For instance, among Argentines of Buenos Aires, "women, more than men, favor indirect aggression . . . respondents tend to agree that women, more than men, judge others, gossip, lie about others, exclude persons from social events, and interrupt conversations."

To summarize, cross-culturally men tend to engage in more physical   10 aggression, and more severe physical aggression, such as homicides, than women. However, women also are reported to engage in physical aggression in many cultures. As will be discussed next, some cultures have very low levels of physical aggression overall, among *both* sexes. Cultural patterns are clearly very influential regarding the expression of both male and female aggression. There are numerous cross-cultural examples of both men and women acting verbally aggressive, but "verbal aggression" is a catch-all label, and more research is needed on the numerous subtypes of verbal aggression and their usage in different cultural contexts. There is tentative evidence from several cultural settings that women may make greater use of indirect aggression than men. Finally, sexual selection and parental investment theory provide an evolutionary explanation for the observed general cross-cultural patterns of sex differences in competition and aggression, a conclusion that in no way denies or minimizes the impact of proximate cultural factors on male and female aggression.

Cross-Cultural Variation in Aggression: Issues and Controversies

Intercultural Variation

11   Montagu notes that the cross-cultural range of variation in aggressive behavior is tremendous, from nonaggressive to highly violent societies. . . . [This] should not imply that all or even most societies can be dichotomized as either violent or nonviolent. As Silverberg and Gray suggest, rather than polarizing societies as either violent or nonviolent types, perhaps it is more realistic to view societies as scalable along a continuum ranging from violent to peaceful. Thus, the previous lists of cultures are intended to provide anthropological citations related to societies that lie toward the extreme ends of a cross-cultural continuum on which many societies occupy intermediate positions.

Intracultural Variation

12   A consideration of the cross-cultural variation in aggression raises several theoretical and conceptual issues. The first issue is that in addition to intercultural variation regarding aggression, *intracultural* variation sometimes exists as well. There is a long-standing yet recently questioned tendency within anthropology—usually based on an implicit assumption of intracultural uniformity, which may or may not be true—to generalize about the characteristics of a culture based on fieldwork in only one or several villages, communities, bands, and so on. When considerable variation exists among intracultural entities, generalizations may lead to misrepresentations about the level of aggressiveness or other features of a culture. For example, it would be incorrect and misleading to generalize that Zapotec culture overall has a low level of aggression based solely on data from one peaceful Zapotec community, "La Paz," in which both O'Nell and I have worked.

In-Group versus Out-Group Aggression

13   A second issue to consider in assessing levels of aggression involves whether to focus on in-group aggression, out-group aggression, or both. Some cultures have very low levels of both in-group and out-group aggression, such as the Buid. For instance, regarding Buid responses to both in-group and out-group conflict: ". . . simple withdrawal is the preferred solution to conflict. The socially approved response to aggression is avoidance or even flight. The Buid language is rich in words for fear, fleeing, and escape from danger, none of which carries negative moral overtones."

On the other hand, as Dentan observes, some societies with very low 14 in-group physical aggression may be willing to engage in externally directed aggression. Ross, e.g., notes that the internally peaceful Papago of southern Arizona and northern Mexico defended themselves against raiding Apaches. Still other societies exhibit moderate to high levels of both in-group and out-group aggression, such as among the Waorani.

Cultural Changes in Aggressiveness/Peacefulness over Time

A third issue to consider in assessing the level of aggression of a culture 15 is that levels of both in-group and out-group aggression can change over time. Sponsel notes that "the transformation of warlike societies into peaceful ones has occurred repeatedly in human history." Similarly, Dentan discusses apparent shifts in levels of aggressivity among the !Kung San over several decades, wherein they seem to have experienced a two-decade period of relative peacefulness, from the mid-1950s to the mid-1970s, which was interspersed between more aggressive periods.

Greenberg describes how a Chatino community in Mexico, which 16 was once fraught with violent murders and maimings, instituted an agrarian reform and, in a movement initiated by the women and later supported by the majority of villagers, banned alcohol consumption— a major social change—which drastically reduced the bloodshed. Greenberg explains that "sick of seeing their men killed in blood feuds, the women of the village had organized and had managed to pass an ordinance prohibiting the sale and consumption of alcohol and the carrying of knives or guns. These measures were effective and put an end to the blood feuding and factionalism in the village." This ban on alcohol was strictly enforced to the point that should a villager be seen drinking in a neighboring town, that person could be jailed and fined upon returning to the village, even if sober.

Besides illustrating a culture with a high level of aggression, the 17 Waorani, who are described by Robarchek and Robarchek also dramatically demonstrate the human capacity to enact cultural change, specifically, to bring about peace. Although not becoming an inherently nonviolent society, the Waorani have managed to reduce their homicide rate by *more than 90%* in a matter of a few years. Robarchek and Robarchek explain: "The killers are still there—many were our friends and neighbors—but with relatively rare exceptions, they have stopped killing. They were not conquered or incarcerated, nor were they incorporated as equals into the socioeconomic system of Ecuadorian society. Rather, new leaders emerged who possessed new information and offered a new set of alternatives."

18   Thus, the level of aggressiveness within a society can change quite markedly, as illustrated by the Chatino, Waorani, and other cases. Implications of this observation are that cultural comparisons regarding aggression should include a specification of the time frames involved. Also, awareness of the potential for culture change may at times account for discrepancies in descriptions of aggression and peacefulness given by different fieldworkers for the same culture but at different times periods. A final implication, relevant for reducing violence, is that cultural transitions toward lower levels of aggression can be both dramatic and rapid.

Aggression as a Multidimensional Construct

19   A fourth conceptual issue related to assessing the aggressiveness of any particular culture as well as to making cross-cultural comparisons is that *aggression* and, more generally, *conflict* are multidimensional concepts. For example, possibly relevant dimensions of physical aggression might include spousal aggression; physical punishment of children; infanticide; homicide; capital punishment; interpersonal fighting with fists, clubs, sticks, and spears; and group raids, ambushes, and battles. By some indicators, a culture could seem quite tranquil while by other indicators, the same society could seem more violent. This observation about multidimensionality is relevant, of course, to any attempts to scale societies along a peaceful-to-violent continuum, as suggested by Silverberg and Gray.

20   Some of the challenges posed by the multidimensionality of aggression are reflected in Fabbro's comparison of seven societies, all of which he characterizes as "peaceful" based on a set of criteria (e.g., no wars, no collective internal violence, little or no structural violence, little or no interpersonal physical violence). Although Fabbro's overall assessment is that all seven societies have a low level of physical violence, the multidimensionality issue comes into play as infanticide is noted in two cultures but not in the other five, the physical punishment of children is noted in three cultures but not in the other four, and spousal aggression is noted in three societies but *not* in one society (and for the remaining three societies, its presence or absence is not directly commented on by Fabbro). In a summary table, Fabbro classifies four societies as having "*little* physical violence," and of those four, "lethal physical violence" is also noted for two; the remaining three societies are classified as having "*some* physical violence," and one of these three is noted to have "lethal physical violence." Finally, Fabbro at times mentions particular cultural beliefs that may directly or indirectly relate to aggression and peacefulness—e.g., noting fear of violence in one society and that vio-

lence is abhorred in another society. It is clear that some aggressive acts, of various types and occurring at various rates, may occur in societies that are at or near the tranquil end of a cross-cultural, peaceful-to-violent continuum. It also follows that arranging societies along a continuum of peaceful to violent, although possible, may not be as clear-cut an undertaking as it might have seemed at first.

The Importance of Cultural Meaning and the Emic-Etic Debate

The challenges of comparing societies due to the multidimensionality of aggression is further illustrated through a consideration of the Gebusi of New Guinea. Also, the Gebusi case simultaneously serves to introduce a fifth conceptual issue, namely, the importance of understanding cultural meaning, belief systems, and the overall cultural context within which aggressive and peaceful behaviors occur.   21

Knauft draws attention to the paradox posed by the Gebusi and certain other societies as well: The Gebusi are very tranquil in everyday life and devalue violence, yet they have a very high homicide rate. Among the Gebusi, the physical punishment of children is extremely rare, anger and aggression are considered unbecoming and antisocial, good-humored camaraderie—"good company"—is a typical feature of interaction and is highly valued, and disputes over land or resources are infrequent. At the same time, the Gebusi homicide rate is at least equivalent to 568 per 100,000 for this culture of about 450 persons. Most homicides entail the killing of sorcerers who are believed to be responsible for illness and death. Thus, the key to a full interpretation of homicide lies within the Gebusi cultural meaning system.   22

> . . . The killing of sorcery suspects by adults is thought to be a communal duty—an act to expunge human malice that cannot be eliminated by any other means. The adult violence that does occur in Gebusi society tends to be quickly over, extreme, and subsequently played down or ignored. Conversely, good company is reasserted and reemphasized. On a day-to-day and week-to-week basis, anger and aggressiveness are strikingly absent; aggression is rare, even though it is extremely violent when it does occur. Homicide tends to occur in a highly delimited and socially sanctioned context: the attribution of sorcery following the sickness death of someone in the community. This context is strikingly and effectively dissociated in Gebusi psychology from normal, everyday life.

While a consideration of the cultural meaning is obviously an important aspect of understanding aggression, some authors have taken extreme positions about the centrality of cultural meanings. Heelas, e.g., sees no value in etic (observer-based) definitions of aggression: "We   23 must resist asserting that Ilongot youths are aggressive simply because they lop off heads; that Samoan fathers are aggressive simply because they beat their children; or, for that matter, that the British were aggressive when they lined up to exterminate the indigenous people of Tasmania." To illustrate his argument, Heelas proposes that Yanomamo wife-beating should *not* be considered aggression because inflicting physical injuries is how a husband shows that he "cares" for his wife. Silverberg and Gray find Heelas' argument unconvincing and see value in both emic (actor-based) and etic (observer-based) perspectives: "Just because beatings may signify 'caring' to some Yanomamo women (how many is unclear) does not negate the etic reality of the beatings as violent acts." Chagnon's ethnographic observations indicate that wives attempt to avoid being beaten by their husbands; in other words, they are not eager recipients of this type of husbandly "care," a point noted by Silverberg and Gray in their critique of Heelas' interpretation. The cultural context of Yanomamo wife-beating also suggests that this so-called "caring" occurs when a husband is angry at his wife and that much of it results from a husband's sexual jealousy. Chagnon writes, for instance: "Some men are given to punishing their wives by holding the glowing end of a piece of firewood against them, producing painful and serious burns. . . . It is not uncommon for a man to injure his sexually errant wife seriously and some men have even killed wives for infidelity by shooting them with arrows."

24   Clearly, there is utility in both emic and etic perspectives. What is the point of arguing for the "correctness" of one approach to the total exclusion of the other? For instance, when the research goals are culturally comparative, then an etic perspective on aggression is critical, and when the goals are culturally interpretive, i.e., oriented toward understanding the belief system within a particular culture, focusing on emic "participant understandings" obviously is of central importance. Furthermore, within a single study, emic and etic approaches need not be polarized to the point of mutual exclusivity. For instance, in studying the child-disciplinary practices employed in two Zapotec communities, I combined ethnographic and ethological methods to address both emic and etic considerations: "Ethnographic observations recorded in field-notes provide information on the cultural context and the cultural meaning of particular actions [i.e., an emic orientation], while the systematic sampling and precise definition of behavior elements employed during ethological observation permit quantitative as well as qualitative analyses to be performed [i.e., an etic approach]." Similarly, to return to the Gebusi case, clear, observer-based etic descriptions of the observable tranquillity of daily life and an objective calculation of homicide rates, when combined with an emic understanding of actor-based

beliefs about maintaining "good company," sorcerers, the reasons why sorcerers should be killed, and other facets of the cultural meaning (belief) system, provide a more complete and a more sophisticated understanding of aggression in this given cultural context than either a purely emic or a purely etic orientation does on its own.

Aggression within the Broader Frame of Conflict Management

Wherever a society lies on the peaceful-to-violent continuum, certain   25
mechanisms exist for dealing with conflict. Black proposes a five-part
typology of conflict management that includes *avoidance* of interaction,
self-help (unilateral aggression), *settlement* (using a nonpartisan third
party), *negotiation* to reach a joint decision, and *toleration.* . . .

In some societies, the emphasis is on punishing wrongdoers, but in   26
many others, conflict management hinges on repairing strained or broken relationships. Some cultures have formal mechanisms for handling conflict, such as courts or arbitration boards, and other cultures rely strictly on informal mechanisms such as teasing, gossip, exclusion, ostracism, witchcraft, and so on. Olson provides an interesting illustration of informal conflict control, used on the Islands of Tonga, when he analyzes the *kava*-drinking circle to demonstrate how elders and other community members reinforce community values and how, through the use of humor and joking, inappropriate behavior can be criticized in a nonviolent manner, sometimes resulting in the reduction of conflict or the solution to a problem as the wayward individual learns of the dissatisfaction of the group and then makes a corrective change in behavior.

Cultures tend to have arrays of informal and sometimes formal con-   27
flict management processes and options. Certain types of aggression, or
what Black labels self-help, may or may not be included in the culturally appropriate menu of conflict management options. Several recent anthropological works demonstrate the diversity of conflict resolution and conflict management strategies and options employed in different cultural settings.

Conclusions

One purpose of this article, and the others in this special issue, is to present a sampling of topics and issues within the anthropology of aggression and conflict. This process has begun with brief considerations of (1) sex differences and (2) the cultural variation in aggression.   28

A cross-cultural consideration of aggression in females and males   29
shows simultaneously that proximate cultural influences strongly affect
the expression of both female and male aggression and that the overall
pattern of sex differences in physical aggression is in congruence with

evolutionary models. Phrasing a conclusion in this way avoids nature-nurture dichotomization. This conclusion is based on cross-cultural observations that (1) females are not always nonaggressive, (2) male physical aggression is more frequent and more severe than female aggression, (3) in no culture is female aggression more lethal than male aggression, and (4) tremendous cultural variation exists in levels of male and female physical aggression and regarding how male and female aggression is expressed—recognizing that in some cultures one or both sexes may not engage in physical aggression at all.

30   The cross-cultural variation in aggression is remarkable. It is clear that nonviolent cultures exist, as do a range of more violent ones. Also, tremendous change can occur in the aggressivity level of a given culture, a point illustrated by the rapid shift toward peacefulness among the Chatino and Waorani. Along the peaceful-to-violent continuum, most cultures have a variety of mechanisms for dealing with conflict other than through aggression. An implication for reducing aggression is to introduce new, and to enhance the use of existing, nonviolent informal and formal mechanisms for dealing with conflict.

Cycles of Violence: The Anthropology of War and Peace

ERIC R. WOLF

It is possible to identify a continuum with interpersonal conflict, then violence, at one end, and intersocietal violence at the other (we have not—yet?—arrived at interplanetary violence). In our concluding selection, Eric Wolf examines this diversity, especially as it is influenced by patterns of resource control, kinship systems, population pressures, and—in a final discussion, deleted for brevity—levels of technological sophistication and hierarchical control. Wolf's contribution is especially valuable in emphasizing the reality of multiple conflicts, operating simultaneously at different levels, subject to being destabilized in many different ways. Although Wolf recognizes the existence of biologically based needs and inclinations, he argues that they do not in themselves determine the occurrence or nonoccurrence of violence, nor the actual details of violence when it occurs.

Another anthropologist, Robin Fox, described the phenomenon of *ethnographic dazzle*, whereby anthropologists—not to mention beginning students—are readily dazzled by the diversity of human patterns, thereby often missing common patterns that might underlie such diversity. The challenge of identifying such patterns remains formidable, not least when it comes to the anthropology of human violence.

Some years ago, a playwright with anthropological proclivities, Robert   1
Ardrey, wrote a book called *The Territorial Imperative* (1966). In this work
he projected for us an image of Homo Sapiens, Man, as a killer-ape,
thirsty for blood and hungry for meat, and ever bent upon murdering
his fellow humans in defense of his home turf, his "territory." The
implication was that man was innately aggressive, that murderous
instincts were imprinted in his nature, and that he was destined therefore to make love incidentally, but war forever. But the evidence of Man
the carnivorous Killer is not all that clear-cut. Early African Pliocene-
Pleistocene sites show us that early man did indeed kill some small
animals, as do our closest primate relatives, the chimpanzees; but there
is also a good deal of evidence to indicate that the mainstay of early
hominids was not steak, but seeds, nuts, and possibly leafy plants.
Whether or not and how frequently these early foragers killed each
other is a moot point. Interpreting fossil finds by drawing analogies
with the behavior of primates like baboons or chimps or that of social
carnivores like lions or wolves have produced conflicting results. Variations in animal behavior—even variations among members of the
same species or of closely related species—go hand in hand with
variations in climate and topography, the presence or absence of competing populations, the nature and distribution of food resources,
dietary preferences or commitments, physical capabilities, sexual dimorphism, social patterns of tracking and foraging, and the distributive
consequence of sociability. No one rudimentary drive or instinct can account for such complex phenomena and their equally complex inter-
linkages. Paleo-anthropologists have appropriately stressed the need to
develop more carefully thought-out models that relate behavioral data
more systematically to variations in bodily form and habitat.

There are good reasons why analogies drawn from the behavior of   2
primates or carnivores—or even more from unrelated species like stickleback fish and greyleg geese—can be applied to the study of human
behavior only with the greatest of caution. Human beings do share their
biology with other organisms; but biology does not only set limits; it
also offers a range of capacities and potentialities. In human beings,
aggression—like food-intake and sexuality—is processed through the
operations of a large and complex orchestra of organs, the human brain.
This brain furnishes the mechanisms through which we subject our drives to cortical control and monitoring; but the messages which release,

3   direct, or inhibit behavior are not biologically implanted, they are learned. They are learned culturally in the course of human interaction and communication.

4   What is learned collectively and how such collective learning is played out varies widely among the peoples of the world. All human drives are subject to cultural transformations that put them at the service of quite different social, economic, political, and ideological arrangements. These arrangements dictate when and how we may fight, eat, sleep, and have sex. They also impose their own specific tensions and frustrations and offer characteristic channels for the release of such tensions and frustrations. The understanding of aggression in humans as opposed to greyleg geese—the wish and drive to injure someone and the ability to do so—must address itself to the specific character of the human condition, and thus to the human ability to generate widely different programs for the harnessing and transformation of biological energy in humans.

5   Such programs, carried within the circuits of collective social communication, free us—"displace" us—from the animal need to respond to each situation in its separate terms. They set up rules on who to treat as friend, ally, or foe; when to fight, how to fight, how to stop fighting, what to do with the fruits of victory or the bitterness of defeat. Since they are not inborn, wired into our organisms, they are also capable of modification and change. The friends of yesterday may become the enemies of tomorrow; the enemies of yesteryear your future bosom pals. Love and hate may be re-directed; means and goals of conflict may be altered; swords may be beaten into plowshares. In the ability to generate such flexible programs lies another human paradox: the program may have false or imaginary premises and involve us in disaster; but it can also be corrected or replaced. There are, however, no guarantees.

6   To move closer to an understanding of war and peace, it will help if we first of all distinguish violence between people, interpersonal violence, from violence mobilized to fuel conflicts between entire groups. Interpersonal violence may be triggered by the wish to interfere with the activities of another person or to avenge some real or imagined wrong. It may result in killing, but it is not war. War proper involves entire social groups organized as political communities, and—intentionally or unintentionally—its outcomes affect the balance of power between such social groups and communities. Thus there are people who exhibit a minimum of interpersonal violence among themselves, but are bloodthirsty and relentless in carrying war to outsiders. The Mundurucu Indians of the Tapajoz River in the Amazon Basin studies by Robert Murphy are a case in point. There was very little conflict within a Mundurucu village, but massed collective violence against external enemies.

Conversely, there are people who do not carry on war in the sense I have defined it above, who do not use massed violence to affect the balance of power among groups, but who nevertheless exhibit a good deal of interpersonal violence.

An exemplary case investigated by an anthropologist are the 470   7
Kung San or Bushmen of the Dobe region in the Kalahari Desert studies by Richard Lee. The Dobe Kung acknowledge no overriding authority to keep people in line; they settle disputes through arguments, discussion, and through individual action in conflict. But just as they do not have an overriding state, so they do not make war. While Lee was in the field between 1963–69 there was little interpersonal violence, but his questions uncovered 81 cases of disputes: 10 major arguments without blows, 34 disputes involving fights without weapons, and 37 interpersonal conflicts with weapons. Arguments and fights without weapons involve both men and women; conflicts with weapons involve only men. Lee also turned up 22 cases of homicide by men and 15 woundings during the period 1920–1955, many of them occasioned by disputes over women. Homicides lead to other homicides; such feuds in fact involved 15 of the 22 killings.

It is thus clear that the Dobe Kung are not the "Harmless People"   8
some have thought them to be: they fight and sometimes injure other individual Kung. They are familiar with individual violence but they do not carry on war; and this can be said of many hunting and gathering groups in the anthropological record. Julian Steward, who studied the food-gathering Shoshoneans of the dry plateaus and mountain ranges of the Western United States, wrote that

> In aboriginal times most of the Shoshonean people had no national or tribal warfare. There were no territorial rights to be defended, no military honors to be gained, and no means of organizing groups of individuals for concerted action. When war parties of neighboring peoples invaded their country, the Shoshoneans ran away more often than they fought. Hostilities generally consisted of feuds, not organized military action, and they resulted largely from the suspicion of witch-craft and from women stealing. They were therefore as often intratribal as intertribal.

There were obligations to avenge the death of a relative, and these   9
might be followed by reprisals and counterreprisals. But "these were purely personal and could not involve definable suprafamilial groups, for such groups did not exist."

Mervyn Meggitt, who studied the foodgathering Walbiri—about   10
1,400 of whom live in small groups in the near desert-like environment of the Northern Territory of Australia—writes in a similar vein. When

a man dies in a duel, his mother's brothers are charged with avenging his death either by seeking out the culprit who has fled to another community or by performing sorcery to kill him. . . .

11   What we learn from these examples is that among some human groups organized conflict between groups is absent or rare, and we can perhaps specify the conditions that account for the absence of war among them. All three populations—San, Shoshoneans, Walbiri—live in environments where strategic resources are widely scattered and seasonally variable. To survive, a person periodically needs to gain access to resources in other locations, and he gains such access through ties of kinship, marriage, friendship, and exchange. The Kung build these networks of friendship and neighborliness with people at different waterholes through marriage, visiting, the good will that comes with being someone's namesake or giving them gifts of ostrich-eggshell bead necklaces or arrows, spears, and knives. But there is no way in which a person can unilaterally live off the labor or resources accumulated by others. There are no surpluses to maintain a permanent leisure class, and no mechanisms other than those of kinship and friendship to gain access to other peoples' services.

12   Yet note that these conditions may not always have obtained in the past and may be subject to change, as environing circumstances change. The San may have been dominated in the past by Bantu-speaking pastoralists, and in the nineteenth century sold ivory, skins, and ostrich feathers to Bantu traders who supplied customers in Europe. It is thus possible that the San do not carry on war not because they live in the desert, but because they are marginals at the low end of a chain of unequal relations of exchange. . . .

13   Two studies from the tropical and relatively well watered northern coast of Australia suggest that massed violence may have been more frequent there than in the desert. W. Lloyd Warner studied the 3,000 or so Murngin people of northeastern Arnhem Land in 1926–29. He noted that in addition to the usual individual or small-team raids to avenge a death or adultery, there were two *gaingar* or "regional fights involving a large number of clans" during the twenty years preceding his stay. These had involved 15 and 14 deaths respectively. In all, he estimated the total number of killings during this twenty-year period at 200 and argued that such removal of young men from the pool of marriage partners multiplied the marriage chances for the survivors and thus constituted a major factor in Murngin polygyny.

14   Hart and Pilling, discussing the 1,000 or so Tiwi of Melville and Bathurst Islands, noted that disputes, fights, and duels were common; the overwhelming number of them were concerned with seduction and adultery. In 1928 a cumulation of cases of seduction and nondelivery on

promises of bestowing daughters in marriage sent about 30 fighting men from the Tiklauila band into armed conflict with about 60 Mandi-imbula. Yet, the authors note, military action remained individual and took place among disputes and arguments; "warfare, in the sense of pitched battles between groups aligned through territorial loyalties, did not occur and could not occur among the Tiwi." The battle ended with the elders of both bands turning on a young trouble-maker and clubbing him unconscious. Among the Tiwi, women's work furnished an abundance of resources, and polygyny underwrote the successful collection and processing of produce. There was consequently much competition for women between elders and unmarried men, with corresponding tensions and conflicts. Hart and Pilling suggest that the unbalanced marriage ratio was due to extensive slave raiding and removal of young men by the Portuguese between 1600 and 1800, and subsequent "blackbirding" or capture in the nineteenth century.

This discussion should tell us that we should not extrapolate directly from examples of arrangements among hunters and gatherers of the present day to reconstruct what life and war might have been like among the first hunters and gatherers of human prehistory. Neither San, nor Shoshoneans, nor Australian aborigines are examples of pristine human kind; they have all been involved in the processes of European expansion and affected by them. What we can do is note the possible correspondence of resource scarcity and scatter and a tendency to expand interpersonal ties to reduce risks and increase survival chances. Under such circumstances there may well exist a motivation to limit violence, since it is unwise to make enemies of potential friends and allies. 15

At the same time, social life in such simple societies is frequently suffused with disputes over women. We must remember that we are dealing with small-scale groups that are often characterized as being "egalitarian," where there are no marked differences among men in their ability to occupy the culturally approved statuses and to reap the rewards that go with them. Yet precisely because a man needs a woman in order to become a fully fledged and recognized adult male, equal to other males, there exists a potential for conflict and inter-personal violence. Thus Jane Collier and Michelle Rosaldo have suggested that violence between men over women may be particularly strong in simple societies where men can become autonomous adults only when they can earn the rights to marry particular women by doing services for their potential fathers-in-law. There male autonomy depends on laying claims to women in competition with other men, and—once established—on being able to defend these claims against other men: "it is as husbands that individuals acquire the independence that makes 16 them equal to other adult men." Thus the striving for equality among men breeds displays of aggression. . . .

17   Where hunters and gatherers like the San or Aborigines disperse population, horticulturists and pastoralists aggregate them. They will do so by multiplying their families and adding new members through marriage. At the same time as long as they are not governed by an over-arching authority, they must rely crucially on armed self-help. Popula-tions that depend importantly on fishing grounds, hunting range, cultivated fields, or grazing lands thus face a double problem: to ag-gregate men to work, but also to aggregate men to defend crucial re-sources. And once you can aggregate men to defend land or range, you can also employ them to make others yield up land, range, or water.

18   The ability to aggregate fighting men for group warfare rather than for individual aggressive encounters is aided in kinship-ordered soci-eties by patterns of social recruitment through marriage. Patrilocal mar-riage, where men separate their wives from their families of origin and bring them to live in the homes of their fathers and brothers, can serve to keep together a related group of males who work and fight together and may easily engage as a unit in disputes with other groups of men. In such groups the team of fighters is in effect an extension of the do-mestic organization of the household and of households related in the male line; and it can function as a cohesive interest group in maximiz-ing the interests of the household cluster. . . .

19   The pressure of population upon the land is not direct, but mediated through a complex interplay of social organization and culturally formed aspirations. In Highland New Guinea a descent group needs land to produce food not only for people, but also for pigs—pigs raised to acquire women in marriage (women who will bear future warriors and care for future pigs), pigs to underwrite ceremonial feasts that will compensate past allies and attract new ones, and pigs to pay compen-sation in the case of homicide. It is pigs that make Mae Enga life go round, and it is the cultural complex of Mae Enga pig-keeping that trig-gers war between rivals but also peace among allies. It is thus possible to envisage a transformation in the nature of warfare through a trans-formation in the social and cultural mechanisms that constitute the pre-sent adaptation of people to their environment. In this regard it is also important to remember that these mechanisms and adaptation are not given for all times. They are themselves the outcome of processes of agricultural intensification and crop changes in the past and they may thus be subject to change or modification in the future.

20   The patterns of warfare we have discussed so far take place between roughly symmetrical partners, between individuals or between groups roughly matched in resources and demographic potential. Such vio-lence is therefore also self-limiting. Individuals may fight, but others

who live with them will strive to defuse or settle the dispute through intervention and mediations. . . . "We marry whom we fight" is an axiom frequently invoked to limit the scope of conflict.

When we turn to consider more complex political entities—entities 21 that are no longer ordered by kinship and affinity, but by commands from a political center—we also confront a marked escalation in the possibility and scope of organized violence. Such political entities are typically divided into surplus-producers and surplus-takers, one part of the population producing surplus in the form of tribute to supply a group of political specialists. These groups of political specialists are chiefs and their staffs and supporters in simpler situations, elite ruling classes in more complex ones. The flow of tribute underwrites a division of tasks and labor between the population at large and the political specialists at the center. At the same time it also creates the structural possibility of assembling a pool of laborers and resources specifically designated to support, widen, and enhance the instrumentalities at the disposal of the ruling group. In such a situation it is evident that the more producers you control, the greater the surpluses at your disposal, and the stronger the drive to aggrandize your fund of people and resources for war and through war. In these cases, therefore, massed violence in order to injure another territorial political entity becomes an important strategy in the pursuit of power.

Keith Otterbein has shown in a cross-cultural study of 46 societies 22 that the less autonomous local groups are and the higher the level of political centralization embracing them, the more advanced the degree of military sophistication. Political entities directed by a central group of chiefs and states governed from a political center are more likely to possess complex military establishments with a professional army and a hierarchy of military authority than are kin-ordered bands and tribes. In addition, such societies are likely to wage war in order to gain political control over other groups. Power thus grows directly out of the barrel of a gun or a massing of the spears.

SUGGESTIONS FOR FURTHER READING

Carman, J., ed. *Material Harm.* Glasgow: Craithne Press, 1997. A collection of articles describing archaeological evidence for ancient violence, an important topic not covered in the present book.

Levinson, David. *Family Violence in Cross-Cultural Perspective.* Newbury Park, CA: Sage Publications, 1989. A description and analysis of family violence in a wide range of societies; important as a demonstration that anthropology can shed light on an aspect of human violence that is less dramatic but more widespread than war.

Nordstrom, Carolyn, and A. C. G. M. Robben, eds. *Fieldwork under Fire: Contemporary Studies of Violence and Culture.* Berkeley, CA: University of California Press, 1995. Harrowing and thought-provoking accounts of the current cross-cultural array of organized international violence, by courageous researchers willing to document it.

Riches, D. *The Anthropology of Violence.* New York: Basil Blackwell, 1986. Selected papers from a conference on violence as a social institution, containing a diverse array of ethnographic descriptions and suggested explanations.

Sponsel, Leslie, and Thomas Gregor, eds. *The Anthropology of Peace and Nonviolence.* Boulder, CO: L. Rienner, 1994. A useful corrective to the impression—which readers of this chapter may have gotten—that human societies are overwhelmingly violent and warlike.

STUDY QUESTIONS

1. Are there any particular insights from the sociology of violence that are unlikely to apply to anthropology? Are there any particular insights from anthropology that are unlikely to apply to sociology? Any from either field that seem especially cogent when applied to the other?

2. To what extent are sociobiological and cultural materialist interpretations compatible? Incompatible?

3. Does anthropology's cross-cultural perspective make you more optimistic or pessimistic about the possibility that human beings might eventually diminish their reliance upon violence?

4. Explain the importance of variation cross-culturally (among different cultures) as well as intraculturally (within the same culture).

5. What sort of evidence might help resolve the controversy represented here by the work of Chagnon and Ferguson? Why is their disagreement important?

6. Discuss similarities and differences between studying the anthropology of war and the anthropology of violence.

7. Look into the phenomenon of dehumanization and discuss how it might help illuminate the anthropology of war and violence.

8. Can you distinguish between the functions (and/or effects) of war among nontechnological people and among technologically advanced societies?

9. To what extent are the personal motivations of individuals typically studied by anthropologists likely to be similar to those of individuals living in technologically advanced societies? Different?

10. To what extent might nonviolent activities effectively be substituted for the various "benefits" proposed by anthropologists as responsible for the maintenance of war and organized violence?

5

Political Science

Politics, it is sometimes said, is the art of the possible. Political science is the study of this art, an attempt to understand how people organize themselves into political entities and how these entities function. Much of political science concerns itself with the process of governing; analysis of elections; assessment of relationships of power, influence, decision making; and so forth. For obvious reasons, the science of politics has also been taken up with some of the Big Questions of human governance, and among these few are bigger than the question: Why does political violence break out, and especially, why war?

It has been said that history is the study of events that have happened one time, whereas political science is an effort to generalize about these events. Few things are more worth generalizing about than organized violence, especially war. Yet ironically, fewer things may be more resistant to such generalizing. It can be argued, for example, that there is no such thing as "war," just individual wars. But the same can be said of people: there are no "general" human beings (the average *Homo sapiens*, for example, would have one ovary and one testicle!). There are only individuals. Yet it is immensely important, useful, and meaningful to speak of humanity in general; there are characteristics shared by humans as a whole that are worth knowing about: our large brains, our susceptibility to certain viruses and other diseases, our penchant for language and symbolic systems.

And the fact that we often constitute a significant threat to each other's health, happiness . . . even survival.

Political scientists have developed many different constructs in attempting to explain the particular kind of violence that is war. Some have focused, for example, on the role of crisis management and decision making, a concern that necessarily involves substantial attention to psychological factors. Others emphasize *systemic* considerations, looking particularly at structural aspects of the international system as a whole (cynics might say: at the anarchic *absence* of structure and *lack* of a system). Another concern is the internal nature of political states: the role of democratic as opposed to totalitarian institutions, for example, or the significance of war making as an intentional effort to achieve domestic tranquility by taking advantage of the "rally round the flag" effect.

Related to this is concern over how domestic opinion not only impacts war making, but vice versa: how involvement in war, or other forms of political and interstate conflict, influences public opinion. At the same time, economic determinists—increasingly in the minority—point to an old chestnut of Leninist tradition: the role of competition for overseas markets (resulting from overproduction by capitalist economies), combined with an ongoing need for new sources of raw materials.

Nor does this catalog exhaust the list of political culprits. One tradition looks especially to the personalities—notably the ambitions and weaknesses—of political and military leaders, while another emphasizes the conflict of differing ethnic and religious affiliations, with a substantial role for long-simmering historical antagonisms. The role of arms races has also come under scrutiny, typically blamed as leading to various degrees of destabilization, as well as the troublesome impact of military budgets themselves. Scholars have investigated—but have not reached any consensus—as to the significance of *bipolarity* (the existence of two "hegemonic" world powers; e.g., the U.S. and the USSR during the Cold War, or England and France through much of the seventeenth and eighteenth centuries) versus *multipolarity* and even *unipolarity* (the U.S. after the fall of the USSR).

A major assumption, widely held by most political scientists, may be called the *rational actor* model. This approach is shared with economists, who maintain that consumers act to maximize their "utility," which is tantamount to a careful calculation of how to achieve the greatest satisfaction. The equivalent among political scientists is the argument that states go to war not by accident but because they (more accurately, their leaders) determine that the outcome of doing so is likely to be more in their interest than the outcome of remaining at peace; if so, then—assuming that each war has a winner and a loser— they are wrong, on average, one-half of the time!

Nonetheless, detailed modeling of such rationality has an honored place in political science, especially in the case of mathematical game theory. In brief, *game theory* applies to situations in which contestants can be assigned payoffs depending on their behavior as well as that of the other player(s). Two kinds of games are especially interesting to analysts of conflict and violence: the Game of Chicken and the Prisoner's Dilemma. The latter is presented in a brief selection by Robert Axelrod. For the former, imagine two autmobiles driving toward each other. Each wants to win, which requires the other to swerve. But if both insist on winning, both lose! Optimum strategies in the Game of Chicken involve convincing the opponent that one is not going to swerve: perhaps by being strongly committed to the outcome (having one's "national interests" directly engaged), by being unable to swerve (announcing that the decision is out of one's control, analogous to throwing the steering wheel out the window!), by cultivating a macho reputation of unwillingness to swerve or even a penchant for irrationality, or by driving a vehicle that is so large and heavy that it intimidates one's opponent (e.g., having huge military forces).

More conspicuously than most other disciplines concerned with human violence, political scientists tend to assume a *value-neutral* approach, contending that their job is to understand, not to judge or prescribe. Often, especially in the field of international relations, political scientists find themselves closely associated with governmental power structures, so that although they oppose war generally and doubtless subscribe to a personal morality of some sort, they are typically reluctant to criticize state-sponsored preparation for war and occasional willingness to partake of it.

Finally, there is the question of whether violence in general—or war in particular—is inevitable. There is no simple answer, but it is important to acknowledge a formulation by W. I. Thomas, one of the deans of American social science: "If men define situations as real, they are real in their consequences." This phenomenon, identified by sociologist Robert Merton as a *self-fulfilling prophecy*, looms over nearly every consideration of violence.

The Melian Dialogue

THUCYDIDES

The Greek historian Thucydides lived during the fifth century B.C.E. Thucydides participated in the Peloponnesian War between Athens and Sparta and, because of his *History of the Peloponnesian War*, is considered the first and greatest critical historian of antiquity. The work of Thucydides is also notable for its psychological and political insights, especially its assessment of the role of power politics or *Realpolitik* in structuring the relationships between contending political entities. For example, Thucydides emphasized that the primary cause of the great and ruinous war between Athens and Sparta was the anxiety that Athens' growing strength generated in Sparta; his point has been generalized into such important geopolitical concepts as *balance of power* and the role of up-and-coming states in precipitating war with preexisting status-quo powers.

In the "Melian Dialogue," reproduced here, Thucydides provides us with the most famous early account of cold-blooded, amoral *Realpolitik* in war. The Athenians, at war with Sparta, demand the capitulation of Melos, a small Spartan ally. When the Melians appeal to morality, the Athenians respond, chillingly, with a straightforward calculus of politics based on power alone. Even 2,500 years later, most people find this "hard-headed realism" in the political calculation of organized violence to be remarkably understandable . . . although usually not admirable.

On the other hand, it is worth considering that the opposite of Athenian *Realpolitik*—that is, morality-based motivations for political and military action—can lead to every bit as much violence (if not more) than an amoral calculation based solely on maximizing one's advantages. Consider the Crusades, for example, or other "Holy Wars," secular no less than religious. It is an interesting question whether a cerebral, power-based calculation of benefit is more or less likely to precipitate suffering than one based on raw emotion and unbending certainty of what is right and what is wrong. (In reading the following selection, note that *Lacedaemon* is another word for Sparta.)

The Athenians made an expedition against the island of Melos with thirty ships of their own, six Chian, and two Lesbian, twelve hundred hoplites and three hundred archers besides twenty mounted archers of their own, and about fifteen hundred hoplites furnished by their allies in the islands. The Melians are colonists of the Lacedaemonians who would not submit to Athens like the other islanders. At first they were neutral and took no part. But when the Athenians tried to coerce them by ravaging their lands, they were driven into open hostilities. The generals, Cleomedes the son of Lycomedes and Tisias the son of Tisimachus, encamped with the Athenian forces on the island. But before they did the country any harm they sent envoys to negotiate with the Melians. Instead of bringing these envoys before the people, the Melians desired them to explain their errand to the magistrates and to the dominant class. They spoke as follows:

'Since we are not allowed to speak to the people, lest, forsooth, a multitude should be deceived by seductive and unanswerable arguments which they would hear set forth in a single uninterrupted oration (for we are perfectly aware that this is what you mean in bringing us before a select few), you who are sitting here may as well make assurance yet surer. Let us have no set speeches at all, but do you reply to each several statement of which you disapprove, and criticise it at once. Say first of all how you like this mode of proceeding.'

Since we are to be closeted with you, let us converse and not make speeches.

THE MELIAN REPRESENTATIVES ANSWERED: 'The quiet interchange of

We do not object. But discussion between you and us is a mockery, and can only end in our ruin.

explanations is a reasonable thing, and we do not object to that. But your warlike movements, which are present not only to our fears but to our eyes, seem to belie your words. We see that, although you may reason with us, you mean to be our judges; and that at the end of the discussion, if the justice of our cause prevail and we therefore refuse to yield, we may expect war; if we are convinced by you, slavery.'

ATH. Nay, but if you are only going to argue from fancies about

In any case you must face the facts.

the future, or if you meet us with any other purpose than that of looking your circumstances in the face and saving your city, we have done; but if this is your intention we will proceed.

MEL. It is an excusable and natural thing that men in our position

It must be as you, and not as we, please.

should neglect no argument and no view which may avail. But we admit that this conference has met to consider the question of our preservation; and therefore let the argument proceed in the manner which you propose.

ATH. Well, then, we Athenians will use no fine words; we will not

No use in talking about right; expediency is the word.

go out of our way to prove at length that we have a right to rule, because we overthrew the Persians; or that we attack you now because we are suffering any injury at your hand. We should not convince you if we did; nor must you expect to convince us by arguing that, although a colony of the Lacedaemonians, you have taken no part in their expeditions, or that you have never done us any wrong. But you and we should say what we really think, and aim only at what is possible, for we both alike know that into the discussion of human affairs the question of justice only enters where there is equal power to enforce it, and that the powerful exact what they can, and the weak grant what they must.

MEL. Well, then, since you set aside justice and invite us to speak of

For your own sakes, then, it is expedient that you should not be too strict.

expediency, in our judgment it is certainly expedient that you should respect a principle which is for the common good; that to every man when in peril a reasonable claim should be accounted a claim of right, and that any plea which he is disposed to urge, even if failing of the point a little, should help his cause. Your interest in this principle is quite as great as ours, inasmuch as you, if you fall, will incur the heaviest vengeance, and will be the most terrible example to mankind.

ATH. The fall of our empire, if it should fall, is not an event to which we look forward with dismay; for ruling states such as Lacedaemon are not cruel to their vanquished enemies. With the Lacedaemonians, however, we are not now contending; the real danger is from our many subject states, who may of their own motion rise up and overcome their masters.

For ourselves we have no fears. It is you who have to learn the lesson of what is expedient both for us and you.

But this is a danger which you may leave to us. And we will now endeavour to show that we have come in the interests of our empire, and that in what we are about to say we are only seeking the preservation of your city. For we want to make you ours with the least trouble to ourselves, and it is for the interests of us both that you should not be destroyed.

MEL. It may be your interest to be our masters, but how can it be ours to be your slaves?

For you, yes. But how for us?

ATH. To you the gain will be that by submission you will avert the worst; and we shall be all the richer for your preservation.

You will suffer less and we shall gain more.

MEL. But must we be your enemies? Will you not receive us as friends if we are neutral and remain at peace with you?

May we not be neutral?

ATH. No, your enmity is not half so mischievous to us as your friendship; for the one is in the eyes of our subjects an argument of our power, the other of our weakness.

Our subjects would not understand that.

MEL. But are your subjects really unable to distinguish between states in which you have no concern, and those which are chiefly your own colonies, and in some cases have revolted and been subdued by you?

But we are not a colony of yours.

ATH. Why, they do not doubt that both of them have a good deal to say for themselves on the score of justice, but they think that states like yours are left free because they are able to defend themselves, and that we do not attack them because we dare not. So that your subjection will give us an increase of security, as well as an extension of empire. For we are masters of the sea, and you who

You are talking about justice again. We say that we cannot allow freedom to insignificant islanders.

are islanders, and insignificant islanders too, must not be allowed to escape us. . . .

MEL.   We know only too well how hard the struggle must be against

Heaven will protect the right and the Lacedaemonians will succour us.

your power, and against fortune, if she does not mean to be impartial. Nevertheless we do not despair of fortune; for we hope to stand as high as you in the favour of heaven, because we are righteous, and you against whom we contend are unrighteous; and we are satisfied that our deficiency in power will be compensated by the aid of our allies the Lacedaemonians; they cannot refuse to help us, if only because we are their kinsmen, and for the sake of their own honour. And therefore our confidence is not so utterly blind as you suppose.

ATH.   As for the Gods, we expect to have quite as much of their

That the stronger should rule over the weaker is a principle common to Gods and men. Therefore the Gods are as likely to favour us as you. And the Lacedaemonians look only to their interest.

favour as you: for we are not doing or claiming anything which goes beyond common opinion about divine or men's desires about human things. For of the Gods we believe, and of men we know, that by a law of their nature wherever they can rule they will. This law was not made by us, and we are not the first who have acted upon it; we did but inherit it, and shall bequeath it to all time, and we know that you and all mankind, if you were as strong as we are, would do as we do. So much for the Gods; we have told you why we expect to stand as high in their good opinion as you. And then as to the Lacedaemonians—when you imagine that out of very shame they will assist you, we admire the innocence of your idea, but we do not envy you the folly of it. . . .

MEL.   On the other hand, we think that whatever perils there may

But they may need our aid, and they are our kinsmen.

be, they will be ready to face them for our sakes, and will consider danger less dangerous where we are concerned. For if they need our aid we are close at hand, and they can better trust our loyal feeling because we are their kinsmen.

ATH.   Yes, but what encourages men who are invited to join in a

The aid which you can give is not sufficient to make them run into danger for your sakes.

conflict is clearly not the good-will of those who summon them to their side, but a decided superiority in real power. . . . We remark that, in this long discussion, not a word has been uttered by you which would give a reasonable man expectation of deliverance. Your strongest grounds are hopes deferred, and what power you have is not to be compared with that which is already arrayed against you. Unless after we have withdrawn you mean to come, as even now you may, to a wiser conclusion, you are showing a great want of sense. For surely you cannot dream of flying to that false sense of Honour which has been the ruin of so many when danger and dishonour were staring them in the face. Many men with their eyes still open to the consequences have found the word "honour" too much for them, and have suffered a mere name to lure them on, until it has drawn down upon them real and irretrievable calamities; through their own folly they have incurred a worse dishonour than fortune would have inflicted upon them. If you are wise you will not run this risk; you ought to see that there can be no disgrace in yielding to a great city which invites you to become her ally on reasonable terms, keeping your own land, and merely paying tribute; and that you will certainly gain no honour if, having to choose between two alternatives, safety and war, you obstinately prefer the worse. To maintain our rights against equals, to be politic with superiors, and to be moderate towards inferiors is the path of safety. Reflect once more when we have withdrawn, and say to yourselves over and over again that you are deliberating about your one and only country, which may be saved or may be destroyed by a single decision.

The Athenians left the conference: the Melians, after consulting among themselves, resolved to persevere in their refusal. . . . *The Melians refuse to yield.*   2

The Athenian envoys returned to the army; and the generals, when they found that the Melians would not yield, immediately commenced hostilities. They surrounded the town of Melos with a wall, dividing *The Athenians blockade Melos.*   3 the work among the several contingents. They then left troops of their own and of their allies to keep guard both by land and by sea, and retired with the greater part of their army; the remainder carried on the blockade. . . . The Melians took that part of the Athenian wall which looked towards the agora by a night assault, killed a few men, and brought in as much corn and other necessaries as they could ; they then retreated and remained inactive. After this the Athenians set a better watch. So the summer ended. . . .

About the same time the Melians took another part of the Athenian wall; for the fortifications were insufficiently guarded. Whereupon the Athenians sent fresh troops. . . . The place was now closely invested, and there was *Melos taken and the male inhabitants put to death.*   4 treachery among the citizens themselves. So the Melians were induced to surrender at discretion. The Athenians thereupon put to death all who were of military age, and made slaves of the women and children. They then colonized the island, sending thither five hundred settlers of their own.

The Evolution of Cooperation

ROBERT AXELROD

One cause of violence appears to be the worry that "if I don't attack, I will be attacked." Fearing that another individual, or another group, may act uncooperatively, even aggressively, can drive an individual or group to be uncooperative or even aggressive . . . which ends up with both sides in a situation that is decidedly disadvantageous compared to how things would be if they could have only figured out a way to cooperate. Social scientists, mathematicians, and even biologists have fastened on a simplified model for this problem, known as the Prisoner's Dilemma.

In the following selection, political scientist Robert Axelrod explains the basic dimensions of the Prisoner's Dilemma. Although Axelrod was concerned with identifying obstacles to cooperation, an identical analysis is often applied to violence itself; just replace *defect* with *attack*, and *cooperate* with *refrain*. The dilemma, accordingly, is that in rational pursuit of maximum individual gain, each side is driven to a strategy of violence, to everyone's disadvantage! The Prisoner's Dilemma is clearly an oversimplification of the real world. Nonetheless, models of this sort help to clarify important problems. (Also note that in his book, from which this material was excerpted, Axelrod went on to identify an important way out of the Prisoner's Dilemma, known as "Tit for Tat" . . . but that's another matter. For now, our focus is on understanding an important dilemma, and the extent to which we might all be prisoners of it.)

1   Under what conditions will cooperation emerge in a world of egoists without central authority? This question has intrigued people for a long time. And for good reason. We all know that people are not angels, and that they tend to look after themselves and their own first. Yet we also know that cooperation does occur and that our civilization is based upon it. But, in situations where each individual has an incentive to be selfish, how can cooperation ever develop?

2   The answer each of us gives to this question has a fundamental effect on how we think and act in our social, political, and economic relations

with others. And the answers that others give have a great effect on how ready they will be to cooperate with us.

The most famous answer was given over three hundred years ago by Thomas Hobbes. It was pessimistic. He argued that before governments existed, the state of nature was dominated by the problem of selfish individuals who competed on such ruthless terms that life was "solitary, poor, nasty, brutish, and short." In his view, cooperation could not develop without a central authority, and consequently a strong government was necessary. Ever since, arguments about the proper scope of government have often focused on whether one could, or could not, expect cooperation to emerge in a particular domain if there were not an authority to police the situation.

Today nations interact without central authority. Therefore the requirements for the emergence of cooperation have relevance to many of the central issues of international politics. The most important problem is the security dilemma: nations often seek their own security through means which challenge the security of others. This problem arises in such areas as escalation of local conflicts and arms races. . . .

This basic problem occurs when the pursuit of self-interest by each leads to a poor outcome for all. To make headway in understanding the vast array of specific situations which have this property, a way is needed to represent what is common to these situations without becoming bogged down in the details unique to each. Fortunately, there is such a representation available: the famous *Prisoner's Dilemma* game.

In the Prisoner's Dilemma game, there are two players. Each has two choices, namely cooperate or defect. Each must make the choice without knowing what the other will do. No matter what the other does, defection yields a higher payoff than cooperation. The dilemma is that if both defect, both do worse than if both had cooperated. This simple game will provide the basis for the entire analysis used in this book.

The way the game works is shown in figure 5.1. One player chooses a row, either cooperating or defecting. The other player simultaneously chooses a column, either cooperating or defecting. Together, these choices result in one of the four possible outcomes shown in that matrix. If both players cooperate, both do fairly well. Both get *R*, the *reward for mutual cooperation*. In the concrete illustration of figure 5.1 the reward is 3 points. This number might, for example, be a payoff in dollars that each player gets for that outcome. If one player cooperates but the other defects, the defecting player gets the *temptation to defect*, while the cooperating player gets the *sucker's payoff*. In the example, these are 5 points and 0 points respectively. If both defect, both get 1 point, the *punishment for mutual defection*.

7   What should you do in such a game? Suppose you are the row player, and you think the column player will cooperate. This means that you will get one of the two outcomes in the first column of figure 5.1. You have a choice. You can cooperate as well, getting the 3 points of the reward for mutual cooperation. Or you can defect, getting the 5 points of the temptation payoff. So it pays to defect if you think the other player will cooperate. But now suppose that you think the other player will defect. Now you are in the second column of figure 5.1, and you have a choice between cooperating, which would make you a sucker and give you 0 points, and detecting, which would result in, mutual punishment giving you 1 point. So it pays to defect if you think the other player will defect. This means that it is better to defect if you think the other player will cooperate, *and* it is better to defect if you think the other player will defect. So no matter what the other player does, it pays for you to defect.

8   So far, so good. But the same logic holds for the other player too. Therefore, the other player should defect no matter what you are expected to do. So you should both defect. But then you both get 1 point which is worse than the 3 points of the reward that you both could have gotten had you both cooperated. Individual rationality leads to a worse outcome for both than is possible. Hence the dilemma.

9   The Prisoner's Dilemma is simply an abstract formulation of some very common and very interesting situations in which what is best for each person individually leads to mutual defection, whereas everyone would have been better off with mutual cooperation. The definition of

		Column Player	
		Cooperate	*Defect*
Row Player	*Cooperate*	$R = 3, R = 3$ Reward for mutual cooperation	$S = 0, T = 5$ Sucker's payoff, and temptation to defect
	Defect	$T = 5, S = 0$ Temptation to defect and sucker's payoff	$P = 1, P = 1$ Punishment for mutual defection

FIGURE 5.1   The Prisoner's Dilemma

Note: The payoffs to the row chooser are listed first.

Prisoner's Dilemma requires that several relationships hold among the four different potential outcomes. The first relationship specifies the order of the four payoffs. The best a player can do is get T, the temptation to defect when the other player cooperates. The worst a player can do is get S, the sucker's payoff for cooperating while the other player defects. In ordering the other two outcomes, R, the reward for mutual cooperation, is assumed to be better than P, the punishment for mutual defection. This leads to a preference ranking of the four payoffs from best to worst as T, R, P, and S. . . .

The second part of the definition of the Prisoner's Dilemma is that the players cannot get out of their dilemma by taking turns exploiting each other. This assumption means that an even chance of exploitation and being exploited is not as good an outcome for a player as mutual cooperation. It is therefore assumed that the reward for mutual cooperation is greater than the average of the temptation and the sucker's payoff. This assumption, together with the rank ordering of the four payoffs, defines the Prisoner's Dilemma.

Thus two egoists playing the game *once* will both choose their dominant choice, defection, and each will get less than they both could have gotten if they had cooperated. If the game is played a known finite number of times, the players still have no incentive to cooperate. This is certainly true on the last move since there is no future to influence. On the next-to-last move neither player will have an incentive to cooperate since they can both anticipate a defection by the other player on the very last move. Such a line of reasoning implies that the game will unravel all the way back to mutual defection on the first move of any sequence of plays that is of known finite length. . . .

The first question you are tempted to ask is, "What is the best strategy?" In other words, what strategy will yield a player the highest possible score? This is a good question, but as will be shown later, no best rule exists independently of the strategy being used by the other player. In this sense, the iterated Prisoner's Dilemma is completely different from a game like chess. A chess master can safely use the assumption that the other player will make the most feared move. This assumption provides a basis for planning in a game like chess, where the interests of the players are completely antagonistic. But the situations represented by the Prisoner's Dilemma game are quite different. The interests of the players are not in total conflict. Both players can do well by getting the reward, R, for mutual cooperation or both can do poorly by getting the punishment, P, for mutual defection. Using the assumption that the other player will always make the move you fear most will lead you to expect that the other will never cooperate, which in turn will lead you to defect, causing unending punishment. So unlike chess, in the

Prisoner's Dilemma it is not safe to assume that the other player is out to get you.

13   In fact, in the Prisoner's Dilemma, the strategy that works best depends directly on what strategy the other player is using and, in particular, on whether this strategy leaves room for the development of mutual cooperation.

The Strategy of Conflict

THOMAS C. SCHELLING

Although war is intensely violent, it is typically not an enterprise of angry men, acting on the spur of the moment and out of control; in psychological terms, it is more likely to involve "instrumental" than "impulsive" violence. Thus, even if—and according to many specialists, *especially* if—the stakes are high, the conduct of international politics often derives from an abundance of cool, rational thought. This is especially true when it comes to nuclear strategy, which, according to many critics, incorporates if anything an *excess* of rationality, dangerous because it anesthetizes the decision makers from the emotion-laden, destructive reality of the carnage they are contemplating.

Speaking of the Nazi defendants at the Nuremberg trials following World War II, chief U.S. prosecutor Telford Taylor noted: "The crimes of these men were not committed in rage, nor under the stress of sudden temptation. One does not build a stupendous war machine in a fit of passion, nor an Auschwitz slave factory during a passing spasm of brutality." The construction of nuclear weapons—a high point in potential violence—represents a similarly high point in "rational" enterprise, although nuclear strategists, not surprisingly, vigorously resist any comparison with intentional mass murder. Instead, they point to the theory of deterrence, whereby nuclear weapons ostensibly exist in order to keep the peace and to prevent their use by other countries or terrorist groups.

In any event, nuclear weapons pose a series of special challenges to rationality, including the following. *Vulnerability of the weapons themselves:* If one side can, even in theory, threaten the retaliatory capacity of another, this might not only embolden the first to attack but could also induce the potential victim, fearing such an attack, to attack preemptively . . . which could lead to pre-preemption, and so forth. *Problems of credibility:* Because of their extreme destructiveness as well as the prospect that they will bring about unacceptable retaliation and/or worldwide ecological catastrophe, the threat to use nuclear weapons lacks credibility, and thus utility . . . unless the weapons are somehow made more usable, as via "limited nuclear war" and "civil defense." But if, in order to bolster their credibility, nuclear weapons must be made more usable, then they are thus more likely to be used . . . which flies in the face of their ostensible purpose, which is *not* to be used!

Such logical contradictions aside, theories of deterrence and coercion have been dominated by *rational actor* models of one sort or another, and one of the most influential theorists has been economist-turned-political-theorist Thomas Schelling. Although he applied his logic especially in the context of nuclear strategy and game theory, Schelling's approach is relevant to most threats of conventional war as well.

Among diverse theories of conflict—corresponding to the diverse meanings of the word "conflict"—a main dividing line is between those that treat conflict as a pathological state and seek its causes and treatment, and those that take conflict for granted and study the behavior associated with it. Among the latter there is a further division between those that examine the participants in a conflict in all their complexity— with regard to both "rational" and "irrational" behavior, conscious and unconscious, and to motivations as well as to calculations—and those that focus on the more rational, conscious, artful kind of behavior. Crudely speaking, the latter treat conflict as a kind of contest, in which the participants are trying to "win." A study of conscious, intelligent, sophisticated conflict behavior—of successful behavior—is like a search for rules of "correct" behavior in a contest-winning sense.

We can call this field of study the *strategy* of conflict.[1] We can be interested in it for at least three reasons. We may be involved in a conflict ourselves; we all are, in fact, participants in international conflict, and we want to "win" in some proper sense. We may wish to understand how participants actually do conduct themselves in conflict situations; an understanding of "correct" play may give us a bench mark for the study of actual behavior. . . .

Strategy—in the sense in which I am using it here—is not concerned with the efficient *application* of force but with the *exploitation of potential force.* It is concerned not just with enemies who dislike each other but with partners who distrust or disagree with each other. It is concerned not just with the division of gains and losses between two claimants but with the possibility that particular outcomes are worse (better) for *both* claimants than certain other outcomes. In the terminology of game

[1]The term "strategy" is taken, here, from the *theory of games,* which distinguishes games of skill, games of chance, and games of strategy, the latter being those in which the best course of action for each player depends on what the other players do. The term is intended to focus on the interdependence of the adversaries' decisions and on their expectations about each other's behavior. This is not the military usage.

theory, most interesting international conflicts are not "constant-sum games" but "variable-sum games": the sum of the gains of the participants involved is not fixed so that more for one inexorably means less for the other. There is a common interest in reaching outcomes that are mutually advantageous.

4   To study the strategy of conflict is to take the view that most conflict situations are essentially *bargaining* situations. They are situations in which the ability of one participant to gain his ends is dependent to an important degree on the choices or decisions that the other participant will make. The bargaining may be explicit, as when one offers a concession; or it may be by tacit maneuver, as when one occupies or evacuates strategic territory. It may, as in the ordinary haggling of the market-place, take the *status quo* as its zero point and seek arrangements that yield positive gains to both sides; or it may involve threats of damage, including mutual damage, as in a strike, boycott, or price war, or in extortion.

5   Viewing conflict behavior as a bargaining process is useful in keeping us from becoming exclusively preoccupied either with the conflict or with the common interest. To characterize the maneuvers and actions of limited war as a bargaining process is to emphasize that, in addition to the divergence of interest over the variables in dispute, there is a powerful common interest in reaching an outcome that is not enormously destructive of values to both sides. A "successful" employees' strike is not one that destroys the employer financially, it may even be one that never takes place. Something similar can be true of war. . . .

6   The idea of deterrence figures so prominently in some areas of conflict other than international affairs that one might have supposed the existence of a well-cultivated theory already available to be exploited for international applications. Deterrence has been an important concept in criminal law for a long time. . . .

7   It is not only criminals, however, but our own children that have to be deterred. Some aspects of deterrence stand out vividly in child discipline: the importance of rationality and self-discipline on the part of the person to be deterred, of his ability to comprehend the threat if he hears it and to hear it through the din and noise, of the threatener's determination to fulfill the threat if need be—and, more important, of the threatened party's conviction that the threat will be carried out. Clearer perhaps in child discipline than in criminal deterrence is the important possibility that the threatened punishment will hurt the threatener as much as it will the one threatened, perhaps more. There is an analogy between a parent's threat to a child and the threat that a wealthy paternalistic nation makes to the weak and disorganized government of a poor nation in, say, extending, foreign aid and demanding "sound" economic policies or cooperative military policies in return.

And the analogy reminds us that, even in international affairs, deterrence is as relevant to relations between friends as between potential enemies. . . .   8

The deterrence idea also crops up casually in everyday affairs. Automobile drivers have an evident common interest in avoiding collision and a conflict of interest over who shall go first and who shall slam on his brakes and let the other through. Collision being about as mutual as anything can be, and often the only thing that one can threaten, the maneuvers by which one conveys a threat of mutual damage to another driver aggressing on one's right of way are an instructive example of the kind of threat that is conveyed not by words but by actions, and of the threat in which the pledge to fulfill is made not by verbal announcement but by losing the power to do otherwise.   9

Finally, there is the important area of the underworld. Gang war and international war have a lot in common. Nations and outlaws both lack enforceable legal systems to help them govern their affairs. Both engage in the ultimate in violence. Both have an interest in avoiding violence, but the threat of violence is continually on call. It is interesting that racketeers, as well as gangs of delinquents, engage in limited war, disarmament and disengagement, surprise attack, retaliation and threat of retaliation; they worry about "appeasement" and loss of face; and they make alliances and agreements with the same disability that nations are subject to—the inability to appeal to higher authority in the interest of contract enforcement. . . .   10

But what configuration of value systems for the two participants—of the "payoffs," in the language of game theory—makes a deterrent threat credible? How do we measure the mixture of conflict and common interest required to generate a "deterrence" situation? What communication is required, and what means of authenticating the evidence communicated? What kind of "rationality" is required of the party to be deterred—a knowledge of his own value system, an ability to perceive alternatives and to calculate with probabilities, an ability to demonstrate (or an inability to conceal) his own rationality?   11

What is the need for trust, or enforcement of promises? Specifically, in addition to threatening damage, need one also guarantee to withhold the damage if compliance is forthcoming; or does this depend on the configuration of "payoffs" involved? What "legal system," communication system, or information structure is needed to make the necessary promises enforceable?   12

Can one threaten that he will "probably" fulfill a threat; or must he threaten that he certainly will? What is the meaning of a threat that one will "probably" fulfill when it is clear that, if he retained any choice, he'd have no incentive to fulfill it after the act? More generally, what are   13 the devices by which one gets committed to fulfillment that he would otherwise be known to shrink from, considering that if a commitment makes the threat credible enough to be effective it need not be carried out. What is the difference, if any, between a threat that deters action and one that compels action, or a threat designed to safeguard a second party from his own mistakes? Are there any logical differences among deterrent, disciplinary, and extortionate threats? . . .

14   There are two points worth stressing. One is that, though "strategy of conflict" sounds cold-blooded, the theory is not concerned with the efficient *application* of violence or anything of the sort; it is not essentially a theory of aggression or of resistance or of war. *Threats* of war, yes, or threats of anything else; but it is the employment of threats, or of threats and promises, or more generally of the conditioning of one's own behavior on the behavior of others, that the theory is about. . . .

15   Second, such a theory is nondiscriminatory as between the conflict and the common interest, as between its applicability to potential enemies and its applicability to potential friends. The theory degenerates at one extreme if there is no scope for mutual accommodation, no common interest at all even in avoiding mutual disaster; it degenerates at the other extreme if there is no conflict at all and no problem in identifying and reaching common goals. But in the area between those two extremes the theory is noncommittal about the mixture of conflict and common interest; we can equally well call it the theory of precarious partnership or the theory of incomplete antagonism. . . .

Risky Behavior and "Compellent" Threats

16   There is typically a difference between a threat intended to make an adversary *do* something (or cease doing something) and a threat intended to keep him from starting something. The distinction is in the timing, in who has to make the first move, in whose initiative is put to the test. To deter by threat an enemy's advance it may be enough to burn the bridges behind me as I face the enemy; to compel by threat an enemy's retreat I have to be committed to move forward, and this requires setting fire to the grass behind me with the wind blowing toward the enemy. I can block your car in the road by placing my car in your way; my deterrent threat is passive, the decision to collide is up to you. If you, however, find me in your way and threaten to collide unless I move, you enjoy no such advantage; the decision to collide is still yours, and I enjoy deterrence. You have to arrange to *have* to collide unless I move, and that is a degree more complicated.

17   The threat that compels rather than deters, therefore, often takes the form of administering the punishment *until* the other acts, rather than

if he acts. This is so because often the only way to become physically committed to an action is to initiate it. Initiating steady pain, even if the threatener shares the pain, may make sense as a threat, especially if the threatener can initiate it irreversibly so that only the other's compliance can relieve the pain they both share. But irreversibly initiating certain disaster, if one shares it, is no good. Irreversibly initiating a moderate *risk* of mutual disaster, however, if the other's compliance is feasible within a short enough period to keep the cumulative risk within tolerable bounds, may be a means of scaling down the threat to where one is willing to set it going. Subjecting the enemy (and oneself) to a 1 per cent risk of enormous disaster for each week that he fails to comply is somewhat similar to subjecting him (and oneself) to a steady weekly damage rate equivalent to 1 per cent of disaster. . . .

"Rocking the boat" is a good example. If I say, "Row, or I'll tip the boat over and drown us both," you'll say you don't believe me. But if I rock the boat so that it *may* tip over, you'll be more impressed. If I can't administer pain short of death for the two of us, a "little bit" of death, in the form of a small probability that the boat will tip over, is a near equivalent. But, to make it work, I must really put the boat in jeopardy; just saying that I may turn us both over is unconvincing. 18

Brinkmanship

The argument of this paper leads to a definition of brinkmanship and a concept of the "brink of war." The brink is not, in this view, the sharp edge of a cliff where one can stand firmly, look down, and decide whether or not to plunge. The brink is a curved slope that one can stand on with some risk of slipping, the slope gets steeper and the risk of slipping greater as one moves toward the chasm. But the slope and the risk of slipping are rather irregular; neither the person standing there nor onlookers can be quite sure just how great the risk is, or how much it increases when one takes a few more steps downward. One does not, in brinkmanship, frighten the adversary who is roped to him by getting so close to the edge that if one *decides* to jump one can do so before anyone can stop him. Brinkmanship involves getting onto the slope where one may fall in spite of his own best efforts to save himself, dragging his adversary with him. 19

Brinkmanship is thus the deliberate creation of a recognizable risk of war, a risk that one does not completely control. It is the tactic of deliberately letting the situation get somewhat out of hand, just because its being out of hand may be intolerable to the other party and force his accommodation. It means harassing and intimidating an adversary by exposing him to a shared risk, or deterring him by showing that if he 20 makes a contrary move he may disturb us so that we slip over the brink whether we want to or not, carrying him with us.

21   The idea that we should "keep the enemy guessing" about our response, particularly about *whether* we shall respond, needs an interpretation along these lines. It is sometimes argued that we need not threaten the enemy with the certainty of retaliation or the certainty of resistance, but just scare him with the possibility that we may strike back. . . . To say that we may or may not retaliate for an invasion of some neutral country, depending on how it suits us at the time, and that we shall not let the enemy make this decision for us, nor let him know just what to expect, may confront the enemy with what appears to be a bluff. But to get so involved in or near a neutral country with troops or other commitments that we are not altogether sure ourselves about whether we could evade a fight in case of invasion, may genuinely keep the enemy guessing.

22   In sum, it may make sense to try to keep the enemy guessing as long as we are not trying to keep him guessing about our own motivation. If the outcome is partly determined by events and processes that are manifestly somewhat beyond our comprehension and control, we create *genuine* risk for him. . . .

War and Misperception

ROBERT JERVIS

At some level, the choice of going to war derives from the actions of a relatively small number of decision makers, often acting in a situation of crisis. It is therefore subject to the vagaries of human error. Although one strand of political thought (typically a right-wing perspective) tends to interpret war as deriving from the misbehavior of individuals and/or countries, another, typically liberal perspective sees it as analogous to an automobile accident: neither side desires the outcome, but because of various blunders accidents happen. The study of such accidents brings together political scientists and psychologists, spawning an important component of the field known as *political psychology*.

Many psychological factors relevant to the politics of wartime decision making have been identified and studied. These include rigidity of thinking and planning; the coercive power of small groups ("groupthink"); a tendency for wishful thinking and excluding bad news; the negative consequences of attempting to process information under conditions of sleep deprivation, time pressures, heavy responsibility, and limited options; inaccurate perception of others (including frequent misreading of an adversary's intentions); and plain old-fashioned miscommunication. The following article points out a few of these considerations.

Possible Areas of Misperception

Although this article will concentrate on misperceptions of intentions of potential adversaries, many other objects can be misperceived as well. Capabilities of course can be misperceived; indeed . . . excessive military optimism is frequently associated with the outbreak of war. Military optimism is especially dangerous when coupled with political and diplomatic pessimism. A country is especially likely to strike if it feels that, although it can win a war immediately, the chances of a favorable diplomatic settlement are slight and the military situation is likely to deteriorate. Furthermore, these estimates, which are logically independent, may be psychologically linked. Pessimism about current diplomatic and long-run military prospects may lead statesmen to exaggerate the possibility of current military victory as a way of convincing themselves that there is, in fact, a solution to what otherwise would be an intolerable dilemma.

Less remarked on is the fact that the anticipated consequences of events may also be incorrect. For example, America's avowed motive for fighting in Vietnam was not the direct goal of saving that country, but rather the need to forestall the expected repercussions of defeat. What it feared was a "domino effect" leading to a great increase in Communist influence in Southeast Asia and the perception that the United States lacked the resolve to protect its interests elsewhere in the world. In retrospect, it seems clear that neither of these possibilities materialized. This case is not unique; states are prone to fight when they believe that "bandwagoning" rather than "balancing" dynamics are at work—that is, when they believe that relatively small losses or gains will set off a self-perpetuating cycle. In fact, such beliefs are often incorrect. Although countries will sometimes side with a state which is gaining power, especially if they are small and can do little to counteract such a menace, the strength and resilience of balancing incentives are often underestimated by the leading powers. Statesmen are rarely fatalistic; they usually resist the growth of dominant powers. A striking feature of the Cold War is how little each side . . . suffered when it . . . had to make what it perceived as costly and dangerous retreats.

At times we may need to distinguish between misperceptions of a state's predispositions—that is, its motives and goals—and misperceptions of the realities faced by the state. Either can lead to incorrect predictions, and, after the fact, it is often difficult to determine which kind of error was made. When the unexpected behavior is undesired, decision-makers usually think that they have misread the other state's motives, not the situation it faced. Likewise, scholars generally focus on misjudgments of intentions rather than misjudgments of situations. We, too, shall follow this pattern, although it would be very useful to explore the proposition that incorrect explanations and predictions concerning other states' behaviors are caused more often by misperceptions concerning their situations than by misperceptions about their predispositions. . . .

4   Because a state which finds the status quo intolerable or thinks it can be preserved only by fighting can be driven to act despite an unfavorable assessment of the balance of forces, it is neither surprising nor evidence of misperception that those who start wars often lose them. For example, Austria and Germany attacked in 1914 largely because they believed that the status quo was unstable and that the tide of events was moving against them. . . .

5   The Japanese made a similar calculation in 1941. Although they overestimated the chance of victory because they incorrectly believed that the United States would be willing to fight—and lose—a limited war, the expectation of victory was not a necessary condition for their decision to strike. According to their values, giving up domination of China—which would have been required in order to avoid war—was tantamount to sacrificing their national survival. Victory, furthermore, would have placed them in the first rank of nations and preserved their domestic values. The incentives were somewhat similar in 1904, when they attacked Russia even though "the Emperor's most trusted advisers expressed no confidence as to the outcome of the war. . . . The army calculated that Japan had a fifty-fifty chance to win a war. The Navy expected that half its forces would be lost, but it hoped the enemy's naval forces would be annihilated with the remaining half." Fighting was justified in light of Japan's deteriorating military position combined with the possibility of increasing its influence over its neighbors. . . .

Misperceptions and the Origins of World Wars I and II

6   Tracing the impact of beliefs and perceptions in any given case might seem easy compared to the problems just presented. But it is not, although even a brief list of the misperceptions preceding the major conflicts of this century is impressive. Before World War I, all of the participants thought that the war would be short. They also seem to have been optimistic about its outcome, but there is conflicting evidence. (For example, both Edward Grey and Theobald von Bethmann Hollweg made well-known gloomy predictions, but it is unclear whether these statements accurately reflected their considered judgments. In addition, quantitative analysis of the available internal mem-

oranda indicates pessimism, although there are problems concerning the methodology employed.)

May argues that the analyses of the intentions of the adversaries during this period were more accurate than the analyses of their capabilities, but even the former were questionable. Some of the judgments of July 1914 were proven incorrect—for example, the German expectation that Britain would remain neutral and Germany's grander hopes of keeping France and even Russia out of the war. Furthermore, the broader assumptions underlying the diplomacy of the period may also have been in error. Most important on the German side was not an image of a particular country as the enemy, but its basic belief that the ensuing events would lead to either "world power or decline." For the members of the Triple Entente, and particularly Great Britain, the central question was German intentions, so brilliantly debated in Eyre Crowe's memorandum and Thomas Sanderson's rebuttal to it. We still cannot be sure whether the answer which guided British policy was correct.   7

The list of misperceptions preceding World War II is also impressive. Capabilities again were misjudged, although not as badly as in the previous era. Few people expected the blitzkrieg to bring France down; the power of strategic bombardment was greatly overestimated; the British exaggerated the vulnerability of the German economy, partly because they thought that it was stretched taut at the start of the war. Judgments of intention were even less accurate. The appeasers completely misread Hitler; the anti-appeasers failed to see that he could not be stopped without a war. For his part, Hitler underestimated his adversaries' determination. During the summer of 1939 he doubted whether Britain would fight and, in the spring of 1940, expected her to make peace.   8

It might also be noted that in both cases the combatants paid insufficient attention to and made incorrect judgments about the behavior of neutrals. To a large extent, World War I was decided by the American entry and World War II by the involvement of the Soviet Union and the United States. But we cannot generalize from these two examples to say that states are prone to make optimistic estimates concerning the role of neutrals; it may be equally true that pessimistic judgments may lead states to remain at peace, and we would have no way of determining the validity of such assessments.   9

Did the Misperceptions Matter?

But did these misperceptions cause the wars? Which if any of them, had they been corrected, would have led to a peaceful outcome? In attempting to respond to such questions, we should keep in mind that they are hypothetical and so do not permit conclusive answers. . . .   10

Not all misperceptions have significant consequences.   11

12   If Britain and France had understood Hitler, they would have fought much earlier, when the balance was in their favor and victory could have been relatively quick and easy. (Managing the postwar world might have been difficult, however, especially if others—including the Germans—held a more benign image of Hitler.) If Hitler had understood his adversaries, the situation would have been much more dangerous since he might have devised tactics that would have allowed him to fight on more favorable terms. But on either of these assumptions, war still would have been inevitable; both sides preferred to fight rather than make the concessions that would have been necessary to maintain peace.

13   The case of 1914 is not as clear. I suspect that the misperceptions of intentions in July, although fascinating, were not crucial. The Germans probably would have gone to war even if they had known that they would have had to fight all of the members of the Triple Entente. The British misjudgment of Germany—if it were a misjudgment—was more consequential, but even on this point the counterfactual question is hard to answer. Even if Germany did not seek domination, the combination of her great power, restlessness, and paranoia made her a menace. Perhaps a British policy based on a different image of Germany might have successfully appeased the Germans—to use the term in the older sense—but Britain could not have afforded to see Germany win another war in Europe, no matter what goals it sought.

14   Capabilities were badly misjudged, but even a correct appreciation of the power of the defense might not have changed the outcome of the July crisis. The "crisis instability" created by the belief that whoever struck first would gain a major advantage made the war hard to avoid once the crisis was severe, but may not have been either a necessary or a sufficient condition for the outbreak of the fighting. . . .

15   Had the participants realized not only that the first offensive would not end the war, but also that the fighting would last for four punishing years, they might well have held back. Had they known what the war would bring, the kaiser, the emperor, and the czar presumably might have bluffed or sought a limited war, but they would have preferred making concessions to joining a general struggle. The same was probably true for the leaders of Britain and France, and certainly would have been true had they known the long-term consequences of the war. In at least one sense, then, World War I was caused by misperception.

Models of Conflict

16   Two possible misperceptions of an adversary are largely the opposites of each other, and each is linked to an important argument about the

causes of conflict. On the one hand, wars can occur if aggressors underestimate the willingness of status quo powers to fight (the World War II model); on the other hand, wars can also result if two states exaggerate each other's hostility when their differences are in fact bridgeable (the spiral or World War I model). These models only approximate the cases that inspired them. As noted earlier, World War II would have occurred even without this perceptual error, and the judgments of intentions before 1914 may have been generally accurate and, even if they were not, may not have been necessary for the conflict to have erupted. Nevertheless, the models are useful for summarizing two important sets of dynamics.

The World War II model in large part underlies deterrence theory. The main danger which is foreseen is that of an aggressive state which underestimates the resolve of the status quo powers. The latter may inadvertently encourage this misperception by errors of their own—for example, they may underestimate the aggressor's hostility and propose compromises that are taken as evidence of weakness. In the spiral model, by contrast, the danger is that each side will incorrectly see the other as a menace to its vital interests and will inadvertently encourage this belief by relying on threats to prevent war, thereby neglecting the pursuit of agreement and conciliation. . . . 17

It is clear that states can either underestimate or overestimate the aggressiveness of their adversaries and that either error can lead to war. Although one issue raised by these twin dangers is not central to our discussion here, it is so important that it should at least be noted. If the uncertainty about others' intentions cannot be eliminated, states should design policies that will not fail disastrously even if they are based on incorrect assumptions. States should try to construct a policy of deterrence which will not set off spirals of hostility if existing political differences are in fact bridgeable; the policy should also be designed to conciliate without running the risk that the other side, if it is aggressive, will be emboldened to attack. Such a policy requires the state to combine firmness, threats, and an apparent willingness to fight with reassurances, promises, and a credible willingness to consider the other side's interests. But the task is difficult, and neither decision-makers nor academics have fully come to grips with it. . . . 18

The existence of a spiral process does not prove the applicability of the spiral model, for increasing tension, hostility, and violence can be a reflection of the underlying conflict, not a cause of it. For example, conflict between the United States and Japan increased steadily throughout the 1930s, culminating in the American oil embargo in 1941 and the Japanese attack on Pearl Harbor four months later. Misperceptions were common, but the spiral model should not be used to explain these 19 events because the escalating exchange of threats and actions largely revealed rather than created the incompatibility of goals. Japan preferred to risk defeat rather than forego dominance of China; the United States preferred to fight rather than see Japan reach its goal. . . .

20   Furthermore, even if the initial conflict of interest does not justify a war and it is the process of conflict itself which generates the impulse to fight, misperception may not be the crucial factor. The very fact that states contest an issue raises the stakes because influence and reputation are involved. To retreat after having expended prestige and treasure, if not blood, is psychologically more painful than retreating at the start; it is also more likely to have much stronger domestic and international repercussions. . . .

Assessing Hostile Intent

21   On balance, it seems that states are more likely to overestimate the hostility of others than to underestimate it. States are prone to exaggerate the reasonableness of their own positions and the hostile intent of others; indeed, the former process feeds the latter. Statesmen, wanting to think well of themselves and their decisions, often fail to appreciate others' perspectives, and so greatly underestimate the extent to which their actions can be seen as threats.

22   When their intentions are peaceful, statesmen think that others will understand their motives and therefore will not be threatened by the measures that they are taking in their own self-defense. Richard Perle, former assistant secretary of defense, once said that if we are in doubt about Soviet intentions, we should build up our arms. He explained that if the Russians are aggressive, the buildup will be needed, and, if they are not, the only consequence will be wasted money. Similarly, when United States troops were moving toward the Yalu River, Secretary of State Dean Acheson said that there was no danger that the Chinese would intervene in an effort to defend themselves because they understood that we were not a threat to them. Exceptions, such as the British belief in the 1930s that German hostility was based largely on fear of encirclement and the Israeli view before the 1973 war that Egypt feared attack, are rare. (The British and the Israeli perceptions were partly generated by the lessons they derived from their previous wars.)

23   This bias also operates in retrospect, when states interpret the other side's behavior after the fact. Thus American leaders, believing that China had no reason to be alarmed by the movement of troops toward the Yalu, assumed the only explanation for Chinese intervention in the Korean War was its unremitting hostility to the United States. India, although clearly seeing the Chinese point of view in 1950, saw the Chinese attack on her in 1962 as unprovoked, and so concluded that fu-

ture cooperation was impossible. Similarly, although all Westerners, even those who could empathize with the Soviet Union, understand how the invasion of Afghanistan called up a strong reaction, Soviet leaders apparently did not and instead saw the Western response as "part of a hostile design that would have led to the same actions under any circumstances." . . .

People tend to overperceive hostility because they pay closest atten-   24
tion to dramatic events. Threatening acts often achieve high visibility because they consist of instances like crises, occupation of foreign territory, and the deployment of new weapons. Cooperative actions, by contrast, often call less attention to themselves because they are not dramatic and can even be viewed as nonevents. . . .

Misperception, Commitment, and Change

In a situation that is similar to the game of chicken (that is, any outcome,   25
including surrender, would be better than war), war should not occur as long as both sides are even minimally rational and maintain control over their own behavior. Both sides may bluster and bluff, but it will make no sense for either of them to initiate all-out conflict. Each side will try to stand firm and so make the other back down; the most obvious danger would result from the mistaken belief that the other will retreat and that it is therefore safe to stand firm.

But if both sides maintain control, war can occur only if either or both   26
sides become irrevocably committed to acting on their misperception. In other words, so long as either state retains its freedom of action, war can be avoided because that state can back down at the last minute. But commitment can inhibit this flexibility, and that, of course is its purpose. Standard bargaining logic shows that if one side persuades the other that it is committed to standing firm, the other will have no choice but to retreat. What is of concern here is that this way of seeking to avoid war can make it more likely.

Whether a commitment—and indeed any message—is perceived as   27
intended (or perceived at all) depends not only on its clarity and plausibility, but also on how it fits with the recipient's cognitive predispositions. Messages which are inconsistent with a person's beliefs about international politics and other actors are not likely to be perceived the way the sender intended. For example, shortly before the Spanish-American War President William McKinley issued what he thought was a strong warning to Spain to make major concessions over Cuba or face American military intervention. But the Spanish were worried primarily not about an American declaration of war, but about American aid for the Cuban rebels, and so they scanned the president's speech with this problem in mind. They therefore focused on sections of the speech

that McKinley regarded as relatively unimportant and passed quickly over the paragraphs that he thought were vital.

28   Furthermore, the state sending the message of commitment is likely to assume that it has been received. Thus one reason the United States was taken by surprise when the Soviet Union put missiles into Cuba was that it had assumed that the Soviets understood that such action was unacceptable. Statesmen, like people in their everyday lives, find it difficult to realize that their own intentions, which seem clear to them, can be obscure to others. The problem is magnified because the belief that the message has been received and understood as it was intended will predispose the state to interpret ambiguous information as indicating that the other side does indeed understand its commitment.

Psychological Commitment and Misperception

29   Misperception can lead to war not only through mistaken beliefs about the impact of the state's policy of commitment on others, but also through the impact of commitment on the state. We should not forget the older definition of the term commitment, which is more psychological than tactical. People and states become committed to policies not only by staking their bargaining reputations on them, but by coming to believe that their policies are morally justified and politically necessary. For example, the process of deciding that a piece of territory warrants a major international dispute and the effort that is involved in acting on this policy can lead a person to see the territory as even more valuable than he had originally thought. Furthermore, other members of the elite and the general public may become aroused, with the result that a postcommitment retreat will not only feel more costly to the statesman; it may actually be more costly in terms of its effect on his domestic power. . . .

Conclusion

30   First, although war can occur in the absence of misperception, in fact misperception almost always accompanies it. To say that statesmen's beliefs about both capabilities and intentions are usually badly flawed is not to say that they are foolish. Rather, errors are inevitable in light of the difficulty of assessing technological and organizational capabilities, the obstacles to inferring others' intentions correctly, the limitations on people's abilities to process information, and the need to avoid excessively painful choices.

31   Second, to say that misperceptions are common is not to specify their content. Statesmen can either overestimate or underestimate the other side's capabilities and its hostility. Wars are especially likely to occur when a state simultaneously underestimates an adversary's strength

and exaggerates its hostility. In many cases, however, estimates of capabilities are the product of a policy, not the foundation on which it is built. Policy commitments can influence evaluations as well as be driven by them. Others' hostility can also be overestimated or underestimated and, although exceptions abound, the former error seems more common than the latter. Similarly, more often than falling into the trap of incorrectly believing that other statesmen are just like themselves, decision-makers frequently fail to empathize with the adversary. That is, they tend to pay insufficient attention to constraints and pressures faced by their opponent, including those generated by the decision-maker's own state.

Third, objective analyses of the international system which are so popular among political scientists are not likely to provide a complete explanation for the outbreak of most wars. To historians who are accustomed to explanations which rely heavily on reconstructing the world as the statesmen saw it, this reality will not come as a surprise. But I would also argue that such reconstructions can both build and utilize generalizations about how people perceive information. Although some perceptions are random and idiosyncratic, many others are not. We know that decision-makers, like people in their everyday lives, are strongly driven by the beliefs that they hold, the lessons that they have learned from history, and the hope of being able to avoid painful choices. **32**

Even if these generalizations are correct, any single case can be an exception. . . . It is particularly important for statesmen to realize the ways in which common perceptual processes can lead to conclusions that are not only incorrect, but also extremely dangerous. **33**

Why Men Rebel

TED GURR

It should be apparent at this point that there is no single overarching explanation for human violence, applicable in all its dimensions: personal, societal, and international. Nonetheless, a legitimate goal of all science is to incorporate the largest amount of facts into the smallest number of hypotheses, each as simple as possible. In this regard, political scientist Ted Gurr has made a major contribution, attempting to identify a simple underlying reason for a wide array of violent behavior. His theory of *relative deprivation* is notable as a simple yet general theory of civil violence, one that is—at least in principle—testable, and that incorporates previous work on sociopsychological causes of violence, especially frustration-aggression theory.

Professor Gurr's approach is academic and "value-neutral"—that is, it seeks to understand a phenomenon (in this case, violence) rather than to promote a particular ideology. Nonetheless, it also might shed some light on violence as an act that can be both personal and political: "It is organized violence on the top," wrote anarchist and political radical Emma Goldman, "which creates individual violence at the bottom. It is the accumulated indignation against organized wrong, organized injustice, which drives the political offender to act."

1   The institutions, persons, and policies of rulers have inspired the violent wrath of their nominal subjects throughout the history of organized political life. A survey of the histories of European states and empires, spanning twenty-four centuries, shows that they averaged only four peaceful years for each year of violent disturbances. Modern nations have no better record: between 1961 and 1968 some form of violent civil conflict reportedly occurred in 114 of the world's 121 larger nations and colonies. Most acts of group violence have negligible effects on political life; but some have been enormously destructive of human life and corrosive of political institutions. Ten of the world's thirteen most deadly conflicts in the past 160 years have been civil wars and rebellions; since 1945, violent attempts to overthrow governments have been more common than national elections. The counterpoise to this grim record is the fact that political violence has sometimes led to the creation of new and more satisfying political communities. The consequences of the American, Turkish, Mexican, and Russian revolutions testify in different ways to the occasional beneficence of violence.

2   In this study political violence refers to all collective attacks within a political community against the political regime, its actors—including competing political groups as well as incumbents—or its policies. The concept represents a set of events, a common property of which is the actual or threatened use of violence, but the explanation is not limited to that property. The concept subsumes revolution, ordinarily defined as fundamental sociopolitical change accomplished through violence. It also includes guerrilla wars, coups d'état, rebellions, and riots. Political violence is in turn subsumed under "force," the use or threat of violence by any party or institution to attain ends within or outside the political order. The definition is not based on a prejudgment that political violence is undesirable. Like the uses of violence qua force by the state, specific acts of political violence can be good, bad, or neutral according to the viewpoint of the observer. Participants in political violence may value it as a means of expressing political demands or opposing undesirable policies. Limited violence also can be useful for rulers and for a political system generally, especially as an expression of social malaise when other means for making demands are inadequate. Ethical judg-

ments are held in abeyance in this study to avoid dictating its conclusions. But it does not require an ethical judgment to observe that intense violence is destructive: even if some political violence is valued by both citizens and rulers, the greater its magnitude the less efficiently a political system fulfills its other functions. Violence generally consumes men and goods, it seldom enhances them. . . .

Political scientists might be expected to have a greater concern with political violence than others. Authoritative coercion in the service of the state is a crucial concept in political theory and an issue of continuing dispute. Some have identified the distinctive characteristic of the state as its monopoly of physical coercion. Max Weber, for example, wrote that violence is a "means specific' to the state and that "the right of physical violence is assigned to all other associations or individuals only to the extent permitted by the state; it is supposed to be the exclusive source of the 'right' to use violence." Thomas Hobbes, dismayed by the brutish anarchy of men living outside the restraint of commonwealths, conceived the sovereign's control of coercion to be the foundation of the state and the social condition. . . . 3

The outlines of the theory can now be sketched briefly. The primary causal sequence in political violence is first the development of discontent, second the politicization of that discontent, and finally its actualization in violent action against political objects and actors. Discontent arising from the perception of relative deprivation is the basic, instigating condition for participants in collective violence. The linked concepts of discontent and deprivation comprise most of the psychological states implicit or explicit in such theoretical notions about the causes of violence as frustration, alienation, drive and goal conflicts, exigency, and strain. . . . 4

Relative deprivation is defined as a perceived discrepancy between men's value expectations and their value capabilities. Value expectations are the goods and conditions of life to which people believe they are rightfully entitled. Value capabilities are the goods and conditions they think they are capable of attaining or maintaining, given the social means available to them. Societal conditions that increase the average level or intensity of expectations without increasing capabilities increase the intensity of discontent. Among the general conditions that have such effects are the value gains of other groups and the promise of new opportunities. Societal conditions that decrease men's average value position without decreasing their value expectations similarly increase deprivation, hence the intensity of discontent. The inflexibility of value stocks in a society, short-term deterioration in a group's conditions of life, and limitations of its structural, opportunities have such effects. . . . 5

We need concepts and hypotheses better suited to analyzing the social and psychological transactions that provide the impetus to political violence among members of a collectivity. "Relative deprivation" (RD) 6 is the term used . . . to denote the tension that develops from a discrepancy between the "ought" and the "is" of collective value satisfaction, and that disposes men to violence. . . .

Relative Deprivation Defined

Hypothesis

7   The potential for collective violence varies strongly with the intensity and scope of relative deprivation among members of a collectivity.

8   *Relative deprivation* (RD) is defined as actors' perception of discrepancy between their value expectations and their value capabilities. Value expectations are the goods and conditions of life to which people believe they are rightfully entitled. Value capabilities are the goods and conditions they think they are capable of getting and keeping. (These concepts are more precisely defined below.) The emphasis of the hypothesis is on the perception of deprivation; people may be subjectively deprived with reference to their expectations even though an objective observer might not judge them to be in want. Similarly, the existence of what the observer judges to be abject poverty or "absolute deprivation" is not necessarily thought to be unjust or irremediable by those who experience it. . . .

9   The *intensity* of RD is the extent of negative affect that is associated with its perception, or in other words the sharpness of discontent or anger to which it gives rise. . . .

10   *Potential for collective violence,* the dependent variable of the hypothesis stated at the outset of this section, is defined as the scope and intensity of the disposition among members of a collectivity to take violent action against others. . . .

11   The frustration-aggression and the related threat-aggression mechanisms provide the basic motivational link between RD and the potential for collective violence. They are not inconsistent with the presence of learned and purposive elements in acts of individual and collective violence, however. Men feel deprived with respect to what they have learned to value and to what they have learned to do. The beliefs and symbols that determine the timing, forms, and objects of violence are learned. If their anger is powerful and persistent, men can employ much reason and inventiveness in devising ways to give it violent expression. Some such men may learn to value violence for its own sake. But much of this learning takes place after anger has already been aroused; individuals who are dispassionately violent often are using techniques that proved useful and satisfying in response to past frustrations.

12   There also is an evident sense of purpose among many of the participants in most outbreaks of collective violence, in the sense that they expect violent action to enhance their value position. Revolutionary leaders put their followers' anger to their purpose of seizing power;

rioters take advantage of disorder to loot stores for food and furniture; demonstrators hope to persuade their rulers to take remedial action. The nature and strength of these purposes are major determinants of the form and tactics of collective violence. But in most instances they appear to reinforce or channel the impetus to violence, and are infrequently an autonomous motive for violence. . . .

For Aristotle the principal cause of revolution is the aspiration for eco-   13
nomic or political equality on the part of the common people who lack it, and the aspiration of oligarchs for greater inequality than they have, i.e. a discrepancy in both instances between what people have of political and economic goods relative to what they think is justly theirs. . . .

Almost all theories that purport to explain violent collective behav-   14
ior assign a central place to a variable or concept that generally and often specifically resembles RD as it is defined here. Some salient characteristics of the RD variable are not necessarily incorporated in these other concepts, however. Some of them, particularly those making use of "want/get" formulations, make no reference to the justifiability or intensity of men's value expectations, nor to the theoretical desirability of taking into account both actual and anticipated discrepancies between goals and attainments. Moreover, while many of them specify by illustration the kinds of societal and political conditions that constitute the variable or increase its magnitude, few include specific propositions about its determinants, and only some suggest categories for classifying the variable's manifestations. Finally, many theories do not provide a motivational rationale for the causal connection they propose between the variables and the violent events toward which it is supposed to dispose men. . . .

There is not much support here for the view that political violence is   15
primarily a recourse of vicious, criminal, deviant, ignorant, or undersocialized people. Men and women of every social background, acting in the context of every kind of social group on an infinite variety of motives, have resorted to violence against their rulers. Nor is political violence "caused" by pernicious doctrines, or at least by doctrines alone. Discontented men are much more susceptible to conversion to new beliefs than contented men. Not all new beliefs provide justifications for violence, and most that do are derived from peoples' own cultural and historical experience rather than alien sources. The belief that some kinds of social arrangements or political institutions are intrinsically immune from violence or capable of satisfying all human desires is only a partial truth. Disruptive violence can and has occurred in every twentieth-century political community. No pattern of coercive control, however intense and consistent, is likely to deter permanently all enraged men from violence, except genocide. No extant or utopian pattern of social and political engineering seems capable of satisfying all human aspirations and

resolving all human discontents, short of biological modification of the species. . . .

16   Some conventional wisdom about the means to the resolution of violent conflict is also fallacious. Coercion alone is demonstrably ineffective, in the long run if not the short, because on balance it is more likely to inspire resistance than compliance. The assumption that discontent has primarily physical origins, hence that satisfaction of material aspirations is its cure, is no more accurate. Men aspire to many other conditions of life than physical well-being, not the least of which are security, status, a sense of community, and the right to manage their own affairs. If basic physical needs are met, provision for these aspirations is at least as important as increased material well-being for minimizing violence. If men have substantially more physical resources than status or freedom, they may well use the former to gain the latter, by violent means if necessary. There also is a fallacy in the assumption that all wants must be satisfied to minimize discontent. Discontent is not a function of the discrepancy between what men want and what they have, but between what they want and what they believe they are capable of attaining. If their means are few or threatened, they are likely to revolt; if they obtain new means they can work to satisfy their wants. Concessions also can have unintended effects, however. Temporary palliatives are likely to reinforce a return to violence once their narcotic effect wears off. If men fight to preserve what they have, concessions that remove the threat to it are sufficient. If they rebel to satisfy new or intensified expectations, the only effective concession is to provide them with means adequate to those expectations.

17   Men's resort to political violence is in part unreasoning, but does not occur without reason. Ignorance is almost always among its causes: sometimes ignorance of its consequences by those who resort to it, more often ignorance by those who create and maintain the social conditions that inspire it. But political violence is comprehensible, which should make it neither necessary nor inevitable, but capable of resolution.

The Wretched of the Earth

FRANZ FANON

There is a significant difference between studying, analyzing, and theorizing about something on one hand, and feeling it in your bones on the other. For this reason, we follow Ted Gurr's important theoretical contribution with the personally intense revolutionary writing of Franz Fanon. Born in Martinique, educated in France, Fanon was a psychiatrist who associated himself particularly with the Algerian struggle for independence. Fanon's writings described the possible functioning of violence as a kind of "social catharsis." Although Fanon was primarily concerned with the liberation of people from colonialism and became one of the classic spokespeople among revolutionary ideologists, his work can be more broadly construed as expressing the anger of the "wretched of the earth" everywhere. Thus, for *decolonization*, substitute *freedom*; for *colonials*, substitute *impoverished, downtrodden,* or *underclass*; and for *settlers*, substitute *wealthy, privileged,* or *upper classes*.

Although it is discomfiting to think of violence as cleansing or purifying, as Fanon does, any attempt to understand violence must come to terms with the fact that this perception—whether conscious or not—is widely shared among potentially violent activists, as well as just plain people.

The naked truth of decolonization evokes for us the searing bullets and 1 bloodstained knives which emanate from it. For if the last shall be first, this will only come to pass after a murderous and decisive struggle between the two protagonists. That affirmed intention to place the last at the head of things, and to make them climb at a pace (too quickly, some say) the well-known steps which characterize an organized society, can only triumph if we use all means to turn the scale, including, of course, that of violence.

You do not turn any society, however primitive it may be, upside 2 down with such a program if you have not decided from the very beginning, that is to say from the actual formulation of that program, to overcome all the obstacles that you will come across in so doing. The native who decides to put the program into practice, and to become its moving force, is ready for violence at all times. From birth it is clear to him that this narrow world, strewn with prohibitions, can only be called in question by absolute violence. . . .

The town belonging to the colonized people, or at least the native 3 town, the Negro village, the medina, the reservation, is a place of ill fame, peopled by men of evil repute. They are born there, it matters little where or how; they die there, it matters not where, nor how. It is a world without spaciousness; men live there on top of each other, and their huts are built one on top of the other. The native town is a hungry town, starved of bread, of meat, of shoes, of coal, of light. The native town is a crouching village, a town on its knees, a town wallowing in the mire. It is a town of niggers and dirty Arabs. The look that the native turns on the settler's town is a look of lust, a look of envy; it expresses his dreams of possession—all manner of possession: to sit at the settler's table, to sleep in the settler's bed, with his wife if possible. The colonized man is an envious man. And this the settler knows very well; when their glances meet he ascertains bitterly, always on the defensive, "They want to take our place." It is true, for there is no native who does not dream at least once a day of setting himself up in the settler's place. . . .

4   The settler's work is to make even dreams of liberty impossible for the native. The native's work is to imagine all possible methods for destroying the settler. On the logical plane, the Manicheism of the settler produces a Manicheism of the native. To the theory of the "absolute evil of the native" the theory of the "absolute evil of the settler" replies.

5   The appearance of the settler has meant in the terms of syncretism the death of the aboriginal society, cultural lethargy, and the petrification of individuals. For the native, life can only spring up again out of the rotting corpse of the settler. This then is the correspondence, term by term, between the two trains of reasoning.

6   But it so happens that for the colonized people this violence, because it constitutes their only work, invests their characters with positive and creative qualities. The practice of violence binds them together as a whole, since each individual forms a violent link in the great chain, a part of the great organism of violence which has surged upward in reaction to the settler's violence in the beginning. The groups recognize each other and the future nation is already indivisible. The armed struggle mobilizes the people, that is to say, it throws them in one way and in one direction.

7   The mobilization of the masses, when it arises out of the war of liberation, introduces into each man's consciousness the ideas of a common cause, of a national destiny, and of a collective history. In the same way the second phase, that of the building-up of the nation, is helped on by the existence of this cement which has been mixed with blood and anger. Thus we come to a fuller appreciation of the originality of the words used in these underdeveloped countries. During the colonial period the people are called upon to fight against oppression; after national liberation, they are called upon to fight against poverty, illiteracy, and underdevelopment. The struggle, they say, goes on. The people realize that life is an unending contest. . . .

8   At the level of individuals, violence is a cleansing force. It frees the native from his inferiority complex and from his despair and inaction; it makes him fearless and restores his self-respect. Even if the armed struggle has been symbolic and the nation is demobilized through a rapid movement of decolonization, the people have the time to see that the liberation has been the business of each and all and that the leader has no special merit. From thence comes that type of aggressive reticence with regard to the machinery of protocol which young govern-

ments quickly show. When the people have taken violent part in the national liberation they will allow no one to set themselves up as "liberators." They show themselves to be jealous of the results of their action and take good care not to place their future, their destiny, or the fate of their country in the hands of a living god. Yesterday they were completely irresponsible; today they mean to understand everything and make all decisions. Illuminated by violence, the consciousness of the people rebels against any pacification.

Man, the State and War

KENNETH WALTZ

We close this chapter with a selection from one of the most wide ranging and influential attempts by a political scientist to come to grips with organized violence, specifically war. In his book *Man, the State and War,* Kenneth Waltz examined what he called three images that dominate thinking about the causes of war: human nature (the first image), the characteristics of political states (the second image), and the nature of the international system itself (the third image). Waltz went on to relate these concepts to some of the classic thinkers of political philosophy, notably Spinoza, Kant, and Rousseau. He concluded that all three images of causation are valid but attributed special importance to the third.

Interestingly, political conservatives are especially likely to focus on the first image, maintaining that war—and violence generally—derives from deep and presumably irrevocable human failings (which requires powerful mechanisms of control such as police and the military), while progressives and liberals generally give particular attention to the second, emphasizing the need for political and socioeconomic reform. Waltz's third image—anarchy in the international or state system—has implications that are potentially congenial for both the political left and the right: the former uses it to argue for world government, or, at minimum, increased influence for international organizations such as the United Nations, whereas the latter point to the same image as demonstrating the need for powerful and effective military forces.

Asking who won a given war, someone has said, is like asking who won   1
the San Francisco earthquake. That in wars there is no victory but only varying degrees of defeat is a proposition that has gained increasing acceptance in the twentieth century. But are wars also akin to earthquakes

in being natural occurrences whose control or elimination is beyond the wit of man? Few would admit that they are, yet attempts to eliminate war, however nobly inspired and assiduously pursued, have brought little more than fleeting moments of peace among states. There is an apparent disproportion between effort and product, between desire and result. . . .

2   Why does God, if he is all-knowing and all-powerful, permit the existence of evil? So asks the simple Huron in Voltaire's tale, and thereby confounds the learned men of the church. The theodicy problem in its secular version—man's explanation to himself of the existence of evil—is as intriguing and as perplexing. Disease and pestilence, bigotry and rape, theft and murder, pillage and war, appear as constants in world history. Why is this so? Can one explain war and malevolence in the same way? Is war simply mass malevolence, and thus an explanation of malevolence an explanation of the evils to which men in, society are prey? Many have thought so.

> For though it were granted us by divine indulgence to be exempt from all that can be harmful to us from without [writes John Milton], yet the perverseness of our folly is so bent, that we should never cease hammering out of our own hearts, as it were out of a flint, the seeds and sparkles of new misery to ourselves, till all were in a blaze again.

Our miseries are ineluctably the product of our natures. The root of all evil is man, and thus he is himself the root of the specific evil, war. This estimate of cause, widespread and firmly held by many as an article of faith, has been immensely influential. . . .

3   If so, attempts to explain the recurrence of war in terms of, let us say, economic factors, might still be interesting games, but they would be games of little consequence. If it is true, as Dean Swift once said, that "the very same principle that influences a bully to break the windows of a whore who has jilted him, naturally stirs up a great prince to raise mighty armies, and dream of nothing but sieges, battles, and victories," then the reasons given by princes for the wars they have waged are mere rationalizations covering a motivation they may not themselves have perceived and could not afford to state openly if they had. . . .

4   There are many who have agreed with Milton that men must look to man in order to understand social and political events, but who differ on what man's nature is, or can become. There are many others who, in effect, quarrel with the major premise. Does man make society in his image or does his society make him? . . .

5   Man's behavior, his very nature, which some have taken as cause, is, according to Rousseau, in great part a product of the society in which

he lives. And society, he avers, is inseparable from political organization. In the absence of an organized power, which as a minimum must serve as the adjudicating authority, it is impossible for men to live together with even a modicum of peace. The study of society cannot be separated from the study of government, or the study of man from either. Rousseau, like Plato, believes that a bad polity makes men bad, and a good polity makes them good. This is not to say that the state is the potter and man a lump of clay posing no resistance to the shape the artist would impart. There are, as Rousseau recognized, similarities among men wherever they may live. There are also differences, and the search for causes is an attempt to explain these differences. The explanation of consequence—whether one is worried about the recurrence of theft or of war—is to be found in studying the varying social relations of men, and this in turn requires the study of politics. . . .

Following Rousseau's lead in turn raises questions. . . . As men live in   6
states, so states exist in a world of states. If we now confine our attention to the question of why wars occur, shall we emphasize the role of the state, with its social and economic content as well as its political form, or shall we concentrate primarily on what is sometimes called the society of states? Again one may say strike the word "or" and worry about both, but many have emphasized either the first or the second, which helps to explain the discrepant conclusions reached. Those who emphasize the first in a sense run parallel to Milton. He explains the ills of the world by the evil in man; they explain the great ill of war by the evil qualities of some or of all states. The statement is then often reversed: If bad states make wars, good states would live at peace with one another. With varying degrees of justification this view can be attributed to Plato and Kant, to nineteenth-century liberals and revisionist socialists. They agree on the principle involved, though they differ in their descriptions of good states as well as on the problem of bringing about their existence. . . .

But what of those who incline to a different estimate of major causes?   7
"Now people," President Dwight Eisenhower has said, "don't want conflict—people in general. It is only, I think, mistaken leaders that grow too belligerent and believe that people really want to fight." Though apparently not all people want peace badly enough, for, on a different occasion, he had this to say: "If the mothers in every land could teach their children to understand the homes and hopes of children in every other land—in America, in Europe, in the Near East, in Asia the cause of peace in the world would indeed be nobly served." . . .

One may seek in political philosophy answers to the question: Where   8
are the major causes of war to be found? The answers are bewildering

in their variety and in their contradictory qualities. To make this variety manageable, the answers can be ordered under the following three headings: within man, within the structure of the separate states, within the state system. . . .

9   The first image [does] not exclude the influence of the state, but the role of the state [is] introduced as a consideration less important than, and to be explained in terms of, human behavior. . . . We say that the state acts when we mean that the people in it act, just as we say that the pot boils when we mean that the water in it boils. . . . To continue the figure: Water running out of a faucet is chemically the same as water in a container, but once the water is in a container, it can be made to "behave" in different ways. It can be turned into steam and used to power an engine, or, if the water is sealed in and heated to extreme temperatures, it can become the instrument of a destructive explosion. Wars would not exist were human nature not what it is, but neither would Sunday schools and brothels, philanthropic organizations and criminal gangs. Since everything is related to human nature, to explain anything one must consider more than human nature. The events to be explained are so many and so varied that human nature cannot possibly be the single determinant. . . .

10   The conclusion is obvious: To understand war and peace political analysis must be used to supplement and order the findings of psychology and sociology. What kind of political analysis is needed? For possible explanations of the occurrence or nonoccurrence of war, one can look to international politics (since war occurs among states), or one can look to the states themselves (since it is in the name of the state that the fighting is actually done). . . .

11   According to the second image, the internal organization of states is the key to understanding war and peace.

12   One explanation of the second-image type is illustrated as follows. War most often promotes the internal unity of each state involved. The state plagued by internal strife may then, instead of waiting for the accidental attack, seek the war that will bring internal peace. . . .

13   Bad states lead to war. As previously said, there is a large and important sense in which this is true. The obverse of this statement, that good states mean peace in the world, is an extremely doubtful proposition. The difficulty, endemic with the second image of international relations, is the same in kind as the difficulty encountered in the first image. There the statement that men make the societies, including the international society, in which they live was criticized not simply as being wrong but as being incomplete. One must add that the societies they live in make men. And it is the same in international relations. The actions of states, or, more accurately, of men acting for states, make up

the substance of international relations. But the international political environment has much to do with the ways in which states behave. The influence to be assigned to the internal structure of states in attempting to solve the war-peace equation cannot be determined until the significance of the international environment has been reconsidered. . . .

With many sovereign states, with no system of law enforceable   14
among them, with each state judging its grievances and ambitions according to the dictates of its own reason or desire—conflict, sometimes leading to war, is bound to occur. To achieve a favorable outcome from such conflict a state has to rely on its own devices, the relative efficiency of which must be its constant concern. This, the idea of the third image, is to be examined [next]. . . . It is not an esoteric idea; it is not a new idea. Thucydides implied it when he wrote that it was "the growth of the Athenian power, which terrified the Lacedaemonians and forced them into war." . . .

A state will use force to attain its goals if, after assessing the prospects   15
for success, it values those goals more than it values the pleasures of peace.. Because each state is the final judge of its own cause, any state may at any time use force to implement its policies. Because any state may at any time use force, all states must constantly be ready either to counter force with force or to pay the cost of weakness. The requirements of state action are, in this view, imposed by the circumstances in which all states exist.

In a manner of speaking, all three images are a part of nature. So fun-   16
damental are man, the state, and the state system in any attempt to understand international relations that seldom does an analyst, however wedded to one image, entirely overlook the other two. Still, emphasis on one image may distort one's interpretation of the others. It is, for example, not uncommon to find those inclined to see the world in terms of either the first or the second image countering the oft-made argument that arms breed not war but security, and possibly even peace, by pointing out that the argument is a compound of dishonest myth, to cover the interests of politicians, armament makers, and others, and honest illusion entertained by patriots sincerely interested in the safety of their states. . . .

Doubling armaments, if everyone does it, makes no state more se-   17
cure and, similarly, that none would be endangered if all military establishments were simultaneously reduced by, say, 50 percent. Putting aside the thought that the arithmetic is not necessarily an accurate reflection of what the situation would be, this argument illustrates a supposedly practical application of the first and second images. Whether by educating citizens and leaders of the separate states or by improving the organization of each of them, a condition is sought in

which the lesson here adumbrated becomes the basis for the policies of states. The result?—disarmament, and thus economy, together with peace, and thus security, for all states. If some states display a willingness to pare down their military establishments, other states will be able to pursue similar policies. In emphasizing the interdependence of the policies of all states, the argument pays heed to the third image. The optimism is, however, the result of ignoring some inherent difficulties. . . .

18   Is force or the threat of force used within or among states because some men or states are evil? Perhaps so, but not only for that reason; even good men and good states resort to force occasionally in their dealings. Is war then brought about by the disagreements that exist among states, be they good or bad? Francis I, when asked what differences accounted for the constant wars between him and his brother-in-law Charles V, supposedly answered: "None whatever. We agree perfectly. We both want control of Italy!" Goodness and evil, agreement and disagreement, may or may not lead to war. Then what explains war among states? Rousseau's answer is really that war occurs because there is nothing to prevent it. Among states as among men there is no automatic adjustment of interests. In the absence of a supreme authority, there is then, constant possibility that conflicts will be settled by force. . . .

19   According to the third image, there is a constant possibility of war in a world in which there are two or more states each seeking to promote a set of interests and having no agency above them upon which they can rely for protection. But many liberals and socialist revisionists deny, or at least minimize, the possibility that wars would occur in a world of political or social democracies. An understanding of the third image makes it clear that the expectation would be justified only if the minimum interest of states in preserving themselves became the maximum interest of all of them—and each could rely fully upon the steadfast adherence to this definition by all of the others. Stating the condition makes apparent the utopian quality of liberal and socialist expectations. The criticism could be extended by questioning as well their interpretations of the first image. But the point as it applies here—that emphasizing one image frequently distorts, though it seldom excludes, the other two—is perhaps sufficiently clear. It may profit us more to shift out attention briefly to similar effects that may follow from concentration upon the third image. . . .

20   It is a final explanation because it does not hinge on accidental causes—irrationalities in men, defects in states—but upon his theory of the framework within which *any* accident can bring about a war. That state A wants certain things that it can get only by war does not explain

war. Such a desire may or may not lead to war. My wanting a million dollars does not cause me to rob a bank, but if it were easier to rob banks, such desires would lead to much more bank robbing. This does not alter the fact that some people will and some will not attempt to rob banks no matter what the law enforcement situation is. We still have to look to motivation and circumstance in order to explain individual acts. Nevertheless one can predict that, other things being equal, a weakening of law enforcement agencies will lead to an increase in crime. From this point of view it is social structure—institutionalized restraints and institutionalized methods of altering and adjusting interests—that counts. And it counts in a way different from the ways usually associated with the word "cause." What causes a man to rob a bank are such things as the desire for money, a disrespect for social proprieties, a certain boldness. But if obstacles to the operation of these causes are built sufficiently high, nine out of ten would-be bank robbers will live their lives peacefully plying their legitimate trades. If the framework is to be called cause at all, it had best be specified that it is a permissive or underlying cause of war.

Applied to international politics this becomes . . . the proposition that wars occur because there is nothing to prevent them. . . . But the structure of the state system does not directly cause state A to attack state B. Whether or not that attack occurs will depend on a number of special circumstances—location, size, power, interest, type of government, past history and tradition—each of which will influence the actions of both states. If they fight against each other it will be for reasons especially defined for the occasion by each of them. These special reasons become the immediate, or efficient, causes of war. These immediate causes of war are contained in the first and second images. States are motivated to attack each other and to defend themselves by the reason and/or passion of the comparatively few who make policies for states and of the many more who influence the few. Some states, by virtue of their internal conditions, are both more proficient in war and more inclined to put their proficiency to the test. Variations in the factors included in the first and second images are important, indeed crucial, in the making and breaking of periods of peace—the immediate causes of every war must be either the acts of individuals or the acts of states. . . .

The obvious conclusion of a third-image analysis is that world government is the remedy for world war. The remedy, though it may be unassailable in logic, is unattainable in practice. The third image may provide a utopian approach to world politics. It may also provide a realistic approach, and one that avoids the tendency of some realists to attribute the necessary amorality, or even immorality, of world politics to the inherently bad character of man. If everyone's strategy depends upon everyone else's, then the Hitlers determine in part the action, or better, reaction, of those whose ends are worthy and whose means are fastidious. No matter how good their intentions, policy makers must bear in mind the implications of the third image, which can be stated in summary form as follows: Each state pursues its own interests, however defined, in ways it judges best. Force is a means of achieving the external ends of states because there exists no consistent, reliable process of reconciling the conflicts of interest that inevitably arise among similar units in a condition of anarchy. A foreign policy based on this image of international relations is neither moral nor immoral, but embodies merely a reasoned response to the world about us. The third image describes the framework of world politics, but without the first and second images there can be no knowledge of the forces that determine policy; the first and second images describe the forces in world politics, but without the third image it is impossible to assess their importance or predict their results.

SUGGESTIONS FOR FURTHER READING

Barash, David P. *Approaches to Peace.* New York: Oxford University Press, 1999. A useful collection of classic and near-classic statements from the discipline of "peace studies," emphasizing various ways of achieving peace . . . including but not limited to the avoidance of war.

Falk, Richard A. *On Humane Governance.* University Park, PA: Penn State University Press, 1995. A prominent world-order theorist develops his vision of the requirements for a realistic system of peace.

Howard, Michael. *The Causes of War.* Cambridge, MA: Harvard University Press, 1984. A renowned military historian argues that wars are primarily caused by rational calculations of national gain and loss.

Sederberg, Peter. *Fires Within.* New York: HarperCollins, 1994. A well-balanced review of the connection between political violence and revolutionary change.

Stoessinger, John. *Why Nations Go to War.* New York: St. Martin's Press, 1990. A readable yet highly informative study of seven major wars in the twentieth century, with special emphasis on the causative role of leaders' misperceptions.

STUDY QUESTIONS

1. Relate "The Melian Dialogue" to one or more examples from current events.

2. In what ways does the Prisoner's Dilemma oversimplify the processes that might lead to violence? That is, to what extent is the real world more complex than is reflected in this simple example of game theory?

3. Give some examples in which *Realpolitik* would seem to lead to more—or less—violence than an alternative politics based on moral or religious judgments.

4. Is there an irrational component to the arguments put forth by Schelling? Is there a rational component to the misperceptions described by Jervis?

5. Describe situations (current or historical) in which Gurr's concept of relative deprivation would appear to be irrelevant or inappropriate; describe others in which it seems especially apt.

6. In what ways are Fanon's arguments limited to the experience of colonized people subjected to domination by foreigners? In what ways are they generalizable to other situations?

7. See if you can develop a three- or four-part scheme of different images, analogous to Waltz's, that might organize our thinking about either the biology, psychology, sociology, or anthropology of violence.

8. It has been argued that democracies do not make war upon other democracies. Suggest some possible reasons for this assertion, using some of the categories and concepts presented in this chapter.

9. None of the selections in this chapter was directly concerned with the role of differing political ideologies in generating war and armed conflict. Do what you can to explore this question, using some of the categories and concepts presented in this chapter.

10. Look into some of these concepts, and how they might relate to the politics of violence: status-quo versus revisionist states, nationalism, state sovereignty, the security dilemma (whereby enhanced security for one country generates diminished security for its neighbor), and the question of national character.

6

Criminology

Not all criminals are violent (take white-collar crime such as forgery, tax evasion, or passing bad checks). And not all perpetrators of violence are criminals (e.g., soldiers during wartime, more likely considered heroes than evildoers). Nonetheless, criminality and violence go together, not only in the public mind but in real life. When asked to consider the subject of violence, most people think of violent crime.

It may be that if anything, they think of violent crime too much. There is a growing horror of street violence, serial killings, schoolyard shootings, and a supposed (but undocumented) epidemic of juvenile "superpredators," even as the actual statistics for violent crime improved to some extent during the 1990s. To be sure, crime is all too real, and its consequences are terrible. Between February 1996 and May 1999, there were thirty-seven shooting deaths in U.S. schools alone, including fifteen in a notorious event at Columbine High School in Littleton, Colorado (thirteen innocent victims plus the two shooters). And yet, as a proportion of the total U.S. population (260 million), such episodes are wonderfully rare; violent crime may well loom larger in the popular imagination than in actual reality.

At the same time, the United States leads all developed countries in its per capita crime and imprisonment rate, with only the most devoted optimists claiming this is the result of more efficient policing and/or uniquely stringent incarceration policies. Only Russia and apartheid South Africa have been in the same league.

The present focus, on criminology, is a bit of a departure from earlier chapters. Thus, compared to biology, psychology, anthropology, sociology, or political science, criminology is less academic and more narrowly focused. Moreover, it is widely considered an applied subdiscipline of sociology, although, as we will see, criminology connects significantly to the various fields we have already considered . . . as well as to others (notably law) that are not addressed in the present book.

Criminals are widely assumed to be a small but important subgroup of any population, individuals whose deviant behavior is a threat to public safety and well-being. Society has a self-interested obligation to understand these people, to prevent or inhibit their activities whenever possible, and to respond effectively when necessary. "Explanations" for criminality abound . . . as they do for violence generally. Thus, criminals are variously seen to be (1) psychologically unbalanced; (2) greedy, lazy, and manipulative; (3) the products of morally lax environments, notably inadequate exposure to and respect for ethical values; (4) the products of economically deprived environments, leading to a dangerous combination of hopelessness and anger; (5) suffering from inadequate impulse control and/or insufficient intelligence to realize the value of delayed gratification; (6) victims of childhood neglect, abuse, and socialization into a "subculture of violence"; and (7) outcasts and rebels who just don't fit in. This is only a partial list. Criminology's Holy Grail—a unifying theory of the causes and prevention of criminal violence along with practical guidelines on how to deal with offenders—has been elusive, as it has been for those seeking to understand violence more generally.

Historically, we can identify the early period of criminology as its classical school. Before that, crime was indeed punished, but with little if any effort at understanding. The initiator of criminology's classical school, eighteenth-century Italian economist and jurist Cesare Beccaria, urged that society undertake a rational approach to crime. Beccaria emphasized that human behavior was motivated by the desire for pleasure combined with the avoidance of pain and that accordingly, for society to prevent crime, it must be prepared to administer pain in an amount appropriate to balance the pleasure presumably derived from crime. For Beccaria, punishment must not be a simple act of violence, revenge, or caprice, but rather "public, prompt, necessary, the least possible in the given circumstances, proportionate to the crimes, dictated by the laws."

In this belief, Beccaria was joined by British philosopher Jeremy Bentham, founder of *utilitarianism*, a school of thought that emphasized rational goals for society, famously summarized as seeking "the greatest good for the greatest number." Criminals, too, were seen by the utilitarians as fundamentally rational people, choosing criminality when its potential returns exceeded its likely costs. For both utilitarians and classical criminologists, the answer, once again, was to make legal punishment suitable to the offense. As a result, the routine torture of offenders was curtailed and in some places abolished, and corporal punishments were replaced by prison sentences proportionate to the crime. Reformitories and penitentiaries were also initiated, intended to be, as their names implied, places of reformation and penitence instead of retribution.

At about the same time, however, the classical school's core assumption that crime—including violence—is a product of rational human choice was challenged by another perspective, that of *positivism*. Under this view, championed especially by Auguste Comte (the nineteenth-century social scientist widely considered to be one of the founders of sociology), much of human behavior is generated by forces beyond individual control. These include social, economic, and historical factors, such as one's class and level of affluence or poverty; the occurrence of wars, famines, rebellions, industrial innovations; and so on. In addition, biological and psychological considerations were deemed important and, for the most part, unchangeable. Positivism aimed at a rigorously scientific explanation of behavior, including criminal violence.

We have already briefly encountered such biological blunderers as the phrenologists, who sought to predict violent criminal tendencies (among other things), from skull shapes and cranial bumps. Cesare Lambroso, the nineteenth-century "father of criminology," was allied to this camp. Lambroso sought to attribute criminality to "congenital factors," notably large jaws and strong canine teeth, which he considered to be "primitive throwbacks" to a time when people were presumably more carnivorous, savage, and violent.

Fortunately, other schools of thought also developed under the positivist influence. These included the work of Belgian statistician L. A. J. Quetelet, who initiated serious data gathering, and Emile Durkheim, who introduced the important concept of *anomie*, confusion of roles and social norms, which occurs when societies undergo transitions from small scale and rural to large scale, industrial, and impersonal. *Anomic* societies are generally thought to be more prone to deviant behavior, including violence toward oneself (suicide) as well as toward others.

Other theoretical approaches to criminology deserve mention, including (1) the Chicago School, which emphasized the importance of *social ecology*, especially the role of living in certain urban neighborhoods within which poverty is rampant and social institutions are disorganized; (2) a renewed appreciation of the role of interpersonal psychological factors: the extent to which people learn criminality from violent peers, role models, and other failures of acceptable socialization; and finally, (3) a radical tradition, deriving from the work of Karl Marx, that emphasizes *social conflict* and the extent to which competitive capitalism generates social structures that are unequal and exploitative. This in turn is believed to generate potentially violent resistance, especially on the part of marginalized individuals and groups.

As with the metaphor of the blind men and the elephant with which we began this book, it seems likely that no single criminological theory encompasses the complex whole, even as each one may capture a part of the truth.

Crime as Choice

JAMES Q. WILSON AND RICHARD J. HERRNSTEIN

Political ideologies loom large in attitudes toward violent crime, with liberals and progressives more likely to look toward social and economic causes while conservatives emphasize the importance of personal choice and thus, individual responsibility. (The former leads to a focus on improving society as a "cure" for crime; the latter to greater concern with courts, mandatory sentences, and more and larger prisons.) Two especially influential books in the late 1970s presaged the election of Ronald Reagan in 1980 and a shift toward right-wing perspectives on crime: In *Beyond Probation* (Beverly Hills, CA: Sage, 1979), Charles Murray and Louis Cox argued that crime would be more effectively prevented by punishment than by rehabilitation and treatment, and in *Thinking about Crime* (New York: Basic Books, 1975), political scientist James Q. Wilson maintained that rather than being a product of poverty—and hence, correctible by government programs—crime results from a failure to deter would-be offenders. This position implies that social engineering should be limited to guaranteeing that "crime does not pay." This perspective, in turn, represents a return of classical criminology, with its emphasis on the rational actor.

In the following selection, Wilson and psychologist Richard J. Herrnstein argue that people *choose* crime just as they might choose a brand of . toothpaste.

Theories of crime abound. The lay reader will wonder whether any theory can be an improvement on common sense, and the scholarly one will groan at the prospect of yet another theory. But what may be irrelevant to the former and redundant to the latter is, to us, important; for theories, whatever else they may do, direct our attention to some features of the situation and away from others. Much of the confusion about the sources of individual differences in criminality arises, we believe, from bad theories—that is, from views about how the world works that are incomplete and thus lead us to attend to some things but not to others.

For example, the theory that unemployment or economic want causes crime can lead us to look for increases in criminality during economic recessions but to overlook the possibility that crime may also be caused by prosperity (if it loosens the social bonds), by the distribution of income (if it causes social envy), or by some underlying factor that happens to cause both criminality and unemployment. More generally, theories that call attention to the social setting in which crime occurs (such as the attitudes of parents and peers, the perceived costs and benefits of crime, the influence of drugs and television) direct our attention away from preexisting individual traits that make people more or less susceptible to such social factors; by the same token, theories that emphasize the preferences of individuals tend to deemphasize the situational factors that determine how, or even whether, those preferences affect behavior. The quarrels among lay persons and scholars about what causes crime are basically quarrels about the relative importance of those factors that occupy a central place in competing theories. . . .

Crime as Choice: The Theory in Brief

3   Our theory rests on the assumption that people, when faced with a choice, choose the preferred course of action. This assumption is quite weak; it says nothing more than that whatever people choose to do, they choose it because they prefer it. In fact, it is more than weak; without further clarification, it is a tautology. When we say people "choose," we do not necessarily mean that they consciously deliberate about what to do. All we mean is that their behavior is determined by its consequences. A person will do that thing the consequences of which are perceived by him or her to be preferable to the consequences of doing something else. What can save such a statement from being a tautology is how plausibly we describe the gains and losses associated with alternative courses of action and the standards by which a person evaluates those gains and losses.

4   These assumptions are commonplace in philosophy and social science. Philosophers speak of hedonism or utilitarianism, economists of value or utility, and psychologists of reinforcement or reward. We will use the language of psychology, but it should not be hard to translate our terminology into that of other disciplines. Though social scientists differ as to how much behavior can reasonably be described as the result of a choice, all agree that at least some behavior is guided, or even precisely controlled, by things variously termed pleasure, pain, happiness, sorrow, desirability, or the like. Our object is to show how this simple and widely used idea can be used to explain behavior.

5   At any given moment, a person can choose between committing a crime and not committing it (all these alternatives to crime we lump together as "noncrime"). The consequences of committing the crime consist of rewards (what psychologists call "reinforcers") and punishments; the consequences of not committing the crime (i.e., engaging in noncrime) also entail gains and losses. The larger the ratio of the net rewards of crime to the net rewards of noncrime, the greater the tendency

to commit the crime. The net rewards of crime include, obviously, the likely material gains from the crime, but they also include intangible benefits, such as obtaining emotional or sexual gratification, receiving the approval of peers, satisfying an old score against an enemy, or enhancing one's sense of justice. One must deduct from these rewards of crime any losses that accrue immediately—that are, so to speak, contemporaneous with the crime. They include the pangs of conscience, the disapproval of onlookers, and the retaliation of the victim.

The value of noncrimes lies all in the future. It includes the benefits   6
to the individual of avoiding the risk of being caught and punished and, in addition, the benefits of avoiding penalties not controlled by the criminal justice system, such as the loss of reputation or the sense of shame afflicting a person later discovered to have broken the law and the possibility that, being known as a criminal, one cannot get or keep a job.

The value of any reward or punishment associated with either crime   7
or noncrime is, to some degree, uncertain. A would-be burglar can rarely know exactly how much loot he will take away or what its cash value will prove to be. The assaulter or rapist may exaggerate the satisfaction he thinks will follow the assault or the rape. Many people do not know how sharp the bite of conscience will be until they have done something that makes them feel the bite. The anticipated approval of one's buddies may or may not be forthcoming. Similarly, the benefits of noncrime are uncertain. One cannot know with confidence whether one will be caught, convicted, and punished, or whether one's friends will learn about the crime and as a result withhold valued esteem, or whether one will be able to find or hold a job.

Compounding these uncertainties is time. The opportunity to commit   8
a crime may be ready at hand (an open, unattended cash register in a store) or well in the future (a bank that, with planning and preparation, can be robbed). And the rewards associated with noncrime are almost invariably more distant than those connected with crime, perhaps many weeks or months distant. The strength of reinforcers tends to decay over time at rates that differ among individuals. As a result, the extent to which people take into account distant possibilities—a crime that can be committed only tomorrow, or punishment that will be inflicted only in a year—will affect whether they choose crime or noncrime. . . .

Reinforcers

All human behavior is shaped by two kinds of reinforcers: primary and   9
secondary. A primary reinforcer derives its strength from an innate drive, such as hunger or sexual appetite; a secondary reinforcer derives

its strength from learning. The line dividing reinforcers that are innate from those that are learned is hard to draw; and people argue, often passionately, over where it ought to be drawn. When we disagree over whether people are innately altruistic, men are innately more aggressive than women, or mankind is innately warlike or competitive, we are disagreeing over whether behavior responds to primary or to secondary reinforcers.

10   In fact, most reinforcers combine primary and secondary elements. Part of the benefit that comes from eating either bread or spaghetti must derive from the fact that their common ingredient, wheat, satisfies an innate drive—hunger. In this sense, both are primary reinforcers. But bread and spaghetti differ in texture, flavor, and appearance; and the preferences we have for these qualities are in part learned.

11   Because of the constant and universal reinforcing power of money, people are inclined to think of crimes for money gain as more natural, and thus more the product of voluntary choice and rational thought, than crimes involving "senseless" violence or sexual deviance. Stealing is an understandable, if not pardonable, crime; bestiality, "unprovoked" murder, and drug addiction seem much less understandable and therefore, perhaps, less voluntary or deliberate. People sometimes carry this line of thought even further: These "senseless" crimes are the result of overpowering compulsions or irrational beliefs. But this is a false distinction. Certain reinforcers may have a steadier, more predictable effect, but all behavior, even the bizarre, responds to reinforcement. It is sometimes useful to distinguish crimes that arise out of long-standing, hard-to-change reinforcers (such as money) from those that stem from short-acting, (possibly) changeable drives (such as sexual deviance), but we must always bear in mind that these are distinctions of degree, not of kind. . . .

The Context of Reinforcement

12   The effect of a reward or punishment is inversely proportional to the strength of all the reinforcements acting on a person at a given time. The more reinforcement a person is receiving, the less the value of any single reinforcement. The relativity of reinforcement has been demonstrated in the laboratory, but it can be illustrated by everyday experience. Ten dollars received just after payday is less reinforcing than ten dollars received just before payday, when money is running low. The gentle pleasures of the elderly or the infirm, for whom rewards have become fewer, may be as reinforcing to them as the more boisterous pleasures of the young and vigorous.

13   When the amount of reinforcement acting on a person increases, the strength of a small reward decreases relatively more than that of a large

one. Since crime and noncrime usually have attached to them reinforcements of different magnitudes, changes in the context of reinforcement—that is, in the total amount of reinforcement operating—will affect the value of crime and noncrime differently. . . .

For example, a person who would commit a crime if the opportunity was sufficiently close in time and space (say, a boy who will grab a purse if he happens to come upon one being carried by a lone woman on the street) may not commit the crime if other reinforcers, having nothing to do with the value of crime or noncrime, start to operate (say, the boy has just fallen in love, is listening to some pleasant music on his portable stereo, and is enjoying a warm spring day).   14

There are other ways in which a changed context of reinforcement might affect the probability of the commission of a crime. Suppose not only that our boy has fallen in love, but that his girl has agreed to marry him. Suddenly he has more to lose from crime—that is, the value of noncrime has increased because now it includes retaining the affection of the girl and the respect of her parents. In this and other ways, the richer the supply of reinforcements operating on a person, the less chance he will commit a crime.   15

The Theory as a Whole

We began . . . by asserting that the chief value of a comprehensive theory of crime is that it will bring to our attention all the factors that explain individual differences in criminality and thus prevent us from offering partial explanations or making incomplete interpretations of research findings. The larger the ratio of the rewards (material and nonmaterial) of noncrime to the rewards (material and nonmaterial) of crime, the weaker the tendency to commit crimes. The bite of conscience, the approval of peers, and any sense of inequity will increase or decrease the total value of crime; the opinions of family, friends, and employers are important benefits of noncrime, as is the desire to avoid the penalties that can be imposed by the criminal justice system. The strength of any reward declines with time, but people differ in the rate at which they discount the future. The strength of a given reward is also affected by the total supply of reinforcers. . . .   16

The connection between crime and impulsiveness is clear, as is the link between (low) intelligence and crime. Those features of family life that produce stronger or weaker internalized inhibitions have a connection to the presence or absence of aggressiveness and criminality. Certain subcultures, such as street-corner gangs, appear to affect the value members attach to both crime and noncrime. The mass media, and in particular television, may affect both aggressiveness directly and   17 a viewer's sense of inequity that can affect crime indirectly. Schooling may affect crime rates by bringing certain persons together into groups that reinforce either crime or noncrime and by determining the extent to which children believe that their skills will give them access to legitimate rewards. The condition of the economy will have a complex effect on crime depending on whether the (possibly) restraint-weakening impact of affluence dominates the restraint-strengthening influence of employment opportunities.

18   Though we will be using, for the most part, examples of rather common criminality to illustrate our argument, the theory is quite consistent with the more bizarre and unusual forms of crime. Psychopathic personalities lack to an unusual degree internalized inhibitions on crime. Persons possessed by some obsessive interest—for example, pyromania—attach an inordinately high value to the rewards of certain crimes. If everyone loved fire too much society would try hard to teach the moral evil of fire, as well as its practical danger. . . .

19   In addition to pathological drives, there are ordinary ones that can, under certain conditions, become so strong as to lead to crime. History and literature abound with normal men and women in the grip of a too powerful reinforcement. Many people have broken the law for love, honor, family and country, as well as for money, sex, vengeance, or delusion. Such criminals may be psychologically unremarkable; they transgressed because as they perceived the situation, the reward for crime exceeded that for noncrime, and an opportunity presented itself.

Crime as Social Control

DONALD BLACK

Criminal violence need not only result from a greedy, selfish, socially deviant pursuit of personal gain, whether narrowly rational or irrational. According to the theory of *social control*, under certain circumstances violence can be the expression of a personal grievance via unilateral aggression, in the service of a kind of self-help. One of the supposed purposes of law and the criminal justice system in modern societies is to replace private self-help—that is, any tendency to take the law into one's own hands—with restrictions, control, and retribution exacted by society instead of the aggrieved individual. It is therefore widely assumed that violent self-help is limited to traditional societies lacking institutions for criminal prosecution. But as Donald Black of the Center for Criminal Justice at Harvard

Law School demonstrates, the concept of violence as social control and self-help may also explain at least some of what is called "crime" in modern, technological societies. Note the relevance of anthropological material in this presentation as well as the complex connection between social factors and the "choice" to behave violently and/or criminally.

There is a sense in which conduct regarded as criminal is often quite   1
the opposite. Far from being an intentional violation of a prohibition, much crime is moralistic and involves the pursuit of justice. It is a mode of conflict management, possibly a form of punishment, even capital punishment. Viewed in relation to law, it is self-help. To the degree that it defines or responds to the conduct of someone else—the victim—as deviant, crime is social control. And to this degree it is possible to predict and explain crime with aspects of the sociological theory of social control, in particular, the theory of self-help. After an overview of self-help in traditional and modern settings, the following pages briefly examine in turn the so-called struggle between law and self-help, the deterrence of crime, the processing of self-help by legal officials, and, finally, the problem of predicting and explaining self-help itself.

Traditional Self-Help

Much of the conduct described by anthropologists as conflict manage-   2
ment, social control, or even law in tribal and other traditional societies is regarded as crime in modern societies. This is especially clear in the case of violent modes of redress such as assassination, feuding, fighting, maiming, and beating, but it also applies to the confiscation and destruction of property and to other forms of deprivation and humiliation. Such actions typically express grievance by one person or group against another. Thus, one anthropologist notes that among the Bena Bena of highland New Guinea, as among most tribes of that region, "rather than being proscribed, violent self-help is prescribed as a method of social control." The same might be said of numerous societies throughout the world. On the other hand, violence is quite rare in many traditional societies, and at least some of it is condemned in all. What follows is not intended as a representative overview, then, since only the more violent societies and modes of self-help are illustrated. First consider homicide.

In one community of Maya Indians in southern Mexico, for example,   3
any individual killed from ambush is automatically labelled "the one who had the guilt." Everyone assumes that the deceased individual provoked his own death through an act of wrongdoing: "Homicide is

considered a *reaction* to crime, not a crime in itself." Similarly, it has been observed that in a number of equatorial African societies homicide is rarely predatory—committed for gain—but is nearly always related to a grievance or quarrel of some kind. Ifugao of the Philippines hold that any "self-respecting man" must kill an adulterer discovered *in flagrante delicto*. Societies such as these have, in effect, capital punishment administered on a private basis. But unlike penalties imposed by the state, private executions often result in revenge or even a feud, a reciprocal exchange of violence that might last months or years. Moreover, the person killed in retaliation may not be himself or herself a killer, since in these societies violent conflicts between nonkin are virtually always handled in a framework of collective responsibility—or, more precisely, collective liability—whereby all members of a family or other group are accountable for the conduct of their fellows. . . .

Modern Self-Help

4   A great deal of the conduct labelled and processed as crime in modern societies resembles the modes of conflict management—described above—that are found in traditional societies which have little or no law (in the sense of governmental social control—Much of this conduct is intended as a punishment or other expression of disapproval, whether applied reflectively or impulsively, with coolness or in the heat of passion. Some is an effort to achieve compensation, or restitution, for a harm that has been done. The response may occur long after the offense, perhaps weeks, months, or even years later; after a series of offenses, each viewed singly as only a minor aggravation but together viewed as intolerable; or as an immediate response to the offense, perhaps during a fight or other conflict, or after an assault, theft, insult, or injury.

5   As in tribal and other traditional societies, for example, most intentional homicide in modern life is a response to conduct that the killer regards as deviant. In Houston during 1969, for instance, over one-half of the homicides occurred in the course of a "quarrel," and another one-fourth occurred in alleged "self-defense" or were "provoked," whereas only a little over one-tenth occurred in the course of predatory behavior such as burglary or robbery. Homocide is often a response to adultery or other matters relating to sex, love, or loyalty, to disputes about domestic matters (financial affairs, drinking, housekeeping) or affronts to honor, to conflicts relating to debts, property, and child custody, and to other questions of right and wrong. Cases mentioned in the Houston study include one in which a young man killed his brother during a heated discussion about the latter's sexual advances toward his younger

sisters, another in which a man killed his wife after she "dared" him to do so during an argument about which of several bills they should pay, one where a woman killed her husband during a quarrel in which the man struck her daughter (his stepdaughter), one in which a woman killed her 21-year-old son because he had been "fooling around with homosexuals and drugs," and two others in which people died from wounds inflicted during altercations over the parking of an automobile. Like the killings in traditional societies described by anthropologists, then, most intentional homicide in modern society may be classified as social control, specifically as self-help, even if it is handled by legal officials as crime. From this standpoint, it is apparent that capital punishment is quite common in modern America—in Texas, homicide is one of the ten leading causes of death—though it is nearly always a private rather than a public affair.

Most conduct that a lawyer would label as assault may also be understood as self-help. In the vast majority of cases the people involved know one another, usually quite intimately, and the physical attack arises in the context of a grievance or quarrel. Commonly the assault is a punishment, such as when a husband beats or otherwise injures his wife because she has not lived up to his expectations. In one case that came to the attention of the police in Boston, for example, a woman complained that her husband had beaten her because supper was not ready when he came home from work—a state of affairs, incidentally, which might have been the woman's own way of expressing disapproval of her husband. Other standards are enforced violently as well. In one instance that occurred in a major northeastern city and that apparently was not reported to the police, a young woman's brothers attacked and beat her boyfriend "for making her a drug addict," and in another a young man was stabbed for cooperating with the police in a burglary investigation. In a case in Washington, D.C., that resulted in an arrest, a boy shot his gang leader for taking more than his proper share of the proceeds from a burglary. Years later, the same individual shot someone who had been terrorizing young women—including the avenger's girlfriend—in his neighborhood. Though he pleaded guilty to "assault with a deadly weapon" and was committed to a reformatory, not surprisingly he described himself as "completely right" and his victim as "completely wrong." 6

Indigenous people arrested for violence in colonial societies are likely to have a similar point of view: They may be proud of what they have done and admit it quite openly, even while they are being prosecuted as criminals by the foreign authorities. Those apprehended in Europe for the crime of duelling—also a method of conflict resolution—have 7 typically lacked remorse for the same reasons. Thus, when asked by a priest to pray for forgiveness before being hanged for killing a man with a sword, one such offender in France exclaimed. "Do you call one of the cleverest thrusts in Gascony a crime?" As in duelling, moreover, violence in modern societies is often prescribed by a code of honor. He who shrinks from it is disgraced as a coward.

8   Many crimes involving the confiscation or destruction of property also prove to have a normative character when the facts come fully to light. There are, for example, moralistic burglaries, thefts, and robberies. Over one-third of the burglaries in New York City resulting in arrest involve people with a prior relationship, and these not infrequently express a grievance the burglar has against his victim. . . .

9   Finally, it might be noted that the practice of collective liability—whereby all of the people in a social category are held accountable for the conduct of each of their fellows—occurs in modern as well as traditional societies. This is most apparent during a war, revolution, or riot, when anyone might suffer for the deeds of someone else, but during peaceful times too, seemingly random violence may often be understood in the same way. Today a police officer might become the victim of a surprise attack by a stranger, for example, because of the conduct of one or more fellow officers in the past. Seemingly random crime of other kinds may involve collective liability as well. Thus, for instance, a black rapist described his selection of white victims as a process of vengeance against white people in general:

> It delighted me that I was defying and trampling upon the white man's law, upon his system of values, and that I was defiling his women—and this point, I believe, was the most satisfying to me because I was very resentful over the historical fact of how the white man has used the black woman. I felt I was getting revenge. . . .

10   The state often imposes the categories of offender and victim upon people who were contesting the proper application of these labels during the altercation in question. Whether there was originally a cross-complaint or not, however, in all of these cases the state defines someone with a grievance as a criminal. The offense lies in how the grievance was pursued. The crime is self-help.

11   It should be apparent from much of the foregoing that in modern society the state has only theoretically achieved a monopoly over the legitimate use of violence. In reality violence flourishes (particularly in modern America), and most of it involves ordinary citizens who seemingly view their conduct as a perfectly legitimate exercise of social control. It might therefore be observed that the struggle between law and

self-help in the West did not end in the Middle Ages, as legal historians claim. . . . It continues. Many people still "take the law into their own hands." They seem to view their grievances as their own business, not that of the police or other officials, and resent the intrusion of law. They seem determined to have justice done, even if this means that they will be defined as criminals. . . .

It might be wondered why so much self-help occurs in a society such   12
as modern America. Why do so many people criminally pursue their own grievances in a society where law is developed to such a high degree? Why, in particular, are they so violent? . . .

The Theory of Self-Help

Several centuries ago, Thomas Hobbes argued that without a sovereign   13
state—without law—a "war of every one against every one" would prevail, and life would be "solitary, poor, nasty, brutish, and short." Many stateless societies have since been observed by anthropologists, however, and Hobbes's theory has proven to be somewhat overstated: Life without law does not appear to be nearly as precarious as he believed. Even so, the idea that violence is associated with statelessness still enjoys considerable support. With various refinements and qualifications, an absence of state authority has been used to explain high levels of violence in settings as diverse as the highlands of New Guinea, and western Sicily. It has also been used to explain war and other violent self-help in international relations. A version of the same approach may be relevant to an understanding of self-help in modern society.

Hobbesian theory would lead us to expect more violence and other   14
crimes of self-help in those contemporary settings where law—governmental social control—is least developed, and, indeed, this appears to fit the facts: Crimes of self-help are more likely where law is less available. This is most apparent where legal protection is withheld as a matter of public policy, such as where a contract violates the law. A gambling debt is not legally enforceable, for example, and the same applies to transactions in illicit narcotics, prostitution, stolen goods, and the like. Perhaps for this reason many underworld businesses find it necessary to maintain, in effect, their own police, such as the "strong-arms" of illegal loan operations and the "pimps" who oversee the work of prostitutes. Furthermore, it appears that social control within settings of this kind is relatively violent.

Lower-status people of all kinds—blacks and other minorities, the   15
poor, the homeless—enjoy less legal protection, especially when they have complaints against their social superiors, but also when conflict erupts among themselves. To the police and other authorities the problems

of these people seem less serious, their injuries less severe, their honor less important. A fight or quarrel among them may even be viewed as itself a "disturbance of the peace," an offense in its own right, regardless of the issues dividing the parties. . . .

16   Before closing, it is possible to specify the relationship between law and self-help more precisely. The likelihood of self-help is not merely a function of the availability of law, and, moreover, crimes of self-help are not always handled leniently by legal officials. Different locations and directions in social space have different patterns. In other words, the relationship between law and self-help depends upon who has a grievance against whom. . . .

Predatory and Dispute-Related Violence: A Social Interactionist Approach

RICHARD B. FELSON

Some of the most productive attempts by criminologists to understand violent crime involve integrating principles from other disciplines, notably social psychology. The following selection is a notable attempt to employ the concepts of goal-directedness and to interpret behavior as deriving from social interactions (as opposed to unilateral "decisions" of individuals, whether conscious or not). It also demonstrates that substantial clarity can be gained by making certain conceptual distinctions, as between predatory and dispute-related violence, and also distinguishing whether the perpetrator is concerned with achieving compliance, justice, or establishing a particular social identity as a result of the violent interaction. Even though real-life situations are nearly always more complicated than the schematic breakdown presented here, reality is so multifaceted that simplifications of this sort—so long as they are not mistaken for reality itself—can be a great aid to understanding.

1   Harm doing is studied under different guises. Social psychologists interested in aggression study shock delivery in laboratory settings. Other social psychologists study competitive choices and contentious tactics in experimental games, but identify their subject as social conflict. Criminologists study physical violence under the rubric of crime, sociologists study family violence, and anthropologists study the sometimes violent expression of grievances in societies with rudimentary

legal systems. All of these scholars are interested in why people purposefully harm each other.

Two theories proposed by social psychologists have been particu- 2
larly influential in the study of physical violence. The frustration-aggression hypothesis suggests that individuals are likely to engage in aggression when their goals have been blocked or—in the most recent version of the theory—when faced with aversive stimuli. This approach has been influential in studies of the effect of stress on criminal and family violence, and in the study of the effects of poverty and social inequity on homicide rates.

Another influential approach—social learning theory—stresses the 3
importance of modeling and rewards in the socialization of violent behavior. Social learning theory provides the rationale for extensive research on the effects of media violence, and on the intergenerational transmission of violence. The claim is made that people engage in violence because they've observed their parents and their TV heros engaging in violence.

These theories parallel the distinction that is generally made between 4
angry aggression and instrumental aggression. Angry aggression refers to involuntary acts that are compelled by aggressive drive or energy—forces inside the person. Harm to the target is an end in itself. In contrast, in instrumental aggression, harm doing is a means to an end. Individuals harm others because it brings them some benefit or reward.

A relatively new approach to aggression and violence challenges this 5
distinction. What might be called a "social interactionist" perspective emphasizes the role of social interaction—as opposed to conditions inside the person—in aggressive behavior. It interprets all aggressive behavior as goal-oriented or instrumental, that is, as an attempt to achieve what people value. Aggressive actions seek to compel and deter others, to achieve a favorable social identity, and to obtain justice, as defined by the actor. While much aggression is done "in anger," anger and aggression reflect a social control reaction to perceived misdeeds rather than involuntary responses to frustration. In contrast to the frustration-aggression hypothesis, people only get angry when they *blame* someone for frustrating or aversive events. While they may behave impulsively in the sense that they fail to consider long-range consequences, their behavior is still the consequence of a decision-making process.

Note that a social interactionist approach is concerned with an 6
actor's point of view, not the truth of any allegations. While the target does play at least some causal role in most incidents of dispute-related violence, I do not use the term *victim precipitation.* This value-laden term confuses cause and blame. Assigning a causal role to targets does not necessarily imply that they were blameworthy. For example, whether

an individual kills someone in self-defense or in response to mild criticism, the target's behavior has an effect. Whether the target is blameworthy may be relevant to the legal system but it is irrelevant to a scientific analysis of violence. . . .

7   I apply a social interactionist approach to criminal violence. Two general types of violence are distinguished: predatory and dispute-related. . . .

Predatory Violence

8   Three general concerns of actors in violent incidents are presented in table 1: generating compliance; pursuing justice; and the achievement of desired social identities. These concerns are relevant to both types of violence. Thus, the table suggests three reasons why individuals might engage in predatory or unprovoked violence. First, they may use coercion to compel the target to engage in some desired behavior. In these incidents, contingent threats or bodily force are used to compel a person to do something they would not otherwise do. For example, threats may be used in order to obtain money or sex. A second form of predatory violence involves an attempt to establish or assert some identity, using what Arkin has described as an assertive form of self-presentation. The person is commonly referred to as a "bully"—someone who preys on a vulnerable target in order to demonstrate his power. The bully's domination of the target demonstrates power and may increase his or her status for some audiences.

9   A third form of predatory violence involves equity restoration. When individuals decide that the distribution of rewards and costs is unfair, they may attempt to restore equity by harming the person perceived as privileged, even when that person is not held responsible for the injustice. By increasing the costs or reducing the rewards of the overbenefited party they can produce equity or distributive justice. The redistribution can be described as predatory rather than dispute-related

TABLE 1   Motives in Predatory and Dispute-Related Violence

Actor's Concern	Type of Violence	
	Predatory	Dispute-Related
Compliance	"Compellence"	Deterrence
Justice	Redistribution	Retribution
Social Identities	Assertive self-presentation	Defensive self-presentation

because the actor does not have a dispute with the target. Such a process helps explain why jealousy might lead to violence. . . .

Gaining Compliance

In these incidents contingent threats or bodily force are used to compel a person to comply with some directive. For example, in the typical blackmail, the offender threatens to reveal information to legal authorities for punishment unless the victim complies. In the typical robbery, the offender threatens to deliver harm themselves unless the victim complies. The offender is usually motivated to obtain money or property and is using the threat of violence as a means of social influence. He usually selects targets who are likely to comply and to provide a good "take."

Most robbery offenders use violence strategically, that is, in order to successfully complete the crime. They make their threat, and if the victim complies, they do not engage in any further violence. Armed offenders rarely attack the victim while unarmed offenders sometimes engage in preemptive strikes designed to give their threats credibility. The minimal, strategic use of force suggests that the purpose of most robbers is to gain compliance and not to harm their victim. It also demonstrates that an actual attack is sometimes a sign of weakness: it is used when the threat of violence fails to influence a target.

Rape involves the use of contingent threats or bodily force to compel a person to engage in sexual intercourse. The three major outcomes in a completed rape are sexual activity, harm to the victim, and domination of the victim. The question of motive involves determining which of these outcomes is the goal of the offender and which are incidental. For a sexually motivated offender, domination and harm to the victim are incidental outcomes; his interest is in influencing the victim to have sexual activity.

In contrast to popular thinking, there is considerable evidence that many rapes are sexually motivated. First, like robbers, rapists generally use violence in a strategic fashion—using only enough force to obtain compliance. They attempt to establish a credible threat but they are unlikely to carry out the threat if the victim complies. Second, there is evidence that men tend to use sexual coercion as a last resort in incidents involving people they know. In other words, they use coercion after other methods of influence have failed. Third, the use of sexual coercion is related to high "sexual aspirations." College men who are dissatisfied with the frequency of their sexual activity, or who indicate that a higher frequency of orgasms was necessary for them to be sexually satisfied, are more likely to engage in coercive sexual behavior. Fourth, "date rapes" usually occur when a male is sexually aroused. In all 71 incidents of date rape studied by Kanin, the rape occurred during an intensive consensual sexual encounter, most commonly involving oral-genital sex. Finally, the targets of rape are almost always young women. There is obviously a strong relationship between age and sexual attractiveness. Felson and Krohn find evidence that the age pattern reflects a *preference* for young women and not just differential opportunity. This is indicated by evidence that a young woman is more likely to be raped during a robbery than an older woman. . . .

14 Bullying involves the unprovoked use of aggression against targets to assert some identity rather than produce a material gain. For the bully, dominating the victim is an accomplishment, a way of demonstrating power to himself and others. The bully's general strategy appears to be to dominate a vulnerable low-status target using coercive means. Research on young bullies shows that they tend to be 1–2 years older than their victims and physically stronger. Typically, they victimize children who are unpopular, physically unattractive, and physically uncoordinated. The role of self-presentation is suggested by evidence that bullies tend to seek out situations in which their behavior can be witnessed by their peers. That bullies sometimes operate in groups also suggests that the attack can confer status on those who use it. Adults, even when they are aware of bullying, are apparently reluctant to intervene, fearing that they might make things worse. Apparently, they expect the victim to stand up to the bully. . . .

Dispute-Related Violence

15 Dispute-related violence occurs as a result of social control reactions to perceived wrongdoing. Individuals feel aggrieved when they believe that they have been wronged, and they are motivated to punish the miscreant. Unlike individuals engaged in predatory violence, antagonists are likely to feel angry in dispute-related violence. Like the criminal justice system, they use punishment either to deter the target and others from repeating the offense, or because of their beliefs about justice. They view their behavior as retribution, that is, as a legitimate and justifiable response to the misdeeds of others. The initial attack is usually verbal, but it can lead to retaliation in the form of physical violence. One of the goals of retaliation is to "save face" (or defend "honor"), and thus it is a defensive form of self-presentation. As indicated in table 1, deterrence, retribution, and defensive self-presentation are central to dispute-related violence. . . .

Transgressions as Sources of Conflict

16 If violence results from attempts at informal social control, then it should be associated with the occurrence of transgressions. When transgres-

sions are serious, one is likely to observe severe forms of punishment in response—the punishment is likely to "fit the crime." Those who are harmed by transgressions are the most likely to feel angry and aggrieved and to attack. However, anyone who observes the misdeed may punish the offender, whether or not they were harmed or whether or not anyone was harmed. Justice demands that a wrongdoer be punished. . . .

Stress and Conflict

Many studies have shown a positive correlation between physical vio-   17
lence and stress. The effects of stress, like the effects of aversive stimuli in the laboratory, are generally assumed to be due to some sort of frustration-aggression mechanism. The social interactionist approach, on the other hand, suggests that stress may be one source of the types of behavior that lead to grievances. There is considerable evidence that stress negatively affects performance in school and and work. In addition, one would expect that people who are stressed are less likely to perform the interaction ritual competently. Because of their mood, they are less likely to be polite and friendly, to feign positive emotions, or to show ritualized support for others. If distressed persons are likely to perform less competently, violate expectations, or annoy others, they are likely to become the object of grievances. This is likely to lead to their involvement in aggressive interactions, often, initially, as targets. As indicated above, evidence suggests that the aggrieved party is more often the first to engage in an aggressive act.

Parents and Police as Agents of Social Control

One would expect dispute-related violence to be particularly likely to   18
occur in incidents involving individuals acting in the role of a social control agent. The best examples are parents and police.

Much of the extralegal use of violence by police can be described as   19
dispute-related. Toch, for example, finds that in the most common sequence of events, the officer gives orders or instructions, the suspect expresses his contempt, which leads the officer to use bodily force. The officer frequently feels that the suspect's behavior challenges his reputation, and after he makes the opening move, he feels that he must persevere. The suspect, on the other hand, perceives police action as arbitrary and unfair and an attack on his identity.

In regard to parents, Goode argues that there is always an element   20
of coercion in parent-child relations, even when parents use other forms of influence. Thus, children may comply when parents reason with them because they are aware that they will be punished otherwise. One can interpret reasoning as the justification parents use when they coerce their children. . . .

Retaliation and Escalation

21   When people think that another person has intentionally harmed them, they are likely to retaliate. Experimental research shows that perceived intentional attack is the most reliable elicitor of aggressive behavior. In fact, subjects tend to retaliate for intended shocks even when they do not actually receive the shock. Note that this is directly counter to the frustration-aggression hypothesis, which, in the most recent version, suggests that aversive stimuli, not "bad intentions," leads to aggression.

22   There are at least three reasons why people retaliate. First, an attack is likely to be perceived as wrongdoing by the target and thus creates a grievance. Second, by retaliating, the target of an attack deters his or her tormentor and others from future attacks. Finally, an initial attack casts the target into a negative identity by making the target appear weak and ineffectual. The target can nullify that image, i.e., can "save face," by a counterattack. . . .

Routine Activities and Dispute-Related Violence

23   The routine activity approach was originally designed as a theory of predatory crime. It suggests that there are three elements necessary to produce a predatory crime: a motivated offender, a suitable target, and the absence of capable guardians. . . .

24   Evidence that the routine activity approach is relevant for dispute-related violence comes from studies of assault victimization. For example, research based on the National Crime Survey indicates that the risk of victimization for assault is greater if people are unemployed and unmarried, and if they live near the central city and low income neighborhoods. Those who frequently go out for nighttime entertainment are also more likely to be the victim of violent crimes. Evidence from the Canadian Urban Victim Survey shows that residents who patronize bars, who work or go to class, or who go out for a walk or drive at night, are more likely to be victims of assault than those who do not engage in these activities.

25   The actions of targets are likely to be important in dispute-related violence. In predatory violence, targets are substitutable: if the situation is not opportune, the offender can choose another target. In a dispute-related crime, the offender is only interested in one target—the person with whom he is aggrieved. The routine activities of targets that lead them to become the object of grievances are therefore important. For example, the behavior of persons who are stressed or intoxicated is likely to elicit social control reactions, as indicated earlier. Many nighttime

and weekend activities away from home involve alcohol, which may help explain why violence is most frequent during these time periods.

The routine activity approach and a social interactionist approach are compatible because both emphasize the importance of situational variables and opportunities for violent behavior. Both theories give particular emphasis to the role of targets and third parties. Further, both theories assume that offenders consider the rewards and costs of their actions and are therefore compatible with rational choice models. 26

The discussion above suggests that the routine activity approach is applicable to dispute-related violence, although alterations in the theory are necessary. Dispute-related violence can be seen as a response to routine rule-breaking and as an alternative to routine forms of social control. For dispute-related violence to occur one might expect the following elements to be present: (1) at least one person with a proclivity toward violence; (2) a provocation; (3) supportive third parties. . . . 27

In conclusion, whether dispute-related or predatory, violence can be interpreted as goal-oriented behavior. The goals of violence are similar to the goals of many other social behaviors—social influence, justice, and favorable social identities. A social interactionist approach emphasizes relative simple processes that are well established in the social psychological literature and helps make sense of a wide variety of violent behaviors. . . . 28

Psychopathy: Theory and Research

ROBERT D. HARE

Are some perpetrators simply incorrigible? Admittedly, there is a (mercifully) small minority of people who are truly psychotic and/or pathologically drawn to violence itself: perpetrators of grotesque and often sadistic murders, mutilations, cannibalism, and the like. But aside from them, what about those—more frequent—who are entirely "sane" but appear to be driven by a total lack of any empathy or conscience? Canadian psychologist Robert Hare is perhaps the world's foremost expert on such individuals, whom he refers to as *psychopaths*. It should be noted that current psychiatric diagnoses do not recognize this category, instead identifying the more wide-ranging *antisocial personality disorder*. However, Hare has established a detailed diagnostic checklist for psychopathy and its possible existence as a distinct behavioral syndrome poses a substantial challenge for criminology, law, and concepts of how to establish a humane society: On one hand, psychopathic individuals—if they exist—are likely to be repeat offenders, currently resistant to all known treatments. On the other, it is imperative not to misdiagnose people as psychopaths if they are in fact treatable and unlikely to pose a threat to society.

Case History of a Psychopath

1   Donald S., 30 years old, has just completed a three-year prison term for fraud, bigamy, false pretenses, and escaping lawful custody. The circumstances leading up to these offenses are interesting and consistent with his past behavior. With less than a month left to serve on an earlier 18-month term for fraud, he faked illness and escaped from the prison hospital. During the ten months of freedom that followed he engaged in a variety of illegal enterprises; the activity that resulted in his recapture was typical of his method of operation. By passing himself off as the "field executive" of an international philanthropic foundation, he was able to enlist the aid of several religious organizations in a fundraising campaign. The campaign moved slowly at first, and in an attempt to speed things up, he arranged an interview with the local TV station. His performance during the interview was so impressive that funds started to pour in. However, unfortunately for Donald, the interview was also carried on a national news network. He was recognized and quickly arrested. During the ensuing trial it became evident that he experienced no sense of wrongdoing for his activities. He maintained, for example, that his passionate plea for funds "primed the pump"— that is, induced people to give to other charities as well as to the one he professed to represent. At the same time, he stated that most donations to charity are made by those who feel guilty about something and who therefore deserve to be bilked. This ability to rationalize his behavior and his lack of self-criticism were also evident in his attempts to solicit aid from the very people he had misled. Perhaps it is a tribute to his persuasiveness that a number of individuals actually did come to his support. During his three-year prison term, Donald spent much time searching for legal loopholes and writing to outside authorities, including local lawyers, the Prime Minister of Canada, and a Canadian representative to the United Nations. In each case he verbally attacked them for representing the authority and injustice responsible for his predicament. At the same time he requested them to intercede on his behalf and in the name of the justice they professed to represent.

2   While in prison he was used as a subject in some of the author's research. On his release he applied for admission to a university and, by way of reference, told the registrar that he had been one of the author's

research colleagues! Several months later the author received a letter from him requesting a letter of recommendation on behalf of Donald's application for a job.

Donald was the youngest of three boys born to middle-class parents. [3] Both of his brothers led normal, productive lives. His father spent a great deal of time with his business; when he was home he tended to be moody and to drink heavily when things were not going right. Donald's mother was a gentle, timid woman who tried to please her husband and to maintain a semblance of family harmony. When she discovered her children engaged in some mischief, she would threaten to tell their father. However, she seldom carried out these threats because she did not want to disturb her husband and because his reactions were likely to be dependent on his mood at the time; on some occasions he would fly into a rage and beat the children and on others he would administer a verbal reprimand, sometimes mild and sometimes severe.

By all accounts Donald was considered a willful and difficult child. [4] When his desire for candy or toys was frustrated he would begin with a show of affection, and if this failed he would throw a temper tantrum; the latter was seldom necessary because his angelic appearance and artful ways usually got him what he wanted. Similar tactics were used to avoid punishment for his numerous misdeeds. At first he would attempt to cover up with an elaborate facade of lies, often shifting the blame to his brothers. If this did not work, he would give a convincing display of remorse and contrition. When punishment was unavoidable he would become sullenly defiant, regarding it as an unjustifiable tax on his pleasures.

Although he was obviously very intelligent, his school years were [5] academically undistinguished. He was restless, easily bored, and frequently truant. His behavior in the presence of the teacher or some other authority was usually quite good, but when he was on his own he generally got himself or others into trouble. Although he was often suspected of being the culprit, he was adept at talking his way out of difficulty.

Donald's misbehavior as a child took many forms including lying, [6] cheating, petty theft, and the bullying of smaller children. As he grew older he became more and more interested in sex, gambling, and alcohol. When he was 14 he made crude sexual advances toward a younger girl, and when she threatened to tell her parents he locked her in a shed. It was about 16 hours before she was found. Donald at first denied knowledge of the incident, later stating that she had seduced him and that the door must have locked itself. He expressed no concern for the anguish experienced by the girl and her parents, nor did he give any indication that he felt morally culpable for what he had done. His parents were able to prevent charges being brought against him. Nevertheless, incidents of this were becoming more frequent and, in an attempt to prevent further embarrassment to the family, he was sent away to a private boarding school. His academic work there was of uneven quality, being dependent on his momentary interests. Nevertheless, he did well at individual competitive sports and public debating. He was a source of excitement for many of the other boys, and was able to think up interesting and unusual things to do. Rules and regulations were considered a meaningless hindrance to his self-expression, but he violated them so skillfully that it was often difficult to prove that he had actually done so. The teachers described him as an "operator" whose behavior was determined entirely by the possibility of attaining what he wanted—in most cases something that was concrete, immediate, and personally relevant.

7   When he was 17, Donald left the boarding school, forged his father's name to a large check, and spent about a year traveling around the world. He apparently lived well, using a combination of charm, physical attractiveness, and false pretenses to finance his way. During subsequent years he held a succession of jobs, never staying at any one for more than a few months. Throughout this period he was charged with a variety of crimes, including theft, drunkenness in a public place, assault, and many traffic violations. In most cases he was either fined or given a light sentence.

8   His sexual experiences were frequent, casual, and callous. When he was 22 he married a 41-year-old woman whom he had met in a bar. Several other marriages followed, all bigamous. In each case the pattern was the same: he would marry someone on impulse, let her support him for several months, and then leave. One marriage was particularly interesting. After being charged with fraud Donald was sent to a psychiatric institution for a period of observation. While there he came to the attention of a female member of the professional staff. His charm, physical attractiveness, and convincing promises to reform led her to intervene on his behalf. He was given a suspended sentence and they were married a week later. At first things went reasonably well, but when she refused to pay some of his gambling debts he forged her name to a check and left. He was soon caught and given an 18-month prison term. As mentioned earlier, he escaped with less than a month left to serve.

9   It is interesting to note that Donald sees nothing particularly wrong with his behavior, nor does he express remorse or guilt for using others and causing them grief. Although his behavior is self-defeating in the long run, he considers it to be practical and possessed of good sense. Periodic punishments do nothing to decrease his egotism and confidence

in his own abilities, nor do they offset the often considerable short-term gains of which he is capable. However, these short-term gains are invariably obtained at the expense of someone else. In this respect his behavior is entirely egocentric, and his needs are satisfied without any concern for the feelings and welfare of others. . . .

The main features of the disorder [are] superficial charm and good   10
intelligence; absence of delusions and other signs of irrational thinking; absence of "nervousness" or neurotic manifestations; unreliability, untruthfulness and insincerity; lack of remorse or shame; antisocial behavior without apparent compunction; poor judgment and failure to learn from experience; pathologic egocentricity and incapacity for love; general poverty in major affective reactions; specific loss of insight; unresponsiveness in general interpersonal relations; fantastic and uninviting behavior with drink and sometimes without; suicide threats rarely carried out; sex life impersonal, trivial, and poorly integrated, failure to follow any life plan. The first three characteristics are positive in nature and serve to emphasize the fact that the psychopath's behavior is not simply the manifestation of disturbed mental functioning. According to Cleckley, the psychopath lacks the ability to experience the emotional components of personal and interpersonal behavior—he mimics the human personality but is unable to really *feel*. Thus, although his verbalizations (for example, "I'm sorry I got you in trouble") appear normal, they are devoid of emotional meaning, a disorder that Cleckley has termed *semantic dementia*. . . . The psychopath knows the words but not the music, with the result that he is unable to show empathy or genuine concern for others. He manipulates and uses others to satisfy his own demands; yet, through a glib sophistication and superficial sincerity, he is often able to convince those he has used and harmed of his innocence or his intentions to change.

Karpman described the psychopath as a callous, emotionally imma-   11
ture, two dimensional person without any real depth, His emotional reactions are simple and animal-like, occurring only with immediate frustrations and discomfort. However, he is able to *simulate* emotional reactions and affectional attachments when it will help him to obtain what he wants from others. He experiences neither the psychological nor the physiological aspects of anxiety or fear, although he may react with something resembling fear when his immediate comfort is threatened. His social and sexual relations with others are superficial but demanding and manipulative. Future rewards and punishments do not exist, except in an abstract manner, with the result that they have no effect on his immediate behavior. His judgment is poor and his behavior is often guided by impulse and current needs; he is therefore constantly

in trouble. His attempts to extricate himself often produce an intricate and contradictory web of blatant lies, coupled with theatrical and often convincing explanations and promises. . . .

12   Most clinical descriptions of the psychopath make some sort of reference to his egocentricity, lack of empathy, and inability to form warm, emotional relationships with others—characteristics that lead him to treat others as objects instead of as persons and prevent him from experiencing guilt and remorse for having done so. After an extensive review of the literature, McCord and McCord concluded that the two essential features of psychopathy are *lovelessness* and *guiltlessness*. Similarly, Craft considered the two primary features of psychopathy to be a lack of feeling, affection, or love for others and a tendency to act on impulse and without forethought. Secondary features, stemming from these two, are aggressiveness, lack of shame or guilt, inability to profit from experience, and a lack of appropriate motivation. . . .

13   Many individuals exhibit aggressive, antisocial behavior, not because they are psychopathic or emotionally disturbed, but because they have grown up in a delinquent subculture or in an environment that fosters and rewards such behavior. Their behavior, although considered deviant by society's standards, is nevertheless consonant with that of their own group, gang, or family. The terms used for these individuals include *dyssocial "psychopath," subcultural delinquent*, and, when children are involved, *sociosyntonic personality disorder*. Unlike the "true" psychopath, these individuals are capable of strong loyalties and warm relationships with members of their own group (for instance, criminal organizations, delinquent gangs). . . .

14   Many investigators find it more appealing to conceptualize behavior, normal and abnormal, in dimensional terms. According to this view, psychopaths as such do not exist, although some individuals may be considered more psychopathic than others if they occupy a more extreme position on some dimension that we choose to label "psychopathy." The difficulty here is that before we can really say that one person is more or less psychopathic than another, we need to know more about the makeup of the dimension. Assume, for example, that Person *A* exhibits all of the characteristics that we feel are relevant to the dimension of psychopathy, and that Person *B* exhibits only two-thirds of these characteristics. Who is the more psychopathic? If the dimension consists of the *number* of relevant characteristics, then Person *A* would be considered more psychopathic than *B*. However, suppose that the characteristics exhibited by *B*, though fewer in number, are more severe than those shown by *A*. Who is the more psychopathic now? The problem becomes even more complicated if we assume that the defining features of psychopathy, or for that matter any other complex dimension of be-

havior, are not equally weighted—that is, that some are more important than others. Under these conditions, an individual's position on the dimension can only be established when we know the number and severity of relevant characteristics exhibited, and the weights assigned them. In principle, it would be possible to use modern statistical techniques to obtain information of this sort, and to use it to yield a single score indicative of a given individual's degree of psychopathy. . . .

Violence: Treatment versus Correction

SEYMOUR HALLECK

As we have seen, there is very little disagreement that violence is a bad thing, and that society ought to minimize it. What to *do* with the violent offender, however, poses a difficult dilemma. Wrongdoers have been punished for literally millennia. But why? There are numerous reasons, not all of them mutually consistent: (1) protect society from future depredations by the same trangsressors; (2) reform the malefactors, by providing training, treatment, and/or opportunity for them to reflect on the wrongness of their behavior; (3) deter their own future violence as well as that of other would-be transgressors by making it clear that "crime does not pay"; (4) provide a morally satisfying response to wrongdoing, thereby reinforcing those who abide by society's rules and expectations; (5) prevent wronged individuals from "taking the law into their own hands"; and finally, (6) buttress the legitimacy of the state, whose authority is thrown into doubt if violent law breaking is allowed to proceed with impunity.

In any event, liberals and progressives generally favor treatment whereas conservatives prefer incarceration. In our final selection, a psychiatrist makes a humane case for treating those offenders who are in fact treatable. Although a wide range of treatment modalities—especially psychoactive drugs—are now available, their effectiveness is debated, just as resources for correction are sorely limited and the argument of *diminished responsibility* has been met with an increasingly jaundiced eye.

It is difficult to precisely define terms such as *treatment* or *correction*. More often than not, treatment and correction serve similar rather than antagonistic goals. When we correct a person's behavior or change his behavior in order to help him, we are in a very real sense treating or helping him. Unfortunately, the term *treatment,* as applied to offenders, is likely to evoke an image of a purely medical approach, and the term *correction* is likely to be associated with a punitive approach. In reality, there is no purely medical or completely corrective approach to violent offenders. Rather, in most dispositional approaches to the violent offender, medical, behavioral, economic, and punitive models are intertwined in a very complex manner.

2   It is far more useful, then, to consider the issue of "what should be done with the violent offender" from the standpoint of the conventional goals of correctional justice. In dealing with known offenders, the law is designed to serve four major purposes: to incapacitate, to deter, to impose retribution, and to rehabilitate. A discussion of these four goals will provide a realistic view of our choices in dealing with the violent offender. . . .

3   A perplexing issue in using incapacitation with violent offenders is determining the extent or length of incapacitation. The surest way to incapacitate offenders is to execute them. Since, in most instances, our society rejects this solution, we must develop some criteria for determining when an offender no longer presents a substantial threat to other citizens. In this area, we have precious little science to guide us. The best we can do is make predictions about the probability of an individual's committing another violent act if incapacitation is removed. As will be elaborated in more detail later, even our ability to make accurate statements about an individual's potentiality for violence is limited.

4   A second function of the criminal law in dealing with offenders is deterrence. If we do things to an offender that he experiences as unpleasant, he may be deterred from committing offenses in the future (this is called specific deterrence). Other citizens who might have been tempted to commit a similar crime will also be deterred by witnessing an example of what might happen to them if they violated the law (this is called general deterrence). All of this has an inherent logic and appeals to our common sense. Yet there is much controversy in the field of criminal justice as to the value of punishment as deterrence. In recent years economists and sociologists have promulgated a theory of crime in which offenders are considered to be rational people who regularly weigh the risks and benefits involved in committing an antisocial act. In this view, potential offenders will be deterred from committing crimes if they are reasonably sure of a punitive response from society. Deterrence theory is frequently invoked to justify the imposition of punitive sanctions, such as imprisonment, against the offender.

5   The actual data on the effectiveness of imprisonment as a deterrent are far from conclusive. Certainly, the high rates of recidivism following imprisonment in our country indicate that imprisonment is not

effective in diminishing the future criminality of many offenders who are subjected to this sanction. The data on general deterrence offer a little more cause for optimism. By comparing crime rates with the number of convictions and prison sentences in a given area, criminologists have been able to determine that *certainty of punishment* diminishes crime rates. They have also noted that *speed of punishment* diminishes crime. There is, however, great uncertainty whether *severity of punishment* has any deterrent effect. Nonetheless, many states in this country are now imposing fixed and long sentences upon violent offenders; some have restored the death penalty for certain crimes, and others are considering such action. These practices are not logically supported by deterrence theory. Some data indicate that the crime of homicide may be deterred by long sentences, but even these data have been seriously questioned and there is no proof that the death penalty deters the crime of homicide. At the same time, there is little evidence that increasing the length of imprisonment deters other offenders. It is certainty and celerity of punishment—not severity of punishment—that deters. The possibility of severe sanctions also diminishes the certainty that any sanctions will ever be imposed. In the crime of rape, for example, the possibility of severe sentences frequently leads to the offender's being given the benefit of the doubt and enables him to avoid conviction and imprisonment. Certainty of punishment is then diminished. The misuse of deterrence theory to justify imposition of lengthy sentences upon offenders has also resulted in a massive and economically unfeasible overcrowding of our prisons.

A third goal of the criminal law in dealing with violent offenders is   6
retribution. Society has a right to punish those who transgress against it. The imposition of legal sanctions, in the form of imprisonment or execution, confirms the moral codes of society and serves to prevent acts of private vengeance. If the society, under a rule of law, did not punish, private citizens would respond to acts of criminal violence by retaliatory acts of violence, and we would live in a lawless society. Those who worry about the courts' being "soft" on criminals sometimes fear that too much leniency will make law-abiding citizens resort to a vigilante form of justice. Their fears are not entirely unfounded.

Retribution or simple punishment is a legitimate goal of the crimi-   7
nal justice system. The problem with this goal is that it is always extremely difficult to decide how much retribution is just and socially useful. It is expensive to incarcerate offenders; and, certainly, when an individual is no longer violent and will not be a risk to others, society loses a great deal by confining that person to prison. Too much emphasis on retribution also may interfere with the fourth goal of the criminal justice system, rehabilitation.

8   If violent offenders are not to be executed or deported (an unlikely disposition in these days), it is both economical and humane to return them to a free society as soon as they are no longer dangerous. Although some violent offenders may cease to be dangerous almost immediately after they have committed a violent act, we have to assume that most of them will retain a propensity toward violence unless something is done to change them. When we try to change offenders so that they will behave in a manner that we believe is good for the rest of society, we are attempting to rehabilitate them. The term *rehabilitation* is similar to, but not identical with, the term *treatment*.

9   Rehabilitation is not a simple concept. When considered in terms of goals, it can be viewed in several ways. One view of rehabilitation is that it simply involves changing some aspect of the offender so that he will be less likely to commit antisocial acts. With this goal rehabilitation is equivalent to diminishing recidivism. An individual may be considered rehabilitated, then, when he loses his motivation to be violent, develops a more benevolent attitude toward society, learns new skills that give him greater psychological and, social strengths, or develops a more benevolent attitude toward society, learns new skills that give him greater psychological and social strengths, or develops religious or moral beliefs that help him control violence. But if we are concerned only with the absence of recidivism, we can also argue that the prisoner who is lobotomized, castrated, or subjected to some form of psychological mutilation has also been rehabilitated. When we think of rehabilitation only as change which diminishes recidivism, there are a large variety of actions we can take to change violent offenders—some of them consistent with the ethical precepts of a humane society, and some of them not.

10   A second way of viewing rehabilitation as a goal takes these ethical precepts into account. That is, the offender is to be changed so as to diminish his recidivism, but such change must not compromise his future physical and psychological potentialities. Under this definition of rehabilitation, drastic physical treatment—such as psychosurgery and castration, as well as certain forms of drug and behavior therapy—might be excluded. Given the current value system of American society, most of our current efforts at rehabilitation are directed toward this second definition. We try to change offenders in ways that will diminish recidivism but will not drastically diminish the offenders future potentialities.

11   A third and more lofty goal of rehabilitation is to change the offender so that his criminalistic tendencies are eliminated and he also becomes a better citizen. Here the goal is not only to stop recidivism without damaging the offender but also to do something to make the offender a more effective and even happier citizen. Unlike the second goal of re-

habilitation, which does not take cognizance of the offender's need for effectiveness or happiness, this third possible goal leads to concern with the offender's personal needs. Rehabilitation under the second goal is good for society but may not necessarily be good for the offender. Rehabilitation under the third goal is good for both the offender and society.

It is important to keep the above three concepts of rehabilitation in mind when we talk about violent offenders. Those who deal with correctional justice often discuss rehabilitation as though it were a unitary concept. Yet each individual in a given dialogue may have a quite different notion of rehabilitation. When we are motivated by punitive and economic values, we talk about rehabilitation solely in terms of diminishing recidivism without too much regard for the offender's well-being. When we pay attention to ethical considerations, we are concerned that rehabilitation not be so drastic that it hurts the offender. When we view the offender more humanistically, we wish not only to stop him from being violent but also to help him improve his life.

Some of the goals involved in changing offenders may have little or nothing to do with rehabilitation. More specifically, many of the services offered to offenders can be viewed as treatments that are helpful to them but will not influence the probability of their recidivating. (For our purposes here, I will define *treatment* as anything that is done to change an offender in a way that will benefit him or benefit society. The term *treatment*, then, covers all aspects of rehabilitation, but it also encompasses something more.) For instance, many individuals in our prisons are mentally ill. Some suffer greatly from the stresses of incarceration and from personal problems which have little to do with their criminality. Psychotherapists and psychiatrists may try to help offenders with these problems, just as they would help any other citizen. Such treatment, however, may not help society.

Still other goals of the correctional system, may actually conflict with the goal of rehabilitation. Rehabilitation is difficult to accomplish, for instance, when there is too much emphasis upon deterrence and retribution. An individual subjected to a lengthy imprisonment in order to set an example for others may develop a profound bitterness that destroys rehabilitative efforts. An offender kept in prison beyond the point at which he might have been safely released may undergo personality changes that increase his criminalistic tendencies. An offender who feels victimized develops an aggressiveness toward society, and such an attitude also is antagonistic to the rehabilitative process. Obviously, it is difficult to punish and help an offender at the same time.

For a number of reasons, the goal of rehabilitation is not widely supported in our correctional system at this time. The increase in crime rates, particularly in crime that is now affecting middle- and upper-class citizens, has led to a societal ethos of "getting tough" with the criminal. Rehabilitative efforts are frequently viewed as "coddling." But it is not only "hardliners" who are skeptical of the merits of rehabilitation. Advocates of deterrence theory argue that we should focus on prevention of crime by swift and certain punishment. A corollary of this thesis is that we should put less effort into trying to change the offender who has already been convicted. . . .

16   A final word should be said about the ethics of rehabilitation. [We] may soon develop drugs that will diminish an offender's potential for violence at much less expense to the offender's future potentialities; that is, the drugs may diminish not only the individual's violent potentialities but other aspects of his humanness as well, but such changes may not be so drastic as to make them immediately distasteful to society. When such technologies are developed, we will have to make excruciating ethical decisions about their use. Recent court decisions have been in the direction of arguing that incarcerated individuals cannot provide informed consent to participating in experimental rehabilitative procedures. It is unlikely, however, that we will hold to such a position if the crime problem becomes worse and if the technologies become less obviously mutilating to the offender. The ethical question of how far society is entitled to go in changing an offender's psychology and physiology in the name of rehabilitation will, in my opinion, eventually become more important than the current simplistic debates as to whether we should punish or treat violent offenders.

SUGGESTIONS FOR FURTHER READING

Butterfield, Fox. *All God's Children: The Bosket Family and the American Tradition of Violence.* New York: Avon, 1996. A chilling yet insightful account of the heritage of violence within one family of psychopathic murderers.

Diaz, Tom. *Making a Killing: The Business of Guns in America.* New York: New Press, 1997. There are nearly 40,000 gun deaths per year in the United States; this book is a powerful indictment of the gun industry and a call for serious gun control.

Jacoby, Joseph E., ed. *Classics of Criminology.* Oak Park, IL: Waveland Press, 1993. A useful collection of fifty-seven classic articles that have helped define the field of criminology, including both theoretical and empirical works.

Skolnick, Jerome H., and James J. Fyfe. *Above the Law: Police and the Excessive Use of Force.* New York: Free Press, 1994. A solid look at an important and emotion-laden issue, spurred by the now infamous Rodney King beating; written with wisdom and insight from the perspective of both police officers and victims.

Zimring, Franklin E. *American Youth Violence.* New York: Oxford University Press, 1998. A sober, unpanicked, fact-filled treatment of an alarming problem, one that is insufficiently treated in the present book.

STUDY QUESTIONS

1. Discuss the political implications of differing theories of violent criminality. In short, why do certain theories appeal to people who espouse particular ideologies?

2. Is a rational choice model of violent crime necessarily incompatible with explanations based on social and economic factors?

3. Why is it important to have reliable statistics about violent crimes? Is there any danger or disadvantage to using statistics?

4. In the concept of crime as social control, what is being controlled? And why?

5. What is the alternative to a social interactionist approach to violent crime?

6. Discuss some of the benefits and liabilities of labeling a person a psychopath.

7. To what extent can you draw parallels between the various selections in this chapter and ideas presented in Chapter 5 on political science? (Try doing so for the earlier chapters as well.)

8. Design a rebuttal to Halleck's argument, one that emphasizes the liabilities of focusing on treatment and makes a case for punishment as such.

9. Which of the selections in this chapter come closest to espousing a radical or Marxist perspective? Why?

10. In what ways are violent crime similar to—and different from—other aspects of violence we have examined in this book?

Sources

1. Biology

Pages 3–13   Niko Tinbergen, "On War and Peace in Animals and Man." *Science* 160: 1411–1418. Copyright © 1968 American Association for the Advancement of Science. Reprinted with permission from *Science.*

Pages 13–20   Edward O. Wilson, *On Human Nature.* Cambridge, MA: Harvard University Press, 1978. Copyright © 1978 by the President and Fellows of Harvard College. Reprinted with permission from the publisher.

Pages 20–30   David P. Barash and Judith Eve Lipton, *Making Sense of Sex.* Washington, DC: Island Press, 1997. Reprinted with permission from David P. Barash.

Pages 31–46   Klaus A. Miczek, Allan F. Mirsky, Gregory Carey, Joseph DeBold, and Adrian Raine, "An Overview of Biological Influences on Violent Behavior." In *Understanding and Preventing Violence,* Vol.2, *Biobehavioral Influences,* ed. A. J. Reiss, K. A. Miczek, and J. A. Roth. Washington, DC: National Academy Press, 1994. Copyright © 1994 by the National Academy of Sciences. Courtesy of the National Academy Press, Washington, DC.

2. Psychology

Pages 49–56   Erich Fromm, *The Anatomy of Human Destructiveness.* New York: Holt, Rinehart & Winston, 1973. Copyright © 1973 by Erich Fromm. Reprinted with permission from Henry Holt and Company, LLC.

Pages 56–66   John Dollard, Neal E. Miller, Leonard W. Doob, O. H. Mowrer, and Robert R. Sears, "Frustration and Aggression." New Haven, CT: Yale University Press, 1939. Copyright © 1939 by Yale University Press. Reprinted with permission from Yale University Press.

Pages 66–77   Albert Bandura, *Aggression: A Social Learning Analysis.* Englewood Cliffs, NJ: Prentice Hall, 1973. Reprinted with permission from Prentice Hall.

Pages 77–83   Leonard Berkowitz, "On the Formation and Regulation of Anger and Aggression." *American Psychologist* 45 (1990): 494–503. Copyright © 1990 by the American Psychological Association. Reprinted with permission.

Pages 84–87   Leonard D. Eron, L. Rowell Huesmann, Monroe M. Lefkowitz, and Leopold O. Walder, "Does Television Violence Cause Aggression?"

American Psychologist 27 (1972): 253–263. Copyright © 1974 by the American Psychological Association. Reprinted with permission.

Pages 88–97   Stanley Milgram, *Obedience to Authority.* New York: Harper & Row, 1974. Copyright © 1974 by Stanley Milgram. Reprinted with permission from HarperCollins Publishers, Inc.

3. Sociology

Pages 102–108   Lewis Coser, "Some Social Functions of Violence." *The Annals of the American Academy of Politics and Social Science* 364 (1966): 8–18. Copyright © 1966 by Sage Publications. Reprinted with permission from Sage Publications, Inc.

Pages 109–117   Muzafer Sherif, O. J. Harvey, B. Jack White, William Hood, and Carolyn W. Sherif, *Intergroup Conflict and Cooperation: The Robbers Cave Experiment.* Norman, OK: University Book Exchange, 1961.

Pages 118–128   Murray A. Straus, R. J. Gelles, and S. Steinmetz, *Behind Closed Doors: Violence in the American Family.* Garden City, NY: Doubleday, 1980. Copyright © 1980 Richard J. Gelles and Murray A. Straus. Reprinted with permission.

Pages 128–140   J. Hanmer, "Violence and the Social Control of Women." *Feminist Issues* 1 (1981): 29–46. Copyright © 1981 by Transaction Publishers. Reprinted with permission from Transaction Publishers. All rights reserved.

Pages 140–146   Gordon Zahn, "War and Religion in a Sociological Perspective." *Social Compass* 21:4 (1974): 421–431. Reprinted with permission from the author.

Pages 146–151   Johan Galtung, "Violence, Peace, and Peace Research." *Journal of Peace Research* 3 (1969): 167–191. Reprinted with permission from the author.

4. Anthropology

Pages 155–165   Robert Murphy, "Intergroup Hostility and Social Cohesion." *American Anthropologist* 59 (1957): 1018–1035. Reproduced by permission of the American Anthropological Association. Not for further reproduction.

Pages 165–174   Napoleon Chagnon, "Life Histories, Blood Revenge, and Warfare in a Tribal Population." *Science* 239 (1988): 985–992. Copyright © 1988 American Association for the Advancement of Science. Reprinted with permission.

Pages 174–182   R. Bryan Ferguson, *Yanomami Warfare.* Santa Fe, NM: School of American Research Press, 1995. Copyright © 1995 by the School of American Research, Santa Fe. Reprinted with permission.

Pages 182–192   Douglas P. Fry, "Anthropological Perspectives on Aggression: Sex Differences and Cultural Variation." *Aggressive Behavior* 24 (1998): 81–95. Copyright © 1988. Reprinted with permission from Wiley-Liss, Inc., a division of John Wiley & Sons, Inc.

Pages 192–199   Eric R. Wolf, "Cycles of Violence: The Anthropology of War and Peace." In *Waymarks: The Notre Dame Inaugural Lectures in Anthropology,* ed.

Kenneth Moore. South Bend, IN: University of Notre Dame Press, 1987. Copyright © 1987 by University of Notre Dame Press. Reprinted with permission from the publisher.

5. Political Science

Pages 204–210   Thucydides, "The Melian Dialogue." From *The Peloponnesian Wars,* trans. B. Jowett. Oxford: Oxford University Press, 1900.

Pages 210–214   Robert Axelrod, *The Evolution of Cooperation.* New York: Basic Books, 1984. Copyright © 1984 by Robert Axelrod. Reprinted with permission from Basic Books, a member of Perseus Books, LLC.

Pages 214–220   Thomas C. Schelling, *The Strategy of Conflict.* Cambridge, MA: Harvard University Press, 1960. Copyright © 1960, 1980 by the President and Fellows of Harvard College. Reprinted with permission from the publisher.

Pages 220–229   Robert Jervis, "War and Misperception." In *The Origin and Prevention of Major Wars,* ed. R. I. Rotberg and T. K. Rabb. New York: Cambridge University Press, 1989. Copyright © 1988 by the Massachusetts Institute of Technology editors of the *Journal of Interdisciplinary History.* Reprinted with permission from Cambridge University Press.

Pages 229–234   Ted Gurr, *Why Men Rebel.* Princeton, NJ: Princeton University Press, 1970. Reprinted with permission from the author.

Pages 234–237   Franz Fanon, *The Wretched of the Earth.* New York: Grove Press, 1963. Reprinted with permission from Grove Atlantic, Inc.

Pages 237–244   Kenneth Waltz, *Man, the State and War.* New York: Columbia University Press, 1959. Reprinted with permission from Columbia University Press.

6. Criminology

Pages 249–254   James Q. Wilson and Richard J. Herrnstein, "Crime as Choice." From *Crime and Human Nature.* Copyright © 1985 by James Q. Wilson and Richard J. Herrnstein. Reprinted with permission from Simon & Schuster.

Pages 254–260   D. Black, "Crime as Social Control." *American Sociological Review* 48 (1983): 34–45. Reprinted with permission from the American Sociological Association.

Pages 260–267   Richard B. Felson, "Predatory and Dispute-Related Violence: A Social Interactionist Approach." *Advances in Criminological Theory* 5 (1994): 189–235. Copyright © 1994 by Transaction Publishers. Reprinted with permission from Transaction Publishers. All rights reserved.

Pages 267–273   R. D. Hare, *Psychopathy: Theory and Research.* New York: John Wiley & Sons, 1970. Adapted with permission from Robert D. Hare, University of British Columbia, Vancouver, Canada.

Pages 273–278   Seymour Halleck, "Violence: Treatment versus Correction." In *Violence: Perspectives on Murder and Aggression,* ed. I. L. Kutash, S. B. Kutash, L. B. Schlesinger, and Associates. San Francisco, CA: Jossey-Bass, 1978. Reprinted with permission.

Index